Drama for Sc

William Shakespeare's
Macbeth

with notes by
Patrick Murray

The Educational Company of Ireland

First published 2011
The Educational Company of Ireland
Ballymount Road
Walkinstown
Dublin 12

www.edco.ie

A member of the Smurfit Kappa Group plc

© Notes and commentaries, Patrick Murray

Design and layout: Metaphor

Copy-editors: Hilary Bell, Kristin Jensen

Cover image: Shutterstock

Printed in the Republic of Ireland by: Colorman

Acknowledgements
Pages 19, 24, 34, 65, 77, 82, 110, 127 copyright Shakespeare Birthplace Trust.
Pages 9, 74, 75 courtesy of Arclight Films.
All other photos Shutterstock and istockphoto.

QUALITY
I.S. EN ISO 9001:2008
NSAI Certified

The paper used in this book comes from Managed Forests in Northern Europe For every tree felled, at least one new tree is planted

Other titles in the series:
Macbeth Companion Notes
Hamlet
Hamlet Companion Notes
King Lear
King Lear Companion Notes

ISBN: 978-1-84536-382-6

CONTENTS

DRAMATIS PERSONAE

DUNCAN, KING OF SCOTLAND

MALCOLM, DONALBAIN, HIS SONS

MACBETH, BANQUO, GENERALS OF THE KING'S ARMY

MACDUFF, LENNOX, ROSS, MENTEITH, ANGUS, CAITHNESS, NOBLEMEN OF SCOTLAND

FLEANCE, SON OF BANQUO

SIWARD, EARL OF NORTHUMBERLAND, GENERAL OF THE ENGLISH FORCES

YOUNG SIWARD, HIS SON

SEYTON, AN OFFICER ATTENDING ON MACBETH

BOY, SON OF MACDUFF

A CAPTAIN

A PORTER

AN OLD MAN

AN ENGLISH DOCTOR

A SCOTTISH DOCTOR

LADY MACBETH

LADY MACDUFF

GENTLEWOMEN ATTENDING ON LADY MACBETH

THE WEIRD SISTERS

HECATE

THE GHOST OF BANQUO

APPARITIONS

LORDS, GENTLEMEN, OFFICERS, MURDERERS, ATTENDANTS AND **MESSENGERS**

Act One
– Scene One –
[An open place.]

PLOT SUMMARY

In an open place, swept by a thunderstorm, three witches (the Weird Sisters) appear. They discuss their impending meeting with Macbeth, which will follow a decisive battle. Accompanied by their familiars or companions, Graymalkin and Paddock, demons in animal form, they depart through the foggy air.

Short as this scene is, it contributes some significant details. The thunder and lightning of the stage direction are symbolic of the moral and spiritual confusion and tumult soon to overtake Macbeth. The power of the witches to control the elements is suggested in the first two lines. The two opening questions posed by the witches imply that they are able to determine the kind of weather that will prevail at their next meeting. Their gift of prophecy is underlined in the answers of the Second Witch and the Third Witch to the routine questions of the First. They know in advance that they are going to meet with Macbeth upon the heath, after the battle and before sunset.

Their sinister significance and intentions are conveyed in the closing two lines of the scene. Their favourite element is the filthy air obscured by fog, another symbol of the confusion they represent and create. Their paradoxical slogan, 'Fair is foul, and foul is fair' (11), is a neat summary of their reversal of all moral values. It is a point of view that is soon to be embraced by the two main characters in the play, Macbeth and Lady Macbeth. Graymalkin and Paddock, who call to the witches, are usually identified as a cat and a toad. The toad was considered to be poisonous as well as ugly, and so has a symbolic function here.

*'When shall we three meet again /
In thunder, lightning or in rain?' (1, 1, 1–2)*

Pathetic fallacy—nature

Thunder and lightning. Enter three WITCHES

chaos in nature

theme of evil

FIRST WITCH

When shall we three meet again } *rhyme*
In thunder, lightning, or in rain? }

1–2 *When shall we three ... or in rain?:* When will our next meeting be, and what kind of weather shall we choose for it? The lines convey the belief that witches could control the weather.

SECOND WITCH *a battle suggests violence and destruction*

When the hurlyburly's done,
When the battle's lost and won.

3 *hurlyburly:* Here it means the confusion and tumult of rebellion.

THIRD WITCH

5   That will be ere the set of sun. *– Prophetic*

5 *That will be ere the set of sun:* This is Shakespeare's economical way of showing the prophetic gifts of witches.

FIRST WITCH

Where the place?

SECOND WITCH

Upon the heath.

Associated with evil from the beginning

THIRD WITCH

There to meet with Macbeth.

FIRST WITCH

I come, Graymalkin!

8–9 *I come, Graymalkin!/Paddock calls:* Graymalkin is usually identified as a grey cat and Paddock as a toad. The evil spirits which were supposed to attend on witches were thought to appear in the forms of cats and toads.

SECOND WITCH

Paddock calls.

THIRD WITCH

10   Anon.

10 *Anon:* The Third Witch's attendant spirit is not named, but she rushes off at its call. 'Anon' means 'Coming!'

ALL

appearance vs. reality theme

Fair is foul, and foul is fair;
Hover through the fog and filthy air. } *images of disease and corruption*

11–12 *Fair is foul, ... and filthy air:* Good is bad and bad is good. This concise summary of the witches' creed has many echoes throughout the play. The fog may be taken to symbolise the moral confusion generated by the witches and felt by Macbeth. 'Hover' may suggest that they leave the stage by flying!

Exeunt.

EXAMINATION-BASED QUESTIONS

- What can be learned from this scene about the extent of the witches' powers?
- Comment on the meaning and significance of the witches' slogan: 'Fair is foul, and foul is fair' (1, 1, 11).
- What is the function of the scene as a whole?

KEY THEMES AND IMPORTANT FACTS

- This scene introduces the theme of the supernatural in *Macbeth*.

Act One
– Scene Two –
[A Camp near Forres.]

PLOT SUMMARY

Duncan, King of Scotland, and his sons, Malcolm and Donalbain, are confronted by a bleeding captain who has just come from the scene of a fierce battle between the royal forces led by the king's cousin, Macbeth, and a rebel army of traitors led by Macdonwald. Macbeth has defeated the rebels and slain Macdonwald, but is locked in another conflict with the forces of the King of Norway. Ross enters to report that the King of Norway and his treacherous ally, the Thane of Cawdor, have been defeated by Macbeth and Banquo.

The main purpose of this scene is to provide information about Macbeth as a warrior and, to a lesser extent, about Banquo. The emphasis, whether we consider the visual impact of a profusely bleeding captain coming on stage or the verbal images of the battle, is on blood and slaughter. Two equally strong impressions of Macbeth are

conveyed here. One is his heroic performance in battle. Both the bleeding captain and Ross emphasise Macbeth's bravery, which extends far beyond the demands of duty. He is 'brave Macbeth' (16), 'with Valour armed' (29), acquitting himself like another Mars ('Bellona's bridegroom', 54) on the battlefield, saving his king and country from traitors and rebels as well as invaders. But there is another, disturbing, side to the energetic account of Macbeth's military achievements. His valour is tinged with what seems like a barbaric enjoyment of slaughter for its own sake. In the battle with Macdonwald's men he has 'carved out his passage' (19) through a host of enemies and 'unseamed' (22) their chief, ripping him open from the stomach upwards. This ferocity is part of Macbeth's nature and will come to the fore again in his dealings with his various victims. Initially, however, he will be reluctant to display it against Duncan.

Alarum within. Enter DUNCAN, MALCOLM,
DONALBAIN, LENNOX, *with Attendants,*
meeting a bleeding Sergeant

[handwritten: commanding voice/authority]

DUNCAN

What bloody man is that? He can report,
As seemeth by his plight, of the revolt
The newest state.

MALCOLM

This is the sergeant
Who like a good and hardy soldier fought
5 'Gainst my captivity. Hail, brave friend!
Say to the King the knowledge of the broil
As thou didst leave it.

CAPTAIN

[handwritten: Interesting simile]

                    Doubtful it stood,
As two spent swimmers that do cling together
And choke their art. The merciless Macdonwald —
10 Worthy to be a rebel, for to that
The multiplying villainies of nature
Do swarm upon him — from the Western Isles
[handwritten: Irish mercenary soldiers]
Of kerns and gallowglasses is supplied,
And Fortune on his damnèd quarrel smiling
15 Showed like a rebel's whore. But all's too weak;
For brave Macbeth — well he deserves that name — *[handwritten: A heroic introduction]*
Disdaining Fortune, with his brandished steel,
[handwritten: heroic] Which smoked with bloody execution, *[handwritten: is Macbeth bloodthirsty?]*
Like Valour's minion, carved out his passage,
20 Till he faced the slave;
[handwritten: clothing imagery] Which ne'er shook hands, nor bade farewell to him,
Till he unseamed him from the nave to th'chops,
And fixed his head upon our battlements.

DUNCAN

O valiant cousin, worthy gentleman! *[handwritten: IRONY MACBETH]*

CAPTAIN

25 As whence the sun 'gins his reflection
Shipwrecking storms and direful thunders break,
So from that spring whence comfort seemed to come
Discomfort swells. Mark, King of Scotland, mark:
No sooner Justice had, with Valour armed,
30 Compelled these skipping kerns to trust their heels,
But the Norweyan Lord, surveying vantage,
With furbished arms and new supplies of men,
Began a fresh assault.

1–3

5

6–7

6
7
8
9

9–12

10
13

14–15

15

17

[handwritten: at the start of this play Macbeth is heroic]
17–18

19

20

What bloody man ... newest state: The bleeding captain is a striking visual image of violent conflict, a recurring theme of the play. Images of blood, both verbal and visual, occur often in *Macbeth*. The captain's condition makes it obvious that he can give the latest news of the rebellion.
'Gainst my captivity: to prevent my being captured
Say to the King ... leave it: Tell the king how the battle was going when you left it.
broil: battle
Doubtful it stood: The result was in doubt.
spent: exhausted
choke their art: hamper each other
The merciless Macdonwald ... upon him: Macdonwald is just the man to be a rebel, since all the evil deeds that human beings are capable of come naturally to him.
for to that: to that end
kerns and gallowglasses: Kerns were lightly armed foot soldiers. Gallowglasses were horsemen armed with sharp axes.
And Fortune ... rebel's whore: Fortune, that fickle woman, first seemed to favour Macdonwald's wicked cause, but then, typically, turned against him.
all's too weak: Even the combination of Macdonwald and an apparently hostile Fortune cannot overcome Macbeth's bravery.
Disdaining Fortune: Regarding Fortune (or fate) with scorn or contempt; not caring that fortune seemed against him.
with his brandished steel, ... execution: The image here is of Macbeth wielding a sword steaming with the blood of his enemies.
brandished steel: Macbeth's sword
minion: Favourite. Macbeth is seen as the favoured son of Valour, or bravery.
the slave: Macdonwald

21	*Which:* who (i.e. Macbeth)
21–2	*Which ne'er shook hands ... to th'chops:* Macbeth did not spend time on formal ceremony or courtesy but ripped his enemy open from the belly to the jaw-bone.
25–8	*As whence the sun ... swells:* Just as storm and thunder can come from the same direction as the comforting sun, so new danger threatens in a place where victory seemed assured.
30	*Compelled these skipping kerns ... heels:* forced these hired soldiers to flee
31	*But the Norweyan Lord, surveying vantage:* the king of Norway, seeing his opportunity (presumably because the troops under Macbeth and Banquo were tired or in disarray after their hard fight)
32	*furbished:* in good condition
36	*say sooth:* tell the truth
37	*As cannons ... cracks:* cannons primed with double charges of powder
39	*Except they meant to bathe in reeking wounds:* unless they intended to immerse themselves in the blood of their enemies
40	*Or memorise another Golgotha:* Macbeth and Banquo seemed determined to make this battlefield as memorable as Golgotha ('the place of the skull'), where Christ was crucified.
43–4	*So well thy words ... of honour both:* Both your words and your wounds stamp you as a man of honour.
45	*Thane:* This is a Scottish title of nobility equivalent to lord or earl.
46–7	*What a haste ... strange:* He seems in a great hurry. He looks like a man about to tell extraordinary news.
49	*Where the Norweyan banners flout the sky:* Norwegian flags are flying high to mock the Scottish enemy. *flout:* mock
50	*And fan our people cold:* make our people cold with fear
51	*Norway:* the king of Norway
53	*a dismal conflict:* a dangerous attack
54–5	*Till that Bellona's bridegroom, ... self-comparisons:* Bellona was the Roman goddess of

DUNCAN
Dismayed not this
Our captains, Macbeth and Banquo?

[handwritten: The first binary pairing of Macbeth & Banquo.]

CAPTAIN
Yes —
As sparrows eagles, or the hare the lion.   35
If I say sooth I must report they were   *[handwritten: multitonistic image]*
As cannons overcharged with double cracks;
So they doubly redoubled strokes upon the foe,
Except they meant to bathe in reeking wounds, *[handwritten: (bloodbath)]*
Or memorise another Golgotha,   *[handwritten: Macbeth associated with Christ.]*   40
I cannot tell —
But I am faint, my gashes cry for help.

DUNCAN
So well thy words become thee as thy wounds,
They smack of honour both. Go get him surgeons.

     Exit CAPTAIN, attended   *[handwritten: Duncan is compassionate and generous.]*

     Enter ROSS and ANGUS

Who comes here?

MALCOLM
            The worthy Thane of Ross.   45

LENNOX
What a haste looks through his eyes! So should he look
That seems to speak things strange.

ROSS
               God save the King!

DUNCAN
Whence camest thou, worthy Thane?

ROSS
               From Fife, great King,
Where the Norweyan banners flout the sky,
And fan our people cold.   50
Norway himself, with terrible numbers,
Assisted by that most disloyal traitor,
The Thane of Cawdor, began a dismal conflict, *[handwritten: Classical image 4]*
Till that Bellona's bridegroom, lapped in proof, *[handwritten: Macbeth]*
Confronted him with self-comparisons,   55
Point against point, rebellious arm 'gainst arm, *[handwritten: → MB skilled warrior]*

Curbing his lavish spirit; and, to conclude,
The victory fell on us.

DUNCAN
Great happiness!

ROSS
56
That now
60 Sweno, the Norways' King, craves composition.
Nor would we deign him burial of his men
Till he disburséd, at Saint Colme's Inch,
57
Ten thousand dollars to our general use.

DUNCAN
59
No more that Thane of Cawdor shall deceive
60
65 Our bosom interest. Go pronounce his present death,
And with his former title greet Macbeth.
61
62
ROSS *Duncan is decisive and generous.*
I'll see it done.

DUNCAN
63
What he hath lost, noble Macbeth hath won.

Exeunt. *Irony*

64–5

65

68

war. Macbeth's warlike
prowess makes him fit to be
her husband. The lines mean
that the courageous Macbeth,
clad in strong armour ('lapped
in proof'), confronted Sweno,
king of Norway, with spirit
and skill equal to his own.
Point against point: sword
against sword. Some editors
prefer a comma after
'rebellious', in which case the
meaning would be 'sword
against rebellious sword'.
Curbing his lavish spirit:
controlling or restraining his
exaggerated display of
insolence
That: so that, or with the result
that
craves composition: begs for
peace terms
deign: allow
disburséd: paid out
Saint Colme's Inch: Inchcomb,
an island in the Firth of Forth,
not Iona, which is in the
Hebrides.
dollars: Dutch coins, current in
England when *Macbeth* was
written, but not in Macbeth's
Scotland
shall deceive … interest: This
can mean either 'shall betray
the trust I placed in him' or
'shall betray my dearest
interests'.
pronounce his present death:
spread the news that he has
been sentenced to immediate
execution
*What he hath lost, noble
Macbeth hath won:* This final
line of the scene is rich in
irony. It anticipates Duncan's
other misguided tributes to
Macbeth. What the king
cannot know is that his choice
of successor to the first
Cawdor will be a much more
successful traitor.

EXAMINATION-BASED QUESTIONS

- Duncan's opening question, 'What bloody man is that?' (1, 2, 1), is only one of the many references to blood and slaughter in this scene. Identify these references and discuss their importance.
- What do we learn about Macbeth's character in this scene?
- Commentators have found the Captain's presentation of Macbeth somewhat disturbing. Do you find any reason for this attitude?
- Discuss the elements of language and imagery that make this a heroic scene.
- Which elements in the dialogue contribute to the development of the plot?

KEY THEMES AND IMPORTANT FACTS

- This scene introduces the themes of deception and false appearance.

Act One

– Scene Three –

[A Heath.]

PLOT SUMMARY

The witches discuss the various kinds of harm they can cause to human beings. A drumbeat heralds the arrival of Macbeth and Banquo. Macbeth is hailed by the witches as Thane of Glamis and of Cawdor and as future King of Scotland. Banquo is greeted as the begetter of kings. The witches vanish and the truth of one of their prophecies is confirmed when Ross gives Macbeth the news that the king has made him Thane of Cawdor. Banquo warns Macbeth against the dangers posed by occult powers. Macbeth, in soliloquy, reveals his troubled mind.

The first scene was devoted exclusively to the witches and the second to human beings. This scene brings the two together. In the first scene the witches were impressive. Here they inspire somewhat less fear and little confidence in their power to do harm. Their malicious deeds have a slightly childish quality. The Second Witch has killed swine apparently because their owner annoyed her. The First Witch came across a sailor's wife who refused to hand over some chestnuts. By way of reprisal, the witch does her utmost to harm the woman's husband. Her efforts in this direction, however, do not say very much for her capacity to harm. She has power over the winds, but cannot destroy the unnamed sailor ('Though his bark cannot be lost, / Yet it shall be tempest-tost', 24–25). Her production of the shipwrecked pilot's thumb scarcely marks her as a serious or dedicated agent of supernatural evil.

Macbeth is a play full of echoes and anticipations. An example is the passage beginning 'I'll drain him dry as hay' (18 ff.). This passage is about the master of the *Tiger*, but most of it can also be read as a comment on Macbeth's fate. Like the anonymous sailor, Macbeth will be 'drained', though morally and spiritually rather than physically. He will also be deprived of sleep (see 3, 2, 17–22). Macbeth, too, will be cursed and ostracised ('a man forbid', 21) and will 'dwindle, peak, and pine' (23; see 5, 2, 20–2). The most significant lines of the First Witch's speech are: 'Though his bark cannot be lost, / Yet it shall be tempest-tost', quoted above. The worst the witches can do to the master of the *Tiger* is to cause the winds to buffet his ship, but he keeps control of his destiny in spite of their utmost efforts. These lines cannot be applied directly to Macbeth, since his 'bark' (his cause, his life, his body, his soul) *is* lost. But the reason for this is that Macbeth will not fight sufficiently hard to resist the destructive forces of temptation. He is partly the agent of his own destruction, unlike the master of the *Tiger*, who will not scuttle his ship. The fate of the pilot, 'Wracked as homeward he did come' (29), is an ironic anticipation of what will happen to Macbeth as he makes his way homeward after the battle.

From the point of view of characterisation, the most interesting feature of this scene is the contrasting attitudes of Banquo and Macbeth to the pronouncements of the witches. As Banquo points out to him, Macbeth ought to respond with pleasure to the prophecies. Instead, he is startled and fearful. When the witches predict a royal crown for him, they nowhere suggest that he should get it by foul means. Macbeth's guilty start reflects guilty thoughts already formed. The witches are merely encouraging Macbeth to do something he has previously been tempted to do. The idea of killing Duncan for his crown has clearly occurred to him before this encounter with the witches. If this were not the case, it would be difficult to account for the vivid and terrifying images of murder in his soliloquy.

Banquo's response to the witches and what they have to say is quite different from Macbeth's in some important respects. His feelings are far less deeply engaged. He is rather sceptical about the significance of their prophecies and is conscious that evil spirits can bring about one's downfall by tempting one initially with 'honest trifles' (125). Macbeth knows this as well as Banquo, but chooses to ignore it because he wants what the witches promise him. Banquo has comparatively little regard for whatever good or ill the witches may intend for him (their 'favours' or their 'hate', 61). Macbeth is very interested and wants to know from what superior authority the witches have derived their information ('this strange intelligence', 76). It is Macbeth, not Banquo, who wants to discuss the matter further ('let us speak / Our free hearts each to other', 154–55). When Macbeth hears the prediction for his own future, he wants to learn more; Banquo does not bother to make further enquiries. It is significant that Macbeth takes refuge in untruth to conceal his intense interest in what he has heard, pretending that his 'dull brain was wrought / With things forgotten' (149–50), when, in fact, he has obviously been meditating, not on the past, but on the future.

the theme of evil is being further elaborated in this scene.

Thunder. Enter the three WITCHES

FIRST WITCH
Where hast thou been, sister?

SECOND WITCH
Killing swine. (pigs) / *This is a bloody act in a blood soaked play*

THIRD WITCH
Sister, where thou?

FIRST WITCH
A sailor's wife had chestnuts in her lap,
5   And munched, and munched, and munched: 'Give me,' quoth I:
'Aroint thee, witch!' the rump-fed ronyon cries.
Her husband's to Aleppo gone, master o' the Tiger:
But in a sieve I'll thither sail,
And, like a rat without a tail, → *zoomorphic simile*
10   I'll do, I'll do, and I'll do.

2   *Killing swine:* Witches were thought to specialise in killing farm animals. The slaughter of pigs is a particularly bloody activity.

6   *Aroint thee:* Go away! *rump-fed ronyon:* overfed, mangy hag

7–10   *Her husband's ... and I'll do:* Witches had the power to sail in sieves. This one proposes to take the form of a rat, creep on board the *Tiger* and cast a vengeful spell. When witches took animal forms there was always some imperfection in the animal involved, hence the rat without a tail.
The Tiger: This ship sailed for the middle East in 1604 and, following a terrible voyage returned to England in the summer of 1606

SECOND WITCH
I'll give thee a wind.

FIRST WITCH
Thou art kind.

THIRD WITCH
And I another.

FIRST WITCH
I myself have all the other,
15   And the very ports they blow,
All the quarters that they know
I' the shipman's card.
I'll drain him dry as hay:
Sleep shall neither night nor day
20   Hang upon his penthouse lid;
He shall live a man forbid;
Weary sev'nights nine times nine
Shall he dwindle, peak, and pine:
Though his bark cannot be lost,
25   Yet it shall be tempest-tost.
Look what I have.

The sleep motif is introduced here. The inability to sleep is associated with evil

poetic language;

SECOND WITCH
Show me, show me.

FIRST WITCH
Here I have a pilot's thumb,
Wracked as homeward he did come.

Drum within.

Marginal notes (left column):

11–18   *I'll give thee ... dry as hay:* The Second and Third Witches offer to raise storms for the First Witch, who herself can raise all the other winds that will prevent the *Tiger* from entering any port. The 'quarters' are those of the compass. The 'shipman's card' is the seaman's compass card. The victim will be 'dry as hay' because the ship cannot put into port to get water for the duration of the storms.

15   *ports they blow:* The wind blowing from the land would make it impossible for a ship at sea to dock at any port.

20   *penthouse lid:* eyelid
21   *forbid:* cursed
22–3   *Weary sev'nights ... peak, and pine:* For 81 weeks he will waste away, becoming thinner and thinner. Seven and nine were considered to be magic numbers.

24   *Though his bark cannot be lost:* The power of the Witches is limited. They cannot sink the ship.

28   *a pilot's thumb:* the thumb of a shipwrecked pilot

'A drum! A drum! / Macbeth doth come.' (1, 3, 30–1)

THIRD WITCH

30 A drum! a drum!
Macbeth doth come.

ALL

The weird sisters, hand in hand,
Posters of the sea and land,
Thus do go about, about:
35 Thrice to thine, and thrice to mine,
And thrice again, to make up nine.
Peace! The charm's wound up.

The characters are paired already

Enter MACBETH and BANQUO

MACBETH

So foul and fair a day I have not seen.

A direct echo of the witches. First words Macbeth says, associated with evil.

BANQUO

How far is't called to Forres? What are these,
40 So withered, and so wild in their attire,
That look not like th'inhabitants o' the earth,
And yet are on't? Live you? Or are you aught
That man may question? You seem to understand me,
By each at once her choppy finger laying
45 Upon her skinny lips: you should be women,
And yet your beards forbid me to interpret
That you are so.

Appearance vs reality

Appearance vs. reality

MACBETH

Speak, if you can: what are you?

Macbeth initiates the witches prophecies

FIRST WITCH

All hail, Macbeth! hail to thee, Thane of Glamis!

SECOND WITCH

All hail, Macbeth! hail to thee, Thane of Cawdor!

THIRD WITCH

50 All hail, Macbeth! that shall be King hereafter.

BANQUO

Good sir, why do you start, and seem to fear
Things that do sound so fair? I'the name of truth,
Are ye fantastical, or that indeed
Which outwardly ye show? My noble partner
55 You greet with present grace, and great prediction
Of noble having and of royal hope,

32 *weird:* This comes from an Old English word meaning fate. The Witches are agents of fate or destiny.
33 *Posters:* travellers
35–6 *Thrice to thine … to make up nine:* Three, as well as seven and nine, was considered to be a magic number.
37 *Peace! The charm's wound up:* The spell is ready.
38 *So foul … not seen:* Here Macbeth unwittingly echoes the witches' utterance: 'Fair is foul, and foul is fair'. For him, the victory is fair and the weather is foul.
39 *How far … Forres?:* how far is Forres supposed to be?
called: thought or believed to be
42–3 *Or are you aught, … question?:* Banquo wonders whether it is safe to question the witches. Questioning evil spirits could lead to perilous consequences.
44–5 *choppy finger … lips:* They want Banquo to be quiet, so that they can turn their attention to Macbeth.

51 *why do you start:* Macbeth may well be startled because the Third Witch has just made him conscious of his strong and secret desire to be king. Should the actor playing Macbeth try to suggest that he was paralysed with guilt even before the action of the play began, having already killed Duncan time and again in his mind?

53 *fantastical:* imaginary
55–6 *You greet … of royal hope:* The witches have greeted Macbeth with the titles Glamis ('present grace'); Cawdor ('great prediction/Of noble having') and King ('royal hope').

57   *rapt withal:* totally preoccupied with the greetings

That he seems rapt withal: to me you speak not.
If you can look into the seeds of time,
And say which grain will grow and which will not,
60   Speak then to me, who neither beg nor fear
Your favours nor your hate.

Benquo is more rational.

FIRST WITCH
Hail!

SECOND WITCH
Hail!

THIRD WITCH
Hail!

FIRST WITCH
65   Lesser than Macbeth, and greater.

these witches "palter" in a double sense i.e paradox

SECOND WITCH
Not so happy, yet much happier.

67   *get kings:* be the father or ancestor of kings

THIRD WITCH
Thou shalt get kings, though thou be none:
So, all hail, Macbeth and Banquo!

FIRST WITCH
Banquo and Macbeth, all hail!

70   *you imperfect speakers:* you who provide insufficient detail
71   *Sinel:* Macbeth's father
72–3   *The Thane of Cawdor … prosperous gentleman:* It is odd that Macbeth does not seem to know of Cawdor's treachery and his punishment (Scene 2: 57–66). Possible explanations are that Shakespeare was careless here or that Cawdor's help to Norway was secret and therefore unknown to Macbeth.
76   *You owe this strange intelligence:* you have this strange news

MACBETH
70   Stay, you imperfect speakers, tell me more:
By Sinel's death I know I am Thane of Glamis;
But how of Cawdor? The Thane of Cawdor lives,
A prosperous gentleman; and to be King
Stands not within the prospect of belief,
75   No more than to be Cawdor. Say from whence
You owe this strange intelligence? Or why
Upon this blasted heath you stop our way
With such prophetic greeting? Speak, I charge you.

Macbeth is greedy for more engagement with these witches

    The WITCHES *vanish.*

BANQUO
The earth hath bubbles, as the water has,
80   And these are of them. Whither are they vanished?

80   *these are of them:* The witches are of the same nature as bubbles – they are insubstantial.
81   *corporal:* having a body

MACBETH
Into the air, and what seemed corporal melted
As breath into the wind. Would they had stayed!

Appearence vs. Reality

BANQUO

Were such things here as we do speak about?
Or have we eaten on the insane root
85   That takes the reason prisoner?

MACBETH

Your children shall be kings.

BANQUO

You shall be King.

MACBETH

And Thane of Cawdor too; went it not so?

BANQUO

To the self-same tune and words. Who's here?

Enter ROSS and ANGUS

ROSS

The king hath happily received, Macbeth,
90   The news of thy success; and when he reads
Thy personal venture in the rebels' fight,
His wonders and his praises do contend
Which should be thine or his. Silenced with that,
In viewing o'er the rest o'the self-same day,
95   He finds thee in the stout Norweyan ranks,
Nothing afeared of what thyself didst make,
Strange images of death. As thick as hail
Came post with post, and every one did bear
Thy praises in his kingdom's great defence,
And poured them down before him.

ANGUS

100   We are sent
To give thee from our royal master thanks;
Only to herald thee into his sight,
Not pay thee.

ROSS

And, for an earnest of a greater honour,
105   He bade me, from him, call thee Thane of Cawdor:
In which addition, hail, most worthy thane!
<u>For it is thine.</u> *Duncans generossity is clear*

BANQUO

<u>What! Can the devil speak true?</u> *Banquo can see the witches for what they are.*

---

84   *the insane root:* a root that makes the person who eats it insane

90   *reads:* This does not mean that Duncan has read an account of what Macbeth has achieved in battle, but that he has observed or taken note of this.
91   *venture:* part played by Macbeth at great risk to himself
the rebels' fight: the fight against the rebels
92–3   *His wonders … thine or his:* Duncan's admiration struggles with his desire to praise Macbeth. The wonder is appropriate to Duncan, the praise due to Macbeth. Some editors find in these lines a suggestion that Duncan feels so inadequate in the face of Macbeth's achievements that he thinks Macbeth more worthy of the throne than he himself is. This last interpretation might explain why Duncan is 'Silenced' by the thought.

94   *viewing o'er:* reading about
95   *stout:* brave

97   *Strange images of death:* the corpses of the enemy
98   *post with post:* messenger after messenger

104   *earnest:* pledge or token

106   *addition:* newly acquired title

109   *borrowed robes:* This is the first of a series of images of inappropriate clothing used in relation to Macbeth. The borrowed robes are tokens of Macbeth's usurpation of what is not rightly his.

110   *heavy judgement:* sentence of death
111   *combined:* in league
112   *line:* support, strengthen
114   *wrack:* wreck, ruin, destruction
115   *treasons capital:* treasons punishable by death
     confessed and proved: the guilty man has confessed his treason and his guilt has been established
117   *behind:* still to come
120   *home:* completely
121   *enkindle you:* entice you to hope for
123–6 *And oftentimes … consequence:* In order to lead us into danger, the powers of evil often tell us the truth about small things so that they may deceive us about great matters.
127   *Cousins:* kinsmen
127–9 *Two truths … imperial theme:* Macbeth sees the accurate statements already made by the witches (Macbeth is now Thane of Cawdor as well as Glamis) as delightful preludes ('prologues') to a magnificent ('swelling') drama in which he will play the part of king ('the imperial theme').
130–1 *This supernatural soliciting … good:* This invitation from the witches cannot be evil and good at the same time.
131–3 *If ill … truth?:* If evil forces are at work, why has the prophecy of my succession to the throne begun with a true statement? Banquo has already dealt with this point (lines 123–6).
134–7 *If good … nature?:* If, on the other hand, good forces are inspiring the prophecy, why do I surrender to the temptation to see myself as Duncan's murderer, a vision so horrible that it makes my hair stand on end and my heart beat uncontrollably?
137–8 *Present fears … imaginings:* The real dangers we have to face are less terrifying than the horrors we imagine. Macbeth's behaviour before and after the murder of Duncan, and during the banquet scene, illustrates the truth of this in his case.
139–42 *My thought … what is not:* The murder (of Duncan) is still only a figment of my imagination ('fantastical'), but the thought of murder so shatters my being that my power to act is

MACBETH
The Thane of Cawdor lives; why do you dress me
In borrowed robes? *The first example of clothing imagery*

ANGUS
              Who was the thane lives yet;
110 But under heavy judgement bears that life
Which he deserves to lose. Whether he was combined
With those of Norway, or did line the rebel
With hidden help and vantage, or that with both
He laboured in his country's wrack, I know not;
115 But treasons capital, confessed and proved,
Have overthrown him.

(SOLILOQUY)
MACBETH
[*Aside.*]   Glamis, and Thane of Cawdor: *He is already hooked*
The greatest is behind. [*To* ROSS *and* ANGUS.] Thanks for
   your pains.
[*Aside to* BANQUO.] Do you not hope your children shall
   be kings, *He already sees Banquo as a threat.*
When those that gave the Thane of Cawdor to me
Promised no less to them?

BANQUO
120   That, trusted home,
Might yet enkindle you unto the crown,
Besides the Thane of Cawdor. But 'tis strange:
And oftentimes, to win us to our harm, *again Banquo*
The instruments of darkness tell us truths, *understands the*
125 Win us with honest trifles, to betray's *way the witches*
In deepest consequence. *work.*
Cousins, a word, I pray you.

MACBETH
[*Aside.*] Two truths are told,
As happy prologues to the swelling act
Of the imperial theme. [*Aloud.*] I thank you, gentlemen.
130 [*Aside.*] This supernatural soliciting *(guidance)*
Cannot be ill, cannot be good. If ill, *an echo of the witches paradox.*
Why hath it given me earnest of success, *contrast with Banquo*
Commencing in a truth? I am Thane of Cawdor:
If good, why do I yield to that suggestion *Macbeth is already considering*
135 Whose horrid image doth unfix my hair *regicide*
And make my seated heart knock at my ribs, *has a conscience'*
Against the use of nature? Present fears
Are less than horrible imaginings.
My thought, whose murder yet is but fantastical,

140 Shakes so my single state of man that function
Is smothered in surmise, and nothing is
But what is not.

BANQUO
Look how our partner's rapt.

MACBETH
[Aside.] If chance will have me King, why, chance may
crown me,
Without my stir.

BANQUO
                    New honours come upon him,
145 Like our strange garments, cleave not to their mould
But with the aid of use.

MACBETH
[Aside.]   Come what come may,
Time and the hour runs through the roughest day.

BANQUO
Worthy Macbeth, we stay upon your leisure.

MACBETH
Give me your favour: my dull brain was wrought
150 With things forgotten. Kind gentlemen, your pains
Are registered where every day I turn
The leaf to read them. Let us toward the King.
[Aside to BANQUO.]
Think upon what hath chanced; and, at more time,
The interim having weighed it, let us speak
Our free hearts each to other.

BANQUO
155 *[Aside to MACBETH.]*   Very gladly.

MACBETH
[Aside to BANQUO.] Till then, enough.
[Aloud.] Come, friends.

    Exeunt.

overwhelmed and nothing is
real to me except imagined
(future) events. The actor should
suggest that Macbeth is so
absorbed in thought that he is
rooted to the spot. Only his
thoughts are real to him and his
body almost ceases to function.
142   *rapt:* in a trance

144–6   *New honours … of use:* Just as
it takes time for the body to get
used to new clothes, so too it
will take Macbeth some time to
adjust to his new title.

146–7   *Come what come … day:*
Even the worst day will end;
everything will take its course.
Compare 5, 5, 19: 'Tomorrow,
and tomorrow, and tomorrow'.

149   *Give me your favour:* Forgive
me.
wrought: agitated, disturbed,
overcome
150   *things forgotten:* memories, or
things of the past being
recalled. Macbeth's soliloquy
just before this shows how
great a lie this is; he is
thinking not of the past but of
the future.

150–2   *your pains … read them:* Your
sacrifices are recorded in my
memory; every day I recall
them to mind. Macbeth is
thinking of memory as a book
which can be opened at will.

154–5   *The interim … each to other:*
When we have thought about
what has happened, let us
speak frankly to each other.

EXAMINATION-BASED QUESTIONS

- This scene extends our knowledge of the nature of the witches and of what they stand for. In what ways?
- How is it suggested here that the witches' powers are limited?
- Should the witches be taken seriously as dangerous agents of evil and harm, or is there an element of childish mischief in their talk and activities?
- There is a considerable difference between Macbeth and Banquo in their reactions to the witches. Examine the differences and explain them.
- What is the significance of the message Ross brings concerning the fate of the Thane of Cawdor?
- Is there anything surprising in Macbeth's reply to Ross, 'The Thane of Cawdor lives' (108)?
- What do we learn about Banquo's character and motives from this scene?
- It is sometimes argued that Macbeth is already a guilty man before he meets the witches, that he has already thought seriously about murdering Duncan. Does this scene confirm or contradict this impression?
- To what extent do the witches actually *tempt* Macbeth?
- This scene develops our understanding of both Macbeth and Banquo. Mention some details that help to do this.
- Macbeth's aside (lines 130–42) is significant. How should the actor's movements, gestures and tone of voice help to give meaning to the lines?

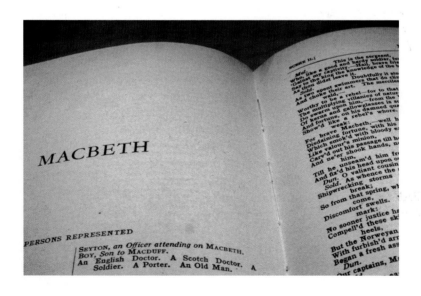

Act One
– Scene Four –
[Forres. The Palace.]

> ### PLOT SUMMARY
>
> Malcolm gives Duncan details of Cawdor's execution. Duncan thanks Macbeth for his services to king and country, then formally makes his son Malcolm successor to the throne. Macbeth responds to this unwelcome news in an aside that reveals his murderous plans.
>
> Malcolm praises the first Thane of Cawdor for ending his rebellious life on a good note. The main point of the reference to Cawdor is to contrast the good ending of the first Cawdor's career and the bad beginning of that of Macbeth, the second Cawdor.
>
> Duncan's commonplace generalisation about the difficulty of deducing the true nature of man from his outward appearance becomes deeply ironic as Macbeth enters. Duncan is regretting the trust he reposed in Cawdor, but at the same time is ready to trust his 'worthiest cousin' (14) and to reward him lavishly. In light of what we know of Macbeth's intentions towards Duncan, everything the latter says by way of praise and gratitude is full of irony, some of it particularly ominous and sinister, as when Duncan tells his potential murderer that 'More is thy due than more than all can pay' (21), not realising that the 'more than all' will be his own life. It is appropriate that a scene so remarkable for its ironies should end on an ironic note. Duncan's last words are a tribute to his 'peerless kinsman', Macbeth (58).
>
> The contrast between the style and tone of Duncan's speeches and those of Macbeth in this scene are worth noting. Duncan is full of joyful enthusiasm, which he expresses without restraint; he sometimes becomes embarrassingly sentimental ('My plenteous joys, / Wanton in fulness, seek to hide themselves / In drops of sorrow', 33–5). Macbeth's replies are forced, formal and conventional, reflecting his inability to pretend he can share in Duncan's happiness. The turning point of the scene, and one of the crucial moments of the play, is Duncan's proud and happy nomination of his son Malcolm as his successor. It is this gesture that, more than anything else, seals his doom. Macbeth's public response to the announcement is curt and ironic: he will make Lady Macbeth 'joyful' (45) with the news that Duncan is to visit them. His short aside just before the end of the scene is full of menace. Duncan has been  talking of titles and honours shining 'like stars' (41) on all who deserve them. Macbeth looks to the extinction of the stars as a prelude to his murderous deed.

Flourish. Enter DUNCAN, MALCOLM,
DONALBAIN, LENNOX, *and Attendants*

DUNCAN

Is execution done on Cawdor? Are not
Those in commission yet returned?

MALCOLM

My liege,
They are not yet come back. But I have spoke
With one that saw him die; who did report
5   That very frankly he confessed his treasons,
Implored your Highness' pardon, and set forth
A deep repentance. Nothing in his life
Became him like the leaving it: he died
As one that had been studied in his death,
10   To throw away the dearest thing he owed
As 'twere a careless trifle.

DUNCAN

There's no art
To find the mind's construction in the face:
He was a gentleman on whom I built
An absolute trust.

Enter MACBETH, BANQUO, ROSS *and* ANGUS

O worthiest cousin!
15   The sin of my ingratitude even now
Was heavy on me. Thou art so far before
That swiftest wing of recompense is slow
To overtake thee. Would thou hadst less deserved,
That the proportion both of thanks and payment
20   Might have been mine! Only I have left to say,
More is thy due than more than all can pay.

MACBETH

The service and the loyalty I owe
In doing it, pays itself. Your Highness' part
Is to receive our duties; and our duties
25   Are to your throne and state, children and servants;
Which do but what they should, by doing everything
Safe toward your love and honour.

Handwritten annotations:
Appearance vs. Reality
This may well have been Duncan's flaw i.e. too trusting
IRONY
Macbeth's falseness is starting to appear

Margin glosses:

2   *in commission:* those entrusted with the duty of seeing to Cawdor's death

3.   *My liege:* my lord

9   *As one that ... his death:* like an actor who had rehearsed the part of a condemned man, so that he could play it to perfection

10–11   *To throw away ... careless trifle:* He threw away his most precious possession, his life, as if it were a worthless thing.

10   *owed:* owned

11–14   *There's no art ... trust:* Nobody can judge the character of a man by looking at his face. As Duncan completes his rueful admission of disillusionment with Cawdor and with human nature, Macbeth enters, to be greeted with fulsome compliments. The irony here is patent.

16–18   *Thou art so far ... overtake thee:* Your good qualities and achievements so far exceed anybody else's that even the most immediate reward cannot do you justice.

18–20   *Would thou ... been mine!:* I wish you had deserved less; in that case I might have been able to reward you in proportion to your merits.

20–1   *Only I have left ... can pay:* All I can say is that you deserve more than I can ever pay you; I do not have enough to reward you adequately.

22–7   *The service ... honour:* My loyal service to you is its own reward. Your only duty is to receive our obedience; our duty is to serve your majesty and the country with childlike affection and the loyalty of servants. Our duties should always be prompted by regard for your welfare and security.

DUNCAN *also intends to nurture*

Plant imagery

Welcome hither:
I have begun to plant thee, and will labour
To make thee full of growing. Noble Banquo,

30 That hast no less deserved, nor must be known
No less to have done so, let me infold thee
And hold thee to my heart.

BANQUO

There if I grow,
The harvest is your own.

DUNCAN

My plenteous joys,
Wanton in fulness, seek to hide themselves
35 In drops of sorrow. Sons, kinsmen, thanes,
And you whose places are the nearest, know
We will establish our estate upon
Our eldest, Malcolm, whom we name hereafter
The Prince of Cumberland; which honour must
40 Not unaccompanied invest him only,
But signs of nobleness, like stars, shall shine
On all deservers. From hence to Inverness,
And bind us further to you.

MACBETH

The rest is labour, which is not used for you:
45 I'll be myself the harbinger, and make joyful
The hearing of my wife with your approach;
So, humbly take my leave. *← The first mention of LMB, his love for her is clear*

DUNCAN

My worthy Cawdor! — *Irony*

MACBETH

[*Aside*] The Prince of Cumberland! That is a step
On which I must fall down, or else o'er-leap, *He's beginning*
50 For in my way it lies. Stars, hide your fires! *to consider evil*
Let not light see my black and deep desires: *images of dark*
The eye wink at the hand; yet let that be *+ light.*
Which the eye fears, when it is done, to see. *poetic language*

Exit.

31
33-5

37

39-42

44

45
45-6

50-1

52-3

54

55-8

The tortured elaboration of this speech reflects Macbeth's uneasy dishonesty.
infold: enfold, embrace
My plenteous joys ... drops of sorrow: My unrestrained happiness finds its outlet in tears. There is irony in the fact that this joyful outburst is followed immediately by the announcement of his successor, which seals his fate.
We will establish our estate upon: We will give the right of succession to. This implies that Duncan might have chosen someone other than Malcolm. If Macbeth has been entertaining expectations of succeeding Duncan, his terrible reaction to the announcement becomes more comprehensible.
which honour ... deservers: Malcolm will not be the only one to be given a title of nobility; others who deserve it will also be honoured.
The rest ... for you: Periods of leisure not used for your benefit seem tedious.
harbinger: forerunner
make joyful ... approach: This is a further irony. Lady Macbeth's joy at Duncan's approach will be far from the kind Duncan imagines it to be.
Stars, hide your fires! ... desires: He is planning to murder Duncan in the dark of night.
The eye wink ... to see: Let the eye ignore what the hand does (so that I may be able to disclaim responsibility for the act), but nevertheless let my hand perform this deed, a deed so terrible that I will shudder at the thought of beholding it when it has been done.
True, worthy Banquo: While Macbeth has been contemplating Duncan's murder, Banquo, Macbeth's next victim, has been praising his future murderer and this praise delights the other victim, Duncan. The irony here is multiplied.
And in ... kinsman: And I take delight in hearing him praised. Let us follow the man who has gone ahead of us to make hospitable arrangements for

58

our arrival. He is an incomparable relative.

peerless: without equal

DUNCAN
True, worthy Banquo: he is full so valiant,

55 And in his commendations I am fed;
It is a banquet to me. Let's after him,
Whose care is gone before to bid us welcome:
It is a peerless kinsman.

Irony

Flourish. Exeunt.

EXAMINATION-BASED QUESTIONS

- This scene contains some striking ironies. Examine the principal ones.
- What impression of Duncan is conveyed in this scene?
- Macbeth obviously has problems when he has to respond to Duncan's kindness and compliments. What are his problems? Is there any evidence that he is ill at ease?
- Duncan's pronouncement, 'We will establish our estate upon / Our eldest, Malcolm' (37–8), is of vital importance to the entire plot. Explain.
- Describe Macbeth's state of mind as revealed in his aside beginning 'The Prince of Cumberland ...' (48 ff.).

KEY THEMES AND IMPORTANT FACTS

- Notice the increase in tension after Duncan announces that Malcolm is to be his successor.
- The scene reinforces the theme of false appearance ('There's no art / To find the mind's construction in the face', 11–12).

Duncan makes Macbeth Thane of Cawdor. (1, 4)

Act One
– Scene Five –
[Inverness. Macbeth's Castle.]

PLOT SUMMARY

Lady Macbeth reads her husband's letter conveying the news of the witches' prophecies. In her analysis of Macbeth's character, she is worried by the thought that he may lack the necessary ruthlessness to take the crown. The announcement of Duncan's imminent visit to her castle excites her to near hysteria. She invokes the aid of evil spirits to strengthen her resolution and harden her heart. Macbeth is unsure of what to do. **Lady Macbeth is resolved that Duncan must die**.

In Act 1, Scene 2 we learn about Macbeth's qualities as a professional soldier. In this scene we are given **an intimate glimpse of Macbeth the private man**, first through the medium of his letter to Lady Macbeth, and then in her significant comments on his character in soliloquy. Another major function of this scene is to throw light on Lady Macbeth's character and motives.

Her speech beginning 'Glamis thou art, and Cawdor' (14 ff.) is a major piece of evidence about Macbeth's character from the person who presumably knows him best. **Lady Macbeth's purpose is to indicate her husband's weaknesses**. Like the witches, however, she has a perverted sense of moral values. For them, 'Fair is foul, and foul is fair' (1, 1, 11). For her, compassion, scrupulousness, humane feeling and integrity are to be deplored in a man who wants to get ahead in the world. She sees it as her function to overcome these 'defects' in his character by pouring her 'spirits' (25) in his ear, **by infecting him with a ruthless inhumanity**.

Her next speech, particularly the invocation of the spirits (39 ff.), must be understood in terms of contemporary theories of witchcraft and demonology. In this passage, **Lady Macbeth is formally and deliberately dedicating herself to evil spirits**, asking them to possess her, body and soul. She is assuming the role of a witch. If we accept this, a good deal of what she says and does, and of what happens to all around her, falls into place. Her prayer to the powers of evil is not an empty formula. This must be recognised by the actress who plays the part. Some of the actresses who have played Lady Macbeth as a woman delivering herself up to the guidance of demons have spoken the prayer in a slow, hollow whisper, like an evil chant. They have made their voices sound supernatural, as if from another world. Costume plays a part in creating this effect. A favoured piece is a long, black robe. Some actresses speak the terrible petition on their knees, hands spread outward as if in prayer.

The spirits 'That tend on mortal thoughts' (40) have a deep significance for students of demonology. 'Tend on' means 'wait on' or 'attend on'. The evil spirits wait for evidence of **evil thoughts** ('mortal thoughts' are thoughts of murder), because **such thoughts will allow them to take possession of the minds and wills** of those who harbour them. What Lady Macbeth does here is to will the evil spirits to take possession of her so that she may become a more effective agent of 'mortal' or murderous deeds. The 'murdering ministers' of line 47 are the same as the 'spirits' of line 39.

If we think of **the demonic spirits as having taken possession of Lady Macbeth**, we will not find it surprising that the Porter of Inverness thinks of himself as letting people into hell when he opens the gate of her home. The influence of these spirits is also felt in the unnatural portents on the night of Duncan's murder (2, 3) and in the unnatural darkness surrounding the castle ('There's husbandry in heaven; / Their candles are all out', 2, 1, 4–5).

In his classic study of the subject, the critic W.C. Curry points out that one of the characteristics of **demoniacal sleepwalking** was that a second personality spoke through the victim's mouth, confessing sins and recalling earlier episodes from his or her life.

Whether or not the 'damned spot' (5, 1, 31) is the devil's mark traditionally supposed to be found on a witch is uncertain, but Lady Macbeth's behaviour during the sleepwalking scene and Macbeth's behaviour at other times (when he sees the phantom dagger and when Banquo's ghost appears) illustrate the traditional belief that 'demons are enabled to induce in the imaginations of men, either waking or asleep, whatever visions or hallucinations they please' (Curry, *Shakespeare's Philosophical Patterns*, p. 75).

Two references to Lady Macbeth make explicit the idea that **she is possessed**: 'More needs she the divine than the physician' (5, 1, 66) says the Doctor, the exorcism of evil spirits being one of the functions of a priest. And she is finally described by Malcolm as Macbeth's 'fiend-like queen' (5, 9, 35).

Lady Macbeth's dealings with the powers of evil may be contrasted with Banquo's. He cannot keep himself from dreaming of the witches, but he prays not to Lady Macbeth's 'spirits / That tend on mortal thoughts', but to the 'Merciful Powers' (2, 1, 7). He is not making a vague appeal to heaven for help against temptation. The 'Powers' he invokes are those good angels whose task it is to restrain and counteract evil spirits. **Banquo's will**, at this point at any rate, **controls his 'cursed thoughts'** (2, 1, 8). **Lady Macbeth's will, by contrast, has fostered hers**. She remains powerfully effective as long as her conscious mind remains in control. But even her will cannot control her unconscious mind, and it is from this source that her final collapse comes. When she admits that a resemblance between her father and the sleeping Duncan prevented her from killing the latter, she betrays her one conscious weakness in the play and her one notable streak of human feeling.

Enter LADY MACBETH, *reading a letter*   2

LADY MACBETH

'They met me in the day of success; and I have learned
by the perfectest report, they have more in them than   6
mortal knowledge. When I burned in desire to question   10
them further, they made themselves air, into which they   11
5   vanished. Whiles I stood rapt in the wonder of it, came   12–13
missives from the King, who all-hailed me, "Thane of   16
Cawdor"; by which title, before, these weird sisters
saluted me, and referred me to the coming on of time, with,
"Hail, king that shalt be!" This have I thought good to   17
10   deliver thee, my dearest partner of greatness, that thou
mightest not lose the dues of rejoicing, by being
ignorant of what greatness is promised thee. Lay it to   18–19
thy heart, and farewell.'
Glamis thou art, and Cawdor; and shalt be
15   What thou art promised. Yet do I fear thy nature,   19–20
It is too full o' th' milk of human-kindness
To catch the nearest way: thou wouldst be great,
Art not without ambition, but without
The illness should attend it; what thou wouldst highly,   20–1
20   That thou wouldst holily; wouldst not play false,
And yet wouldst wrongly win; thou'dst have, great Glamis,   21–4
That which cries 'Thus thou must do', if thou have it,
And that which rather thou dost fear to do
Than wishest should be undone. Hie thee hither,
25   That I may pour my spirits in thine ear,
And chastise with the valour of my tongue
All that impedes thee from the golden round,   22
Which fate and metaphysical aid doth seem
To have thee crowned withal.   24
                                                                          26–9
        Enter an ATTENDANT

                        What is your tidings?
                                                                          30
ATTENDANT
The King comes here tonight.

LADY MACBETH
30   Thou'rt mad to say it.   34
Is not thy master with him? Who, were't so,   37–9
Would have informed for preparation.

Marginal glosses:

the perfectest report: the most reliable source. This implies that Macbeth has made careful enquiries about the powers of the Weird Sisters.

missives: messengers

deliver thee: tell you

dues of rejoicing: your proper share of happiness at the news

Lay it to/thy heart, ...: ponder it and keep it secret

th' milk of human-kindness: humane and tender feelings that human beings have in common

To catch the nearest way: to seize what you want in the most ruthless, direct manner

thou wouldst be great, ...: you would like to be great

Art not without ambition, ... attend it: Your ambition is not accompanied by the wickedness that must accompany all ambition.

what thou wouldst ... holily: If you greatly desired something, you would like to get it by fair and honest means.

wouldst not play false ... win: You would not like to cheat, and yet you would like to have what is not rightly yours.

thou'dst have, great Glamis, ... undone: You would like the crown, for which you will be forced to commit murder; your fear of committing this murder is greater than any desire you might feel to undo it once it is done.

That which cries: here 'that' is the crown; the 'that' in line 23 is the murder.

Hie: hurry

And chastise ... withal: and drive out with strong bold words whatever hinders you from gaining the crown, which fate and supernatural help seem prepared to grant you

Thou'rt mad to say it: Lady Macbeth is so startled by the attendant's news that she loses control. In lines 31–2 she recovers immediately to make a reasonable point.

had the speed of him: rode faster than him

The raven ... battlements: The raven, traditionally a bird of ill omen with a hoarse cry, will sound even hoarser than usual as it heralds the entrance of Duncan to Macbeth's castle (the place of his murder). The raven's unusual hoarseness will come from its repeated cries emphasising the determination of Lady Macbeth to leave no doubt about Duncan's fate.

39–40 *Come, you spirits ... thoughts:* Lady Macbeth is formally asking the evil spirits who support those with murderous intentions to take away her womanly qualities. *mortal thoughts:* thoughts of death

42–6 *Make thick ... and it!:* Thicken my blood so that the natural feelings of pity and kindness will not be able to flow through my veins and reach my heart and that no kindly sentiments will weaken my deadly resolution or hinder its achievement.

47 *And take my milk for gall:* Take my milk and replace it with gall. This is the commonly accepted meaning. Gall is a bitter substance which was supposed to induce anger. But 'take' can also have the meaning of 'infect', and if it does here, the sense is 'Infect, bewitch my milk so that it may become gall'. *murdering ministers:* agents of murder

48–9 *Wherever ... mischief!:* The reference is to invisible ('sightless') evil spirits who preside over or attend upon unnatural and wicked deeds in the world of man or nature.

50 *pall:* shroud
dunnest: darkest

51 *That my keen knife ... makes:* The use of 'my' here has caused some editors to suppose that at this point Lady Macbeth intends to murder Duncan herself.

52 *the blanket of the dark:* This is an image of darkness covering the earth like a blanket. She is praying for a darkness so intense that the powers of Heaven will not be able to see the deed or to cry halt.

54 *the all-hail hereafter:* (Macbeth's) future kingship

55–7 *Thy letters ... instant:* Your heart has given me an anticipation of the future and its promises which would otherwise be unknown to me. The kind of future she contemplates here is not the one that is actually in store for them.

59 *as he purposes:* At least he intends to leave tomorrow.

ATTENDANT

So please you, it is true: our Thane is coming;
One of my fellows had the speed of him,
35 Who, almost dead for breath, had scarcely more
Than would make up his message.

LADY MACBETH

Give him tending:
He brings great news. *[Exit Attendant.]* The raven himself
is hoarse
That croaks the fatal entrance of Duncan
Under my battlements. Come, you spirits
40 That tend on mortal thoughts, unsex me here,
And fill me from the crown to the toe top full
Of direst cruelty! Make thick my blood,
Stop up th'access and passage to remorse,
That no compunctious visitings of nature
45 Shake my fell purpose, nor keep peace between
The effect and it! Come to my woman's breasts,
And take my milk for gall, you murdering ministers,
Wherever in your sightless substances
You wait on nature's mischief! Come, thick night,
50 And pall thee in the dunnest smoke of hell,
That my keen knife see not the wound it makes,
Nor heaven peep through the blanket of the dark,
To cry 'Hold, hold!'

Enter MACBETH

Great Glamis! Worthy Cawdor!
Greater than both, by the all-hail hereafter!
55 Thy letters have transported me beyond
This ignorant present, and I feel now
The future in the instant.

MACBETH

My dearest love,
Duncan comes here tonight.

LADY MACBETH

And when goes hence?

MACBETH

Tomorrow, as he purposes.

[Handwritten annotations:] soliloquy — she has already decided to kill the old men — she has no idea what she is asking for — moral blindness — this is an unnatural request — IRONY (she asks for light later) — Diabolical imagery. — she obviously means a lot to him

LADY MACBETH

O, never
60 Shall sun that morrow see!
Your face, my Thane, is as a book where men
May read strange matters. To beguile the time,
Look like the time; bear welcome in your eye,
Your hand, your tongue: look like the innocent flower,
65 But be the serpent under't. He that's coming
Must be provided for; and you shall put
This night's great business into my dispatch;
Which shall to all our nights and days to come
Give solely sovereign sway and masterdom.

Appearance vs. reality

Appearance vs. reality

MACBETH

We will speak further.

LADY MACBETH

70   Only look up clear:
To alter favour ever is to fear.
Leave all the rest to me.

Exeunt.

62–3

65–7

69

70

70–1

The words have sinister overtones if the actor pauses after 'Tomorrow', but this can reduce the effectiveness of Lady Macbeth's next line.
To beguile ... like the time: To deceive those around you, look like everybody else; do not look as if you were planning a terrible deed (see 1, 7, 81–2).
He that's coming ... my dispatch: Provision must be made for our visitor, and you shall leave the management of the affair to me. 'Provided for' and 'dispatch' have cruel double meanings, the first suggesting both the arrangements a hostess would make for her guest and the provision she will make for his murder; the word 'dispatch' means both 'management' and 'to kill'.
Give solely ... masterdom: give absolute power
We will speak further: Macbeth hesitates; he has his doubts.
Only look ... fear: Try to appear free of guilt, because if you show a worried expression, this may arouse suspicion and then you will have something to worry about.

'Come, you spirits / That tend on mortal thoughts, unsex me here, /
And fill me from the crown to the toe top full / Of direst cruelty!'
(1, 5, 39–42)

EXAMINATION-BASED QUESTIONS

- What exactly does Lady Macbeth think of her husband's character in her opening soliloquy? Why is she worried?
- Do Lady Macbeth's impressions of her husband's character match those we get from the earlier scenes?
- What do we learn about Lady Macbeth from her two soliloquies in this scene?
- What is the relationship between husband and wife at this point in the play?
- Deception, concealment and hypocrisy are key themes in the play. How are they conveyed in this scene?
- The knife and blanket referred to by Lady Macbeth have more than one significance. Explain.
- 'He that's coming / Must be provided for' (65–6). What is implied here?
- Suggest how Lady Macbeth should read the letter from Macbeth – for example, refer to her facial expressions, tone of voice and gestures. Using the same headings, suggest how she might deliver her speech to comment on the news contained in the letter.

KEY THEMES AND IMPORTANT FACTS

- The continuing theme of false appearance is strongly reinforced in this scene by Lady Macbeth ('look like the innocent flower / But be the serpent under't', 64–5).
- The imagery used by Lady Macbeth to describe her proposed reception of Duncan into her home reflects the perversity of her character at this point. She speaks of her 'keen knife' and 'the blanket of the dark' as images of murder. A normal hostess would think of a blanket as an image of hospitality.
- Lady Macbeth's 'Come, you spirits' (39) advances the supernatural theme.

Act One
– Scene Six –
[Inverness. Before Macbeth's Castle.]

PLOT SUMMARY

Duncan, accompanied by his courtiers, arrives at Macbeth's castle and is greeted with excessive expressions of courtesy and flattery by Lady Macbeth.

This is a gentle, peaceful scene, suggesting an unruffled calm before a great storm. The speeches of Duncan and Banquo feature images of fruitful natural life and order, the kind of order Macbeth and Lady Macbeth reject in their speeches and deeds. Irony predominates throughout. The chief victim, Duncan, enters the place of his execution full of praise for the beauty of its setting and

surroundings. He compliments the chief architect of his murder. She in turn is eloquently convincing in her protestations of loyalty to her victim. Her mention of their 'service' (14) to Duncan, of the 'honours deep and broad wherewith / Your Majesty loads our house' (17–18), is touched with its own macabre irony. She is certainly much more accomplished at concealing her real feelings and intentions than Macbeth appeared to be in the similar circumstances of Act 1, Scene 4. Duncan's position as the pathetic victim of deceitful appearance is underlined to the very end. He interprets Macbeth's haste in reaching the castle before him as a sign of great love. The irony of Duncan's situation is visually expressed at the close of the scene when Lady Macbeth leads him by the hand into the castle and to his doom.

Hautboys: oboes

Hautboys and torches. Enter DUNCAN, MALCOLM,
DONALBAIN, BANQUO, LENNOX, MACDUFF,
ROSS, ANGUS, *and Attendants*

DUNCAN *Dramatic irony - audience knows what character does not*

This castle hath a pleasant seat; the air
Nimbly and sweetly recommends itself
Unto our gentle senses.

BANQUO *Bird motif - this contrasts with raven already mentioned*   This guest of summer,
The temple-haunting martlet, does approve
5 By his loved mansionry that the heaven's breath
Smells wooingly here: no jutty, frieze,
Buttress, nor coign of vantage, but this bird
Hath made his pendent bed and procreant cradle.
Where they most breed and haunt, I have observed
The air is delicate. *Banquo does not seem to suspect that evil is afoot*

Enter LADY MACBETH

DUNCAN *more dramatic irony*
10   See, see, our honoured hostess.
The love that follows us sometime is our trouble,
Which still we thank as love. Herein I teach you,
How you shall bid God 'ield us for your pains,
And thank us for your trouble.

LADY MACBETH
She is clearly being a hypocrite here All our service,
15 In every point twice done, and then done double,
Were poor and single business to contend
Against those honours deep and broad wherewith
Your Majesty loads our house. For those of old,
And the late dignities heaped up to them,
We rest your hermits.

DUNCAN
20   Where's the Thane of Cawdor?
We coursed him at the heels, and had a purpose
To be his purveyor; but he rides well,
And his great love, sharp as his spur, hath holp him
To his home before us. Fair and noble hostess,
We are your guest tonight. *more dramatic irony*

Macbeth's love for his wife is clear too all

---

1 *seat:* situation, position
1–3 *the air ... senses:* The
freshness and sweetness of the
air calms our senses.
3–6 *This guest ... here:* The house-
martin, who likes to nest in
churches, proves ('does
approve') by choosing this
place for his nest ('his loved
mansionry') that the air is
pleasant.
4 *temple-haunting:* frequenting
places of worship
5 *mansionry:* nests
6 *wooingly:* enticingly
8 *pendant:* hanging
procreant: fertile
10 *delicate:* delightful
6–10 *no jutty ... delicate:* This bird
has used every available
projection for nesting; its
favourite nesting places are
associated with fresh, clear air.
10–14 *See, see ... trouble:* Note the
contrast between the natural,
unaffected exchanges between
Duncan and Banquo and the
complex formality of these
lines. Duncan is saying: 'The
love my subjects show me can
be a bother to me, but I still
accept it with gratitude. I am
showing you that you should
ask God to reward me for the
inconvenience I am causing
you and that you should be
grateful to me for my visit,
which, though it may be
troublesome to you, is inspired
by my love for you.'
19 *late dignities:* most recent
honours
20 *We rest your hermits:* We
remain in your debt. A hermit
is a mendicant and therefore a
debtor to those giving alms.
21 *We coursed ... heels:*
We were close behind him.
22 *To be his purveyor:* A purveyor
was an officer who went ahead
of the king to arrange his
accommodation. Notice that it
is Duncan who sees himself as
Macbeth's purveyor, as if the
latter were already king – one
of the many ironies in a scene
remarkable for irony.
23 *holp:* helped

LADY MACBETH

25   Your servants ever
Have theirs, themselves, and what is theirs, in compt,
To make their audit at your Highness' pleasure,
Still to return your own.

DUNCAN
                              Give me your hand;
Conduct me to mine host. We love him highly,
30   And shall continue our graces towards him.
By your leave, hostess.

   Exeunt.

25–8   *Your servants … your own:*
We, your servants, keep our own servants, ourselves and everything we have at your majesty's disposal, since everything we are and have derives from you.

26   *in compt:* in readiness, in trust (for the king)

27   *To make their audit:* to render an account of all that they have

---

EXAMINATION-BASED QUESTIONS

- How would you describe the tone of the opening speeches of Duncan and Banquo?
- This scene, like Act 1, Scene 4, is full of irony. Identify some examples.
- Duncan is the central figure in this scene. What kind of impression does he make?
- How would you describe Lady Macbeth's treatment of Duncan here? Compare her speeches with those of Macbeth to Duncan in Act 1, Scene 4. In what respect do the two sets of speeches differ?

KEY THEMES AND IMPORTANT FACTS

- This scene characterises Duncan on his last appearance before his death. It also emphasises the pitiful contrast between the guest and his hosts – Duncan's total trust set against Lady Macbeth's shocking reference to 'your Highness' pleasure' (27).

Act One
– Scene Seven –
[Inverness. Macbeth's Castle.]

PLOT SUMMARY

Macbeth detaches himself from the company and displays much confusion of mind and spirit over the plan to murder Duncan. By the time Lady Macbeth joins him, he has decided not to proceed. In a remarkable exercise of will, she overcomes his doubts and scruples.

The scene opens with **Macbeth's remarkable soliloquy**. Here he analyses the implications for himself of the murder he is contemplating. What is most significant about this speech is its clear analysis of the reality behind what he is about to do and its frank acknowledgement of the evil involved in the murder of the king. Not even Macbeth's worst enemies could come up with a more powerful condemnation of his deed than the one he himself sets out here. He gives all the right reasons for not proceeding to kill Duncan: such deeds, he knows, tend to plague those who perform them; Duncan is his relative as well as his anointed king; he will be violating the sacred laws of hospitality if he kills the man he should be protecting against harm; Duncan has been a just and good king, and heaven will cry out in condemnation of his murder. Against such overwhelming reasons for not killing Duncan, **he can think of only one reason for carrying out the deed**: an inordinate ambition of the kind that often leads to disaster. This soliloquy is a splendidly reasoned argument against the murder. It closes on a note of irony, with Macbeth telling himself that ambition is his only 'spur' (25). With the entry of Lady Macbeth, he has another spur to goad him on, as we soon discover.

The part of the scene following this soliloquy is of critical importance, since what happens in it **launches Macbeth firmly on the path of self-destruction**. Lady Macbeth is the active agent throughout this scene (note her dominance again in the banquet scene). Macbeth's defences against her varied assaults are hopelessly inadequate; the chief dramatic interest in the scene is her brilliant deployment of her great resources of will against her weaker partner. The nature of her triumph is illustrated in the short time that elapses (only 50 lines of dialogue) between Macbeth's determination to 'proceed no further in this business' (31) and 'I am settled, and bend up / Each corporal agent to this terrible feat' (79–80).

It is interesting to watch her at work as she batters down his defences one by one. Lady Macbeth's arguments, all in the form of rebukes, are of four kinds: her husband is changeable and lacking in resolution (35–8); his love for her is not what she thought it was if he will not do this much for her (38–9); his determination is no better than that of a drunkard, 'green and pale' after a hangover (37–9); and he lacks courage and manliness (39–54). The last rebuke is her most effective **method of attack** because it is the most deeply wounding, since courage and physical prowess are Macbeth's major claims to self-esteem and public respect; without them, he is nothing. Her cries of 'coward', 'poor cat', 'then you were a man', 'you would / Be so much more the man' (43, 45, 49, 50–51) ring in his ears until resistance is no longer possible. The turning point in the scene, and in the play, comes with his words, 'If we should fail?' (59).

Up to this, Macbeth's counter-arguments have been moral ones. He does not want to show base ingratitude to his recent benefactor who has so honoured him (32) and the deed would be unworthy of a human being (46–7). But now **Lady Macbeth has succeeded in transferring the argument from the moral plane to that of mere expediency and planning**. Macbeth has given in on principle. All that remains for her to do is to suggest some practical scheme – or at least one that will temporarily convince him – and he will be ready to proceed. Her plan is not a very convincing one and would scarcely pass muster in real life. His enthusiastic comments on it (72–7) are almost simple-minded; that he can accept such a plan and even admire it shows the extent of his submission and mental captivity at this point. His 'Bring forth men-children only!' (72) is an endorsement of her ideas on 'manliness' (39–54).

The scene has many echoes and anticipations of other parts of the play. The clothing image that Macbeth uses to express pride in his newly won honours ('Golden opinions ... worn now in their newest gloss ... cast aside', 33–5) is one of a series beginning with his incredulous 'why do you dress me / In borrowed robes?' (1, 3, 108–9) and culminating in the picture of kingship as 'a giant's robe / Upon a dwarfish thief' (5, 2, 21–2). Lady Macbeth sarcastically takes up the clothing image in one of Shakespeare's most astonishing mixed metaphors, reminding her husband that he had dressed himself in the garment of hope as well as those of 'Golden opinions' and that the former garments now seem in a sorry state (as well as looking like a newly awakened drunkard). The references to 'act and valour' (40) on the one hand and 'desire' (41) on the other are often paralleled elsewhere. In this scene we are made vividly aware of a **great gap between Macbeth's desire to be king and his willingness to act in order to make himself so**. Later, the gap is closed. He will seal the fate of Macduff's family with: 'Strange things I have in head that will to hand, / Which must be acted ere they may be scanned' (3, 4, 139–40).

The lines 'What beast was't then / That made you break this enterprise to me?' (47–8) have been the subject of much editorial comment. It is clear that the dramatic force of 'beast' lies in its powerful juxtaposition with 'man' in lines 46 and 49–51. **Macbeth wants to be a man, not the subhuman brute that murdering Duncan would make him**; what subhuman force, then, his wife asks, made him discuss with her the possibility of the murder? Most of the critical debate has centred on the significance of 'break this enterprise', which seems to suggest that Macbeth has already talked of the murder to her. Since there is no sign of this in the text as we have it, it is possible that Lady Macbeth is referring to the contents of his letter (1, 5, 1–13) and is now reading more into it, for her own purposes, than is actually there. We must remember that people arguing excitedly, as she is doing here, often go beyond the facts of the situation in order to make their point.

Lady Macbeth's reference to her child (54–9) has often been interpreted to suggest that she is a totally unnatural and unwomanly creature. She has, it is true, prayed to be filled with 'direst cruelty' and to be freed from all 'remorse' (1, 5, 42–3). It has already been suggested that she is to be seen, after this invocation, as the willing victim of demoniacal possession (see the commentary on Act 1, Scene 5). But the passage about the child cannot be used as further evidence for this. Indeed, far from suggesting that she is unnaturally cruel, it may readily be interpreted in the opposite sense.

Lady Macbeth is not saying that she has murderous feelings towards her infant, but rather, she is suggesting that to kill her infant is the most horrible act that she can conceive of and the most revolting to her own feelings. Her point is to convince Macbeth that he should not break his solemn oath. **She is making a wildly exaggerated comparison between the evil of breaking an oath and the evil of killing her own infant**, in effect saying that she could not contemplate either of these.

	Enter a Sewer: This is a servant who must sample the food before it is eaten by the guests.
1–7	*If it were done ... life to come:* The general sense of these lines is as follows: If, when it is committed, the murder is really over and done with, then the sooner it is committed, the better. If there are no adverse consequences for me in this life, I shall be satisfied, since I am prepared to ignore the possible consequences for me in a future life.
3	*trammel:* trap in a net
4	*his surcease:* Duncan's death
5–6	*here:* in this life
6	*bank and shoal of time:* this narrow stretch of human life as opposed to the vastness of eternity
7	*jump:* risk
7–12	*But in these cases ... our own lips:* In the case of crimes such as murder, the criminal always faces punishment even in this life, in that by murdering he teaches others to murder and he in turn may become a victim. There is a strict justice governing human affairs which ensures that those who perpetrate crimes will be repaid in kind. Macbeth's sentiments are a variation of Christ's words in Matthew: 'All who draw the sword will perish by the sword.'
17–18	*Hath borne ... office:* Duncan has used his royal powers gently and mercifully and has been free from wrongdoing in the discharge of his duties.
18–25	*his virtues ... wind:* Duncan's virtues, enumerated above, will

Hautboys and torches. Enter a Sewer, and divers Servants with dishes and service over the stage.
Then enter MACBETH — a key soliloquy

MACBETH — a key soliloquy

If it were done, when 'tis done, then 'twere well
It were done quickly: if the assassination
Could trammel up the consequence, and catch,
With his surcease, success; that but this blow
5   Might be the be-all and the end-all; here —
But here upon this bank and shoal of time —
We'd jump the life to come. — there is a fear of hell here *(risk)*
                    But in these cases
We still have judgement here, that we but teach
Bloody instructions, which being taught return
10   To plague the inventor. This even-handed justice
Commends the ingredients of our poisoned chalice
To our own lips. — This is exactly what happens to him.
                    He's here in double trust:
First, as I am his kinsman and his subject —
Strong both against the deed; then, as his host,
15   Who should against his murderer shut the door,
Not bear the knife myself.
                    Besides, this Duncan
Hath borne his faculties so meek, hath been   more divine
So clear in his great office, that his virtues   imagery used to
Will plead like angels, trumpet-tongued, against   describe Duncan
20   The deep damnation of his taking-off;
And pity, like a naked new-born babe,
Striding the blast, or heaven's cherubin, horsed
Upon the sightless couriers of the air,
Shall blow the horrid deed in every eye,
That tears shall drown the wind.

25   I have no spur
To prick the sides of my intent, but only
Vaulting ambition, which o'er-leaps itself
And falls on the other — *A central flaw in*
Macbeths character
Enter LADY MACBETH   *He has a high degree*
of self-knowledge
How now! What news?   25–8

LADY MACBETH
He has almost supped: why have you left the chamber?

MACBETH
Hath he asked for me?

LADY MACBETH   29
30   Know you not he has?   34

MACBETH
We will proceed no further in this business: 35–8
He hath honoured me of late; and I have bought
Golden opinions from all sorts of people,
Which would be worn now in their newest gloss,
Not cast aside so soon. *Clothing imagery*

LADY MACBETH
35   Was the hope drunk
Wherein you dressed yourself? Hath it slept since,
And wakes it now, to look so green and pale   37
At what it did so freely? From this time   39
Such I account thy love. Art thou afeared
40 To be the same in thine own act and valour   42
As thou art in desire? Wouldst thou have that
Which thou esteem'st the ornament of life,
And live a coward in thine own esteem, *Belloncs bridegroom*
wont like
Letting 'I dare not' wait upon 'I would',   *this*
Like the poor cat i'the adage?   44–5

MACBETH
45   Prithee, peace:
I dare do all that may become a man; *Macbeth is vulnerable*
Who dares do more, is none. *to attacks on his*
masculinity

LADY MACBETH
What beast was't then
That made you break this enterprise to me?   47–8
When you durst do it, then you were a man;

cry out in horror at his damn-
able murder. Pity, in the guise of
an innocent child, and the
angels of heaven ('cherubin')
will ride on the winds ('sightless
couriers') and blow Macbeth's
deed into every eye, and tears
of pity will drown the storm,
just as wind abates in a shower
of rain.
I have no spur … the other:
I have no incentive to carry out
the projected murder except
ambition, which is like an over-
eager rider who vaults so
eagerly into the saddle that he
falls on the other side of the
horse. Lady Macbeth enters at
this point, however, and
provides him with another spur.
almost supped: almost finished
supper
worn … gloss: The golden
opinions are like new clothes,
which should be enjoyed in all
their novelty.
Was the hope drunk …
freely?: Lady Macbeth is
referring to his hope of being
king. She is suggesting that
this hope was inspired by
drunkenness and that
Macbeth, now fully awake to
reality like a man with a
hangover, is afraid to pursue
the plans he made when he
was drunk. The clothing
metaphor of line 34 is
continued in these lines.
green and pale: sickly
Such I account thy love: I will
think your love is liable to
change in the same way.
the ornament of life: The
meaning of this is not certain.
Most editors take it to refer to
the crown. However, it may
also refer to Macbeth's desire
to enjoy the approval of others
(the 'Golden opinions' above)
or to his desire for self-esteem.
Letting … adage: The adage in
question is an old proverb which
went: 'The cat would eat fish,
and would not wet her feet.'
Applied to Macbeth, the image
is of a pathetic individual,
hopelessly torn between wanting
the crown desperately and
fearing equally desperately to
take the only course of action
that will give it to him.
What beast was't then … to
me?: The force of Lady
Macbeth's question depends
on the two previous lines.

Macbeth has flatly declared that he dares not do what is contrary to his manly nature. Lady Macbeth is arguing in reply that if murder is not a manly thing, then a beast must have prompted Macbeth to suggest the killing of Duncan to her in the first place. One problem critics have found in her question is that there is nothing in the play so far to indicate that it was, in fact, Macbeth who had suggested the murder. Whether this is an example of Shakespeare's carelessness or is due to the absence from the present text of a scene that was once there does not really matter. We may take it, if we wish, that at some point Macbeth has raised the subject of murdering Duncan.

49–51 *When you durst ... the man:* If you dared become king through murder, you would show yourself to be a really brave man.

51–4 *Nor time nor place ... unmake you:* When you originally planned to murder Duncan, neither a suitable time nor a suitable place was available, and still you were eager to provide both; now that both are available, their appropriateness reduces you to unmanly weakness.

54–9 *I have given suck ... done to this:* She would be prepared to dash out the brains of her own infant rather than break the kind of solemn resolution that she claims Macbeth has made.

59 *We fail?:* These two words can have a variety of meanings depending on the inclusion or omission of the question mark. Include it, as in this edition of the text, and put the emphasis on 'we', and Lady Macbeth is asking: 'how could we fail?' Take away the question mark, and she is saying: 'Then we fail, and there is no more to be said.'

60–1 *But screw ... fail:* Strengthen your courage to its utmost limit. Some editors think the image is of a soldier tightening his crossbow, others that Shakespeare was thinking of the strings of a viol.

63 *chamberlains:* attendants on the royal bedchamber

50 And, to be more than what you were, you would
Be so much more the man. Nor time nor place
Did then adhere, and yet you would make both:
They have made themselves, and that their fitness now
Does unmake you. I have given suck, and know
55 How tender 'tis to love the babe that milks me —
I would, while it was smiling in my face,
Have plucked my nipple from his boneless gums,
And dashed the brains out, had I so sworn as you
Have done to this.

MACBETH

If we should fail?

LADY MACBETH

We fail?
60 But screw your courage to the sticking-place,
And we'll not fail. When Duncan is asleep
(Whereto the rather shall his day's hard journey
Soundly invite him) his two chamberlains
Will I with wine and wassail so convince
65 That memory, the warder of the brain,
Shall be a fume, and the receipt of reason
A limbeck only; when in swinish sleep
Their drenched natures lie as in a death,
What cannot you and I perform upon
70 The unguarded Duncan? What not put upon
His spongy officers, who shall bear the guilt
Of our great quell?

MACBETH

Bring forth men-children only!
For thy undaunted mettle should compose
Nothing but males. Will it not be received,
75 When we have marked with blood those sleepy two
Of his own chamber and used their very daggers,
That they have done't?

LADY MACBETH

Who dares receive it other,
As we shall make our griefs and clamour roar
Upon his death?

MACBETH

I am settled, and bend up

33

80   Each corporal agent to this terrible feat.
     Away, and mock the time with fairest show:
     False face must hide what the false heart doth know.

       Exeunt.   Appearance vs.
               reality

EXAMINATION-BASED QUESTIONS

- Describe Macbeth's state of mind in his opening soliloquy.
- Macbeth is making a strong case in this soliloquy. What is the nature of this case?
- Macbeth is often described as a reluctant murderer. Does this soliloquy confirm this description? Explain.
- Discuss the relationship between husband and wife in this scene.
- This scene marks a considerable change in Macbeth's attitude to killing Duncan. How is this change brought about?
- Lady Macbeth dominates this scene. How?
- What outstanding qualities does Lady Macbeth display here?

KEY THEMES AND IMPORTANT FACTS

- This scene exhibits powerful suspense and tension, as Macbeth's future hangs in the balance.
- The suspense arises from the uncertain outcome of a battle of wills between Macbeth and his wife, as she wants to undermine his resistance to murdering Duncan.
- Shakespeare keeps the suspense alive by letting the audience initially think that Macbeth will probably not proceed with the murder. His great soliloquy ('If it were done…', 1–28) and his speech beginning 'We will proceed no further in this business' (31–5) confirm this impression.
- The vital dramatic conflict in the scene is brief but impressive. Lady Macbeth exerts her mighty willpower to undermine Macbeth's moral objections to the murder. Macbeth's 'If we should fail?' (59) shows how well she has succeeded. Her success is complete when Macbeth readily accepts her plan for the murder and comments on the plan with enthusiasm (72–7).

64   *wassail:* festive carousing
      convince: overcome, overpower
65–7 *That memory … A limbeck only:* so that memory, which guards and preserves the consciousness, will be engulfed in fumes, and the part of the brain where reason is lodged will become little better than a mere vessel for distilling alcohol ('limbeck')
70   *put upon:* attribute blame to
72   *quell:* murder, seen here by Lady Macbeth as a magnificent enterprise
72–4 *Bring forth … Nothing but males:* Your children should all be males, since your unconquerable spirit makes you the natural begetter of offspring having manly virtue. Macbeth's view of manly qualities has changed since lines 46–7 of this scene.
74   *received:* accepted by those who come to know of the murder
77   *Who … other:* Who will dare to think of any other explanation?
79–80 *I am settled … feat:* I am determined and will exert all my powers to perform the murder.
81–2 *Away … know:* Let us go and deceive those around us with a false outward show; guilty people must be careful to conceal their feelings by putting on a mask of innocence. Macbeth is now using his wife's kind of language, and reflecting her thoughts (see 1, 5, 62–5).
81   *the time:* the outside world

'Bring forth men-children only! / For thy undaunted mettle should compose / Nothing but males.' (1, 7, 72–4)

Act Two

– Scene One –

[Inverness. Courtyard of Macbeth's Castle.]

PLOT SUMMARY

Banquo enters the dark courtyard with his son, Fleance. Macbeth's entry is heralded by a servant with a torch. There is some polite but uneasy discussion between Macbeth and Banquo about their future prospects and their relationship. Macbeth sends a servant to arrange for the ringing of the bell as a signal that all is in readiness for the murder. Alone, Macbeth has a vision of a dagger, draws his own weapon to test the vision against the reality, and then imagines his visionary dagger covered with blood. The vision fades and Macbeth prepares himself for his murderous task, moving towards the king's bedchamber as the bell rings.

The scene begins on a note of foreboding. The starless night has a symbolic significance; the world is given over to the powers of darkness. Banquo has been troubled by cursed dreams. The relationship between Macbeth and Banquo seems no longer that of loyal comrades or friends. Banquo is on his guard, sword at the ready, in a place where he should feel like a secure and honoured guest. He acts like a sentinel on duty and challenges Macbeth ('Who's there?', 10) in Macbeth's own castle. The latter responds to the incongruous challenge without, apparently, noticing anything odd. Their discussion of their meeting with the Weird Sisters is inconclusive. Macbeth is less than honest in his comments; Banquo dismisses the notion that Macbeth might be tempted to gain advancement at the expense of his (Banquo's) honour.

It is clear from this scene that Banquo, like Macbeth, has been disturbed by what the witches have promised. But his response is to struggle manfully against whatever temptations beset him as a result. He calls on the 'Merciful Powers' (7), those spirits assigned by God to restrain demons, to protect him from giving way to evil thoughts. Macbeth and Lady Macbeth, on the other hand, enlist the aid of evil powers in pursuing their aims. Macbeth's imagination and his conscience have already told him emphatically what he must not do; his failure lies in his lack of will to follow these promptings. Banquo, on the other hand, has the will to avoid what he knows is wrong and to seek supernatural aid in doing so.

The dagger soliloquy is important for the impression it conveys of Macbeth's state of mind just before the murder of Duncan. The phantom dagger is not to be regarded as an additional temptation, since it is clear from the soliloquy that Macbeth has already decided on the murder. When he says that the dagger is marshalling him 'the way that I was going' (42), he is imagining the dagger pointing towards Duncan's room; he is also conscious of the fact that the dagger is indicating a deed that he has already decided on.

Enter BANQUO, *and* FLEANCE *with a torch before him*

BANQUO
How goes the night, boy?

FLEANCE
The moon is down; I have not heard the clock.

BANQUO
And she goes down at twelve.

FLEANCE
I take't, 'tis later, sir.

BANQUO
Hold, take my sword. There's husbandry in heaven;
5   Their candles are all out. Take thee that too. *pathetic*
fallacy
A heavy summons lies like lead upon me,
contrast to Macbeth, the sleep motif
And yet I would not sleep. Merciful Powers,
Restrain in me the cursed thoughts that nature
Gives way to in repose!

Enter MACBETH, *and a* SERVANT *with a torch*

Give me my sword —
10   Who's there?

MACBETH
A friend. *IRONY*

BANQUO
What, sir, not yet at rest? The king's a-bed:
He hath been in unusual pleasure, and
Sent forth great largess to your offices.
15   This diamond he greets your wife withal,
By the name of most kind hostess; and shut up
In measureless content.

MACBETH
                              Being unprepared,
Our will became the servant to defect,
Which else should free have wrought.

BANQUO
                                   All's well.
20   I dreamt last night of the three Weird Sisters:
To you they have showed some truth.

4	*husbandry:* thrift
5	*Their candles:* the stars
	Take thee that too: Banquo is handing Fleance another piece of equipment, probably his dagger and belt.
6	*A heavy summons:* a call to sleep, weariness
7	*I would not sleep:* I do not want to sleep. This is because Banquo fears the bad dreams which haunt his sleep. (See line 20 of this scene.)
	Merciful Powers: The 'Powers' in question are those angels whose function it is to combat and restrain the activities of evil spirits.
14	*largess to your offices:* generous gifts to your servants' quarters
15–17	*This diamond ... content:* Duncan has given your wife this diamond as a tribute to her kindness as a hostess and has finished his day in a state of unbounded happiness.
16	*shut up:* retired to bed
17–18	*Being unprepared ... defect:* The 'defect' here is the lack of preparation for Duncan's visit. Macbeth is saying that since he and his wife were unprepared, their desire to extend more generous hospitality to the king could not be fulfilled.
19	*Which else should free have wrought:* otherwise our hospitality would have been unlimited

MACBETH

a deliberate lie

I think not of them:
Yet, when we can entreat an hour to serve,
We would spend it in some words upon that business,
If you would grant the time.

22	*entreat an hour to serve:* find a suitable time

BANQUO

At your kind'st leisure.

MACBETH

25 If you shall cleave to my consent, when 'tis,
It shall make honour for you.

25–6	*If you shall cleave ... for you:* If you follow my lead or fit in with my plans when the time is right, it will mean advancement for you.
26–9	*So I lose none ... counselled:* If I do not suffer any loss of honour in seeking to add to my honours or titles, but can keep a clear conscience and an untarnished loyalty, then I am ready to listen to what you have to say.

BANQUO

So I lose none
In seeking to augment it, but still keep
My bosom franchised and allegiance clear,
I shall be counselled.

MACBETH

Good repose the while.

BANQUO

30 Thanks, sir: the like to you.

Exeunt BANQUO *and* FLEANCE.

MACBETH – SOLILOQUY

Go bid thy mistress, when my drink is ready
She strike upon the bell. Get thee to bed.

Exit SERVANT.

31	*drink:* The drink is the posset (hot milk curdled by wine or ale) for the servants drugged by Lady Macbeth (see 2, 2, 7 – note).
32	*bell:* The bell will be the signal for the murder.
36–7	*sensible ... sight:* Can you be felt as well as seen?
39	*heat-oppressed:* fevered
40	*palpable:* capable of being felt, tangible
41	*As this which now I draw:* Macbeth here draws his dagger.
42	*Thou marshall'st ... going:* Macbeth imagines the dagger pointing the way to Duncan's chamber. He is saying to the dagger: 'You are inciting me to commit an act which I had already decided on.'
44–5	*Mine eyes ... rest:* Either the dagger is an illusion, in which case my eyes are fooling me, or it is real, in which case my eyes are able to grasp realities outside the scope of the other senses.
46	*dudgeon:* hilt *gouts:* drops

Is this a dagger which I see before me,
The handle toward my hand? Come, let me clutch thee.
35 I have thee not, and yet I see thee still. *Appearance*
Art thou not, fatal vision, sensible *vs.*
To feeling as to sight? Or art thou but *reality*
A dagger of the mind, a false creation,
Proceeding from the heat-oppressed brain?
40 I see thee yet, in form as palpable
As this which now I draw.
Thou marshall'st me the way that I was going;
And such an instrument I was to use.
Mine eyes are made the fools o'th'other senses,
45 Or else worth all the rest: I see thee still;
And on thy blade and dudgeon gouts of blood,
Which was not so before. There's no such thing:

It is the bloody business which informs   48

Thus to mine eyes. Now o'er the one half-world   49

50 Nature seems dead, and wicked dreams abuse

The curtained sleep; witchcraft celebrates   51

Pale Hecate's offerings; and withered Murder,

Alarumed by his sentinel, the wolf,   51-2

Whose howl's his watch, thus with his stealthy pace,

55 With Tarquin's ravishing strides, toward his design

Moves like a ghost. Thou sure and firm-set earth,   52-6

Hear not my steps which way they walk, for fear

Thy very stones prate of my whereabout,

And take the present horror from the time,

60 Which now suits with it. Whiles I threat, he lives:

Words to the heat of deeds too cold breath gives.

A bell rings.

I go, and it is done: the bell invites me.   56-8

Hear it not, Duncan, for it is a knell

That summons thee to heaven, or to hell.

Exit.

    58

    59-60

    60-1

Right column glosses:

informs/Thus: takes this particular form or shape

the one half-world: this hemisphere

curtained sleep: The imagined sleeper is in a four-poster bed with curtains.

witchcraft ... offerings: Witches are taking part in rituals in honour of their goddess Hecate.

withered Murder ... a ghost: The murderer (personified as Murder), alerted by his watchman, the wolf, whose howl serves as a watchword, steals silently and stealthily towards his victim, as the infamous Roman Tarquin once crept towards his virtuous victim, Lucretia, to rape her. The rape of Lucretia is the subject of a poem by Shakespeare.

Thou sure ... whereabout: Macbeth is afraid that the particular direction his steps will take towards Duncan's chamber will cause the stones of the earth to reveal all. This is the significance of 'which way they walk'.

prate: prattle, chatter

And take ... with it: If the stones cry out, they will break the horrible silence which now prevails, a silence which suits the occasion.

Whiles I threat ... gives: While I am here threatening to kill him, he is still alive; speaking too long about a proposed action tends to postpone its performance (see 4, 1, 146–8).

Handwritten annotations: The language here is ghostly and diabolical — also the classical reference (TARQUIN)

EXAMINATION-BASED QUESTIONS

- The opening of the scene is tense and troubled. How is this impression conveyed?
- Describe Banquo's state of mind in this scene.
- How would you describe the Macbeth–Banquo relationship here?
- Macbeth's soliloquy gives us a final glimpse of his mind before the murder. What does it reveal about his thoughts and feelings?

KEY THEMES AND IMPORTANT FACTS

- The passage in this scene that gives the most scope to the actor is Macbeth's dagger soliloquy (33–61). The actor's movements, gestures and facial expressions help to illustrate the meaning of the passage. For example, Macbeth imitates the 'stealthy pace' of murder (54) by taking stealthy steps across the stage.

Act Two

– Scene Two –

[Inverness. Macbeth's Castle.]

PLOT SUMMARY

The murder of Duncan is enacted offstage. The fact that we do not actually see Macbeth killing Duncan is significant; it inevitably makes the deed less appalling to the feelings and to the imagination than it would otherwise have been.

A tense, distraught Lady Macbeth comes into the courtyard. Macbeth, carrying the daggers in bloodstained hands, returns from the scene of his crime to undergo questioning from his wife. He becomes increasingly hysterical; she acts as a calming influence. A knocking on the gate poses a new threat. She deals with this by telling him to appear as if he has just risen from sleep.

The chief interest of the scene is not in the murder itself but in the reactions of the two main characters to it. Even Lady Macbeth is nervous and uncertain. She is momentarily startled by a shriek, which turns out to be the cry of an owl. As Macbeth calls out, she fears that something has gone seriously wrong with their plans.

Macbeth's horrified response to what he has done unsettles and disturbs his wife further. As he looks at his 'hangman's hands' (29), he loses control. His outbursts of self-reproach become hysterical and leave his more practical, rational, calculating wife at a loss. She can only plead for a reasonable approach to what has been done ('Consider it not so deeply ... so, it will make us mad', 31–5). She pleads in vain. Her efforts are so concentrated on calming the tempest in Macbeth's mind that it takes her quite a long time to notice that he has carried the daggers with him from the scene of the crime. Her suggestion that 'A little water clears us of this deed' (68) is one of the many powerful ironies of the play, an irony echoed in the sleepwalking scene (5, 1), when we find her wondering if her hands will ever be clean again. As she goes back to Duncan's chamber with the daggers, Macbeth is still overwhelmed by guilt and remorse. She, the practical one, has to rouse him from his trance if they are to face those who are knocking so insistently at the gate.

The contrast here between the two chief characters is remarkable. Macbeth's uncontrolled outbursts of anguish make him appear indifferent to his fate and leave him open to detection. He has committed the murder in a kind of trance and has neglected to take even the most basic precautions against discovery. It is left to Lady Macbeth to take care of such vital practical details as leaving the daggers back in the bedchamber and making sure that she and Macbeth will not appear as if they have been up and about at the dead of night ('Get on your nightgown, lest occasion call us / And show us to be watchers', 71–2).

Enter LADY MACBETH

LADY MACBETH
That which hath made them drunk hath made me bold:
What hath quenched them hath given me fire. Hark!
Peace!   bird motif
It was the <u>owl</u> that shrieked, the fatal bellman,
5 Which gives the stern'st good-night. He is about it:
The doors are open; and the surfeited grooms
Do mock their charge with snores: I have drugged their
        possets,
That death and nature do contend about them,
Whether they live or die.

MACBETH
10 *[Within.]* Who's there? What, ho!

LADY MACBETH
Alack! I am afraid they have awaked,
And 'tis not done: the attempt and not the deed
Confounds us. Hark! I laid their daggers ready;
He could not miss 'em. <u>Had he not resembled</u>
15 <u>My father as he slept, I had done't.</u>

        Enter MACBETH

                        My husband!

MACBETH
I have done the deed. Didst thou not hear a noise?

LADY MACBETH
I heard the owl scream and the crickets cry.
Did not you speak?

MACBETH
                When?

LADY MACBETH
                        Now.

MACBETH
                        As I descended?

LADY MACBETH
Ay.

---

1   them: the chamberlains
2–5   Hark! … good-night: Lady
         Macbeth is momentarily
         startled by a shriek, and
         realises with relief that the cry
         is not a human one but that of
         an owl. The owl was long
         associated with death, and is
         here compared to the hired
         bellman who rang his bell
         outside the cells of condemned
         prisoners on the night before
         their execution (hence 'stern'st
         good-night').
5   He is about it: Macbeth is
         killing Duncan.
6–7   surfeited … snores: The drunken
         snores of the servants make a
         mockery of their duty as
         guardians of the royal person.
7   possets: hot milk laced with
         wine or ale
8–9   That death … die: So that life
         and death seem to be
         struggling for possession of
         them, i.e. the chamberlains are
         so heavily drugged that their
         lives are in the balance.
10   Who's there? What, ho!:
         Macbeth thinks he hears a
         noise.
12–13   the attempt … Confounds us:
         An unsuccessful attempt on
         Duncan's life will destroy us.
18   Did not you speak?: She is
         referring to his cry in line 10.
21   Who lies … Donalbain: The
         second chamber is the room
         next to Duncan's. The two
         grooms are with Duncan in the
         guestroom, while, according to
         Lady Macbeth, Donalbain is
         occupying the adjoining room.
24–7   There's one did laugh …
         Again to sleep: It is generally
         assumed that Macbeth is
         referring to Malcolm and
         Donalbain's nightmarish
         behaviour in the room next to
         Duncan's. One objection to
         this is that Lady Macbeth has
         just said that Donalbain is in
         the room, making no mention
         of Malcolm. However, when
         she says at line 27, 'There are
         two lodged together', perhaps
         she is correcting her earlier
         omission of Malcolm and
         remembering that both princes
         are sleeping in the second
         chamber. Some editors have
         argued that Macbeth is talking
         here about the grooms in
         Duncan's bedchamber.

26–7	*addressed them … to sleep:* settled down once again to sleep
29	*As they had seen me:* as if they had seen me
	these hangman's hands: Macbeth is not thinking of the hangman as the manipulator of a rope. The hangman in Shakespeare's day had to draw and quarter the victim, and his hands, like Macbeth's, would be covered with fresh blood. Macbeth is also carrying daggers at this point.
30–4	*I could not say 'Amen' … in my throat:* It was commonly believed that the inability to pray was a token of demonic possession.
34–5	*These deeds … make us mad:* We must not become obsessed as you now are with what we have done; if we do, we will go mad. This is an ironic forecast of her own destiny.
36–44	*Methought I heard … sleep no more!:* An inner voice is telling Macbeth that having murdered the sleeping king, who personifies innocent, natural sleep, neither he nor his house will ever again enjoy the benefits of sleep.
38	*Sleep that knits … care:* sleep which smooths out the tangled threads of worry and anxiety
40–1	*great nature's … life's feast:* 'Course' means round. Life's first round is our waking hours which are passed in strenuous labour; sleep is the second round. The second meaning arises from the comparison between life and a meal, in which sleep is seen as the second, or main course, because it is the most sustaining one.

MACBETH
20 Hark!
Who lies i' the second chamber?

LADY MACBETH
Donalbain.

MACBETH
[Looking at his hand.] This is a sorry sight.

LADY MACBETH
A foolish thought to say a sorry sight.
she just doesnt get it.

MACBETH
There's one did laugh in's sleep, and one cried 'Murder!'
25 That they did wake each other: I stood and heard them;
But they did say their prayers, and addressed them
Again to sleep.

LADY MACBETH
There are two lodged together.

MACBETH
One cried 'God bless us!' and 'Amen' the other:
As they had seen me with these hangman's hands.
30 Listening their fear, I could not say 'Amen' *Macbeth by now has crossed to the side of evil.*
When they did say 'God bless us!'
(He cannot say Amen)

LADY MACBETH
Consider it not so deeply.
This is her problem. she is morally shallow (no moral debt)

MACBETH
But wherefore could not I pronounce 'Amen'?
I has most need of blessing, and 'Amen'
Stuck in my throat.

LADY MACBETH
These deeds must not be thought
35 After these ways: so, it will make us mad. *This is ironic*

MACBETH
Methought I heard a voice cry 'Sleep no more!
Macbeth does murder sleep' — the innocent sleep,
Sleep that knits up the ravelled sleave of care, *another clothing image*
The death of each day's life, sore labour's bath,
40 Balm of hurt minds, great nature's second course,
Chief nourisher in life's feast, —

LADY MACBETH

What do you mean?

MACBETH

Still it cried 'Sleep no more!' to all the house:
'Glamis hath murdered sleep, and therefore Cawdor
Shall sleep no more — Macbeth shall sleep no more!'

the inability to sleep is a sign of moral guilt

LADY MACBETH

45 Who was it that thus cried? Why, worthy Thane,
You do unbend your noble strength to think
So brainsickly of things. Go get some water
And wash this filthy witness from your hand. *ironic*
Why did you bring these daggers from the place?
50 They must lie there: go carry them, and smear
The sleepy grooms with blood.

MACBETH

I'll go no more:
I am afraid to think what I have done;
Look on't again I dare not.

LADY MACBETH

Infirm of purpose!
Give me the daggers. The sleeping and the dead
55 Are but as pictures; 'tis the eye of childhood   *Appearance*
That fears a painted devil. If he do bleed,   *vs.*
I'll gild the faces of the grooms withal,   *reality*
For it must seem their guilt.

Exit. Knocking within.

MACBETH

Whence is that knocking?
How is't with me, when every noise appals me?
60 What hands are here! Ha! They pluck out mine eyes.
Will all great Neptune's ocean wash this blood
Clean from my hand? No; this my hand will rather
The multitudinous seas incarnadine,
Making the green one red.

Re-enter LADY MACBETH

LADY MACBETH

65 My hands are of your colour; but I shame
To wear a heart so white. *[Knocking within.]* I hear a knocking
At the south entry; retire we to our chamber.
A little water clears us of this deed: *IRONY*

---

46 *unbend:* slacken
47 *brainsickly:* feverishly, hysterically
48 *witness:* evidence
49 *Why ... place?:* In the earlier part of the scene she has been so taken up with Macbeth's emotional state that it is only now that she notices the daggers.
54–6 *The sleeping ... devil:* Dead people and sleeping people are pictures of living, conscious people; your fears are as those of a child who is frightened by the representation of the devil (by an actor in a morality play or fairground).
56–8 *If he do bleed ... their guilt:* In the previous lines Lady Macbeth has tried to dismiss the murdered Duncan as a mere picture of a living man. Now her reference to his bleeding body contradicts the impression she has been trying to convey. She is playing on the words 'gild', 'guilt' and 'gilt'. In using 'gild' to mean 'paint with blood', Shakespeare is relying on the common association between gold and red.
60 *Ha! They pluck out mine eyes:* Most editors are reminded here of St. Matthew 18: 9: 'And if thine eye cause thee to offend, pluck it out, and cast it from thee: it is better for thee to enter into life with one eye, than having two eyes to be cast into hell fire.'
61–4 *Will all ... red:* Will all the water of the oceans of the world clear my hand of this blood and of this guilt? No, but instead my hand will turn the green of all the oceans into one red mass.
61 *Neptune:* the god of the sea
63 *multitudinous:* limitless, countless
     incarnadine: dye blood-red
64 *Making the green one red:* The 'green' is the ocean; 'one red' means one expanse of red water.

66 *white:* innocent
68 *A little water clears us of this deed:* Note the contrast between this attitude and Macbeth's at lines 61–4. See also the sleepwalking scene, Act 5, Scene 1.

| 69–70 | *Your constancy ... unattended:* Your resolution has deserted you. |

How easy is it then! Your constancy
70 Hath left you unattended. *[Knocking within.]* Hark!
   More knocking.
Get on your nightgown, lest occasion call us
And show us to be watchers. Be not lost
So poorly in your thoughts.

| 71–2 | *Get on your nightgown ... watchers:* Put on your dressing-gown in case we are needed quickly and look like people who are still up and about. |

MACBETH
To know my deed, 'twere best not know myself.

    Knocking within.

| 74 | *To know my deed ... myself:* Macbeth is answering Lady Macbeth's rebuke that he is lost in thought. He is saying that he has every reason to be, since if he is to think of what he has done, he will need to forget who he is to dissociate himself from his deed. |

75 Wake Duncan with thy knocking! I would thou couldst!

   Exeunt.

Macbeth regrets what he has done immediately

EXAMINATION-BASED QUESTIONS

- Contrast the attitudes of the two main characters in this scene.
- How is Lady Macbeth's dominance suggested?
- Describe the effects of the murder on Macbeth.
- How would you describe Lady Macbeth's response to her husband's behaviour after the murder?
- Can you think of anything earlier in the play that might have prepared us for Macbeth's outburst in this scene?
- What is the significance of Macbeth's reference to sleep?
- What details suggest Macbeth's loss of control?
- What is the dramatic significance of the knocking at the gate?
- The scene as a whole is tense and exciting. In what ways?

KEY THEMES AND IMPORTANT FACTS

- This is a scene of great dramatic power. The actor playing Macbeth must express extreme horror at what he has done. He should emerge from the scene of the crime as if he were being pursued. He should stand as if paralysed, unconscious of anything around him.
- His 'brainsickly' comments after the murder (47), which reveal his imaginative nature, are mirrored in the torment and horror depicted on his face and in his agitated movements and gestures.
- By contrast, Lady Macbeth remains in control, moving quickly to quell Macbeth's hysteria and carrying the daggers back to the scene of the murder. When the knocking at the gate revives the tension, she again calms the situation.

Act Two

– Scene Three –

[Inverness. Macbeth's Castle.]

PLOT SUMMARY

In response to the continued knocking on the gate, a drunken porter admits Macduff and Lennox. Macbeth greets them and talks to Lennox, while Macduff goes straight to Duncan's chamber. Seeing what has happened, **he calls in horror for the alarm bell to be sounded**. Macbeth tells Malcolm and Donalbain of their father's death and reports that he himself has slain the grooms in a fit of vengeance. Lady Macbeth faints and Malcolm and Donalbain make plans to flee the country.

The porter episode that opens this scene cannot be regarded simply as comic relief, nor is there any need to dismiss it as a piece of nonsense unworthy of Shakespeare and inserted by actors. Its inclusion in the play can be defended on theatrical grounds, since there has to be a scene between Macbeth's exit and Macduff's entry. The last few lines of Act 2, Scene 2 make it clear that Macbeth must change his clothes and wash his hands. **The old idea that the scene was inserted by Shakespeare to provide comic relief is no longer taken seriously.** For one thing, it would be difficult to see why Shakespeare would have introduced a light-hearted episode merely to dissipate the tension he had steadily built up in the previous nine scenes.

The images and themes of the Porter's speeches are part of a pattern extending through much of the play. His talk of hell and the devil, for example, appears singularly appropriate against the background of the evil forces at work in the castle, and particularly in light of Lady Macbeth's self-dedication to evil in Act 1, Scene 5. **The Porter's references to the equivocator's treason remind us of Cawdor's betrayal of his country**, and are, in turn, echoed in Macbeth's equivocal answers to Lennox and Macduff on his next appearance. Equivocation is to become an important theme in the play. Macbeth is led on to his doom when the witches give him 'earnest of success, / Commencing in a truth' (1, 3, 132–3). At the end he will have every reason 'To doubt th' equivocation of the fiend, / That lies like truth' (5, 5, 43–4). Again, the Porter's images of the farmer and the tailor may be related to the images drawn from natural growth and clothing, which recur throughout the play.

With the exit of the Porter, the focus of attention shifts to Macbeth. There is much significance in the brevity of his replies and comments to Macduff and Lennox. He says as little as he can ('Good morrow, both ... Not yet ... I'll bring you to him', 42–5). To account for this economy of words on Macbeth's part, we must consider his state of mind. Everything he says in these circumstances will invoke **deceit and equivocation**, which can only intensify his already extreme suffering and make him feel even worse about what he has done. His **guilty conscience** betrays itself in his quick correction of his own answer to the question put to him by Lennox about Duncan's plans to leave Inverness: 'He does: he did appoint so' (52).

The discovery of Duncan's murder comes as a relief to Macbeth, since he is then able to speak more freely and more eloquently, and actually means what he is saying: 'Had I but died an hour before this chance / I had lived a blessed time' (90–1). In this most moving speech he is condemning himself, whether consciously or unconsciously; he is also saying things to which all his hearers must subscribe. **His eloquent explanation of the killing of the grooms is cunningly devised**. (The murder of the grooms marks yet another step in Macbeth's moral decline. Note that these are the first murders that he plans and executes without consulting with his 'partner', Lady Macbeth.)

It is difficult to know exactly how one should interpret **Lady Macbeth's fainting fit**. One explanation is that she stages it in order to draw attention away from her husband, because she fears that he may betray both of them in some rash outburst. Against this, it is sometimes argued that her fainting is all too genuine, the earliest hint that the strain of events is beginning to prove too great for her.

Banquo's silent role in much of this scene nevertheless gives some scope to the actor playing the part. Much can be suggested by the way in which he looks at Macbeth as the latter makes his self-justifying speeches. **Banquo's two main interventions in the scene are impressive**. One is a sharp rebuke to Lady Macbeth following her expression of concern that Duncan should have been murdered in *her* home – 'Too cruel anywhere' (87) is Banquo's comment. The other is a firm and unequivocal commitment to the cause of right ('In the great hand of God I stand ...', 129). Later in the play, however, there will be reason to question the strength of Banquo's determination here to fight against 'the undivulged pretence' (130) of treason.

2	*old:* plenty, or more than enough of
4	*Beelzebub:* The Prince of Devils, Satan's second-in-command.
4–5	*Here's a farmer ... plenty:* The farmer had hoarded grain, expecting the price to rise, but the prospect of a good harvest and a fall in prices confronted him with ruin, so he hanged himself. These words have a double meaning. The Porter is suggesting that the Jesuit priest Father Garnet, who also called himself Farmer (see note for line 9 below), was hanged because he was part of the Gunpowder Plot which would have brought prosperity to English Catholics had it been successful.
5–6	*time-server:* One who adapts his opinions to suit the prevailing ones; one who

Knocking within. Enter a PORTER

IRONIC

PORTER
Here's a knocking indeed! If a man were porter of hell-gate, he should have old turning the key. [*Knocking within.*] Knock, knock, knock! Who's there, i'the name of Beelzebub? Here's a farmer that hanged
5 himself on the expectation of plenty: come in, time-server; have napkins enough about you; here you'll sweat for't. [*Knocking within.*] Knock, knock! Who's there, i'the other devil's name? Faith, here's an equivocator, that could swear in both the scales against
10 either scale; who committed treason enough for God's sake, yet could not equivocate to heaven: O, come in, equivocator. [*Knocking within.*] Knock, knock, knock! Who's there? Faith, here's an English tailor come hither for stealing out of a French hose: come in, tailor; here

15 you may roast your goose. *[Knocking within.]* Knock,
knock; never at quiet! What are you? But this place is
too cold for hell. I'll devil-porter it no further: I had
thought to have let in some of all professions that go the
primrose way to the everlasting bonfire. *[Knocking within.]*

20 Anon, anon! *[Opens the gate]* I pray you,
remember the porter.

Enter MACDUFF *and* LENNOX

MACDUFF

Was it so late, friend, ere you went to bed,
That you do lie so late?

PORTER

Faith, sir, we were carousing till the second cock; and

25 drink, sir, is a great provoker of three things.

MACDUFF

What three things does drink especially provoke?

PORTER

Marry, sir, nose-painting, sleep, and urine. Lechery,
sir, it provokes and unprovokes: it provokes the desire,
but it takes away the performance. Therefore, much

30 drink may be said to be an equivocator with lechery: it
makes him, and it mars him, it sets him on, and it takes
him off; it persuades him, and disheartens him; makes
him stand to, and not stand to; in conclusion, equivocates
him in a sleep and, giving him the lie, leaves him.

MACDUFF

35 I believe drink gave thee the lie last night.

PORTER

That it did, sir, i'the very throat on me; but I requited
him for his lie; and, I think, being too strong for him,
though he took up my legs sometime, yet I made a shift
to cast him.

MACDUFF

40 Is thy master stirring?

Enter MACBETH

Our knocking has awaked him; here he comes.

serves a term of imprisonment,
as in the Porter's hell; one
who, like the farmer, is at the
service of the seasons. The
word 'server' also means
'waiter', and this links the
word with 'napkins' (line 6).
The Porter's speech is filled
with such puns.

9 *equivocator:* One who relies
on ambiguities in word
meanings in order to conceal
the truth.
The reference here is probably
to a Jesuit priest, Father
Garnet, who was hanged in
1606 for his part in the
Gunpowder Plot. At his trial,
he used equivocation as a
means of defending himself.
Father Garnet also called
himself Farmer, another pun
(see lines 4–5).

9–10 *that could ... either scale:* He
would swear so ambiguously
that if challenged on a
statement he could always say
that he meant the opposite.

13–14 *here's an English tailor ...
hose:* The English tailor has
imitated the French style in
breeches. There were many
jokes about tailors who
cheated their customers by
skimping their work and
keeping the material they
saved.

15 *roast your goose:* heat your
smoothing-iron

19 *primrose way ... bonfire:* the
pleasant road to hell

24 *the second cock:* about three
o'clock in the morning

27 *Marry:* by Mary
nose-painting: redness of the
nose, a common feature of
those who drink too much
Lechery: lust

30 *equivocator:* deceiver

31–2 *it sets ... off:* gives him
encouragement and then
discourages him

33 *stand to:* prepare

33–4 *equivocates/him in a sleep:*
tricks him into sleeping

34 *giving him the lie:* throwing
him down, also saying that he
is telling lies. This is another of
the Porter's puns, taken up by
Macduff in the next line.

36–9 *That it did ... cast him:*
The lines describe a struggle
between the Porter and drink,
in the manner of a wrestling
match. Drink made his legs
weak, but the Porter managed

('made a shift') to 'cast' his drink, a final pun, since cast could mean either a throw given to the opponent in wrestling, or vomit, in which case the suggestion would be that he threw up his drink.

41 *Our knocking ... comes:* Macbeth looks as if he has just risen from sleep (see 2, 2, 71–2).

LENNOX
Good morrow, noble sir.   *IRONY*

MACBETH
                    Good morrow, both.

MACDUFF
Is the King stirring, worthy Thane?

MACBETH
                          Not yet.

44 *timely:* early

MACDUFF
He did command me to call timely on him;
45 I have almost slipped the hour.

MACBETH
                    I'll bring you to him.

MACDUFF
I know this is a joyful trouble to you;
But yet 'tis one.

MACBETH
The labour we delight in physics pain.
This is the door.

48 *The labour ... pain:* The pleasure we derive from work we enjoy doing takes away whatever hardship the work involves.
physics: acts as a medicine for
50 *For ... service:* I have been given the duty of wakening the king.

MACDUFF
          I'll make so bold to call,
50 For 'tis my limited service.

          Exit.

LENNOX
Goes the King hence to-day?

MACBETH
He does: he did appoint so.

LENNOX   *nature has been disturbed*
The night has been unruly: where we lay,
Our chimneys were blown down; and, as they say,
55 Lamentings heard i'the air, strange screams of death,
And — prophesying with accents terrible
Of dire combustion, and confused events,   *bird image*
New hatched to the woeful time — the obscure bird
Clamoured the livelong night: some say the earth
Was feverous and did shake.

53–62 *The night ... fellow to it:* The disturbances in the natural world reflect the civil disorder in the kingdom.

57 *dire combustion:* dreadful disruption in the state
58 *New hatched ... time:* newly arrived to the present miserable time
the obscure bird: the owl, portent of death

MACBETH

60   'Twas a rough night.

LENNOX

My young remembrance cannot parallel
A fellow to it.

Re-enter MACDUFF

MACDUFF

O horror! horror! horror! Tongue nor heart
Cannot conceive nor name thee!

MACBETH, LENNOX

                What's the matter?

MACDUFF

65 Confusion now hath made his masterpiece!
Most sacrilegious murder hath broke ope
The Lord's anointed temple, and stole thence
The life o'the building. *religious imagery is used to describe Duncan*

MACBETH

            What is't you say? The life?

LENNOX

Mean you his Majesty?

MACDUFF

70 Approach the chamber, and destroy your sight
With a new Gorgon: do not bid me speak;
See, and then speak yourselves.

       Exeunt MACBETH *and* LENNOX

                Awake! Awake!
Ring the alarum-bell. Murder and treason!
Banquo and Donalbain! Malcolm! Awake!
75 Shake off this downy sleep, death's counterfeit,
And look on death itself! Up, up, and see
The great doom's image! Malcolm! Banquo!
As from your graves rise up, and walk like sprites,
To countenance this horror!

      Bell rings.

      Enter LADY MACBETH

66 *sacrilegious murder:* Since the king was regarded as God's deputy, the murder of a king was seen as sacrilege, an offence against a sacred person.

67 *The Lord's anointed temple:* This refers to Duncan's body, which was anointed with holy oil at his coronation. This may also be a reference to the destruction of English monasteries in the reign of Henry VIII, which involved wholesale robbery of their contents and the murder of several monks.

71 *Gorgon:* a mythological figure who turned beholders to stone

72–9 *Awake! Awake! ... horror!:* The full impact of this passage becomes evident only in the acting. As Macduff calls the sleeping occupants of the castle to rise and witness an image of the Last Judgement, they come on stage in their night attire by every entrance, looking like spirits rising from their graves on the Last Day.

75 *downy sleep:* 'Down' means soft feathers, hence 'downy' suggests a peaceful sleep.

77 *The great doom's image!:* This is a picture of the Judgement Day, or Doomsday, with all its horrors.

79 *To countenance this horror!:* This can mean either to confront this horror or to match or suit this horror.

81 *hideous trumpet:* She is talking about the tolling of the great alarm bell of the castle, but 'trumpet' suits the atmosphere of the Judgement Day suggested in lines 72–9.
calls to parley: A parley is a discussion between opposing armies in battle. To Lady Macbeth's ears the bell sounds like the trumpet that was used to call a parley.

NB

83–5 *'Tis not for you … fell:* This is a splendid example of dramatic irony. Macduff is telling Lady Macbeth that the news he has is too frightful for a woman to hear; it would prove fatal to her.

86–7 *Woe, alas! … house?:* A totally innocent Lady Macbeth might well have uttered these words as if thinking, why did such a shocking thing have to happen in our house, of all places? Either she forgets herself for the moment, or else thinks she is convincingly covering her tracks.

87 *Too cruel anywhere:* The actor playing Banquo can take this in two ways: either he can speak the words in mournful tones, to reflect despair, or he can face Lady Macbeth and deliver them as a sharp rebuke to her insensitivity at lines 86–7.

90–5 *Had I but died … to brag of:* However we take them, these lines are deeply ironic. Macbeth intends his words to deceive his hearers, to convey nothing but empty platitudes. The irony is that he is, in fact, speaking the sober truth. The irony of this speech is completed towards the end of the play when he can declare, quite sincerely, that life has, for him, become a tale told by an idiot, 'Signifying nothing'.

90 *chance:* unexpected disaster

92 *mortality:* human life, also death

93 *toys:* things of minor importance

93–5 *renown … to brag of:* Two meanings are present here. (a) Now that the renowned and gracious Duncan is dead, this world is an empty wine cellar holding nothing but dregs ('the mere lees'). (b) The 'vault' carries the suggestion of a burial chamber as well as of a wine cellar, and of the earth under the vault of the sky.

96–8 *What is amiss? … stopped:* Macbeth, of course, has to put on a show of concern, but the tone and movement of these lines indicate more than a hypocritical display of false emotion; he seems genuinely and passionately carried away by the horror of what he has caused.

LADY MACBETH

80 What's the business,
That such a hideous trumpet calls to parley
The sleepers of the house? Speak, speak!

MACDUFF

IRONY

O gentle lady!

'Tis not for you to hear what I can speak:
The repetition in a woman's ear
Would murder as it fell.

Enter BANQUO

85 O Banquo! Banquo!
Our royal master's murdered!

LADY MACBETH

Woe, alas!

What, in our house?

BANQUO

Too cruel anywhere.
Dear Duff, I prithee contradict thyself,
And say it is not so.

Re-enter MACBETH and LENNOX

MACBETH

90 Had I but died an hour before this chance
I had lived a blessed time; for, from this instant,
There's nothing serious in mortality: *This will really come*
All is but toys; renown and grace is dead, *true for him*
The wine of life is drawn, and the mere lees
95 Is left this vault to brag of.

Enter MALCOLM and DONALBAIN

DONALBAIN
What is amiss?

MACBETH

You are, and do not know't:
The spring, the head, the fountain of your blood
Is stopped — the very source of it is stopped.

MACDUFF
Your royal father's murdered.

MALCOLM

O! By whom?

LENNOX

100 Those of his chamber, as it seemed, had done't: *(guards)*
Their hands and faces were all badged with blood;
So were their daggers, which unwiped we found
Upon their pillows:
They stared and were distracted; no man's life
105 Was to be trusted with them.

MACBETH

O, yet I do repent me of my fury
That I did kill them.

MACDUFF

The first sign of opposition from Macbeth

NB Wherefore did you so?

MACBETH

Who can be wise, amazed, temperate and furious,
Loyal and neutral, in a moment? No man:
110 The expedition of my violent love
Outran the pauser, reason. Here lay Duncan,
His silver skin laced with his golden blood; *vivid image*
And his gashed stabs looked like a breach in nature *simile captures the very essence of murder*
For ruin's wasteful entrance: there, the murderers,
115 Steeped in the colours of their trade, their daggers
Unmannerly breeched with gore: who could refrain,
That had a heart to love, and in that heart
Courage to make's love known?

LADY MACBETH

NB Help me hence, ho! *taking attention off MB*

MACDUFF

Look to the lady.

MALCOLM

[*Aside to* DONALBAIN.] Why do we hold our tongues,
   that most may claim
This argument for ours?

DONALBAIN

120 [*Aside to* MALCOLM.] What should be spoken
Here, where our fate, hid in an auger-hole,
May rush and seize us? Let's away
Our tears are not yet brewed.

101 *badged with blood:* clearly marked, as if blood was the symbol of their trade
108 *amazed, temperate and furious:* bewildered, self-controlled and madly angry
110–11 *The expedition ... reason:* My over-powering love for Duncan could not be restrained or controlled by my reason.
111–12 *Here lay ... golden blood:* Duncan is pictured here dressed in the precious royal blood which covers his body like a richly ornamented garment.
113–14 *And his gashed stabs ... entrance:* Duncan's body is imagined as a fortified building; the wounds made by the daggers are like breaches in the walls to allow invaders to enter and cause ruin.
115–16 *their daggers ... gore:* 'Unmannerly' means 'indecently'. The daggers should have been decently covered in their sheaths; instead, these daggers were indecently covered with blood, wearing red breeches. Shakespeare's common habit of word association is illustrated here. Breeches are suggested by 'breach' at line 113.
116–18 *who could refrain ... known?:* What man who loved Duncan, and had the courage to express his love in deeds, could refrain from killing Duncan's murderers?
118 *Help me hence, ho!:* Either Lady Macbeth is overcome by the emotional and physical strain of the occasion and really feels faint, or she is causing a strategic diversion to draw attention away from Macbeth because she is afraid he will say too much and betray himself.
119–20 *Why ... for ours?:* Why are we silent, we who are most concerned with what is being discussed?
120–2 *What should be ... seize us?:* What is the point in our speaking up in a place such as this, when treacherous individuals may well be concealing their plans to

MALCOLM

[Aside to DONALBAIN.]   Nor our strong sorrow
Upon the foot of motion.

BANQUO

                              Look to the lady …

          LADY MACBETH *is carried out.*

121 *auger-hole:* A carpenter bores holes with an auger. Here the term means spy-hole.

123 *Our tears … brewed:* Malcolm and Donalbain are too shocked and grieved to weep, unlike Macbeth and his wife, who can shed false tears at will.

123–4 *Nor our strong sorrow … motion:* Our genuine sorrow has not yet begun to express itself.

125 *And when … hid:* when we have put on clothes

125 And when we have our naked frailties hid,
That suffer in exposure, let us meet,
And question this most bloody piece of work,
To know it further. Fears and scruples shake us:
In the great hand of God I stand, and thence
130 Against the undivulged pretence I fight
Of treasonous malice.

128 *scruples:* doubts

129–31 *In the great hand … treasonous malice:* I place myself under God's protection, and with this as my support, I am ready to fight against any hidden plots or treacherous enemies yet to emerge.

MACDUFF

                    And so do I.

ALL

                              So all.

MACBETH

Let's briefly put on manly readiness,
And meet i'the hall together.

132 *Let's briefly put on manly readiness:* Let us quickly clothe ourselves in a way befitting men and be ready to face our situation like men.

134 *consort:* have anything to do
135 *office:* job, duty

ALL

Well contented.

          Exeunt all but MALCOLM *and* DONALBAIN.

MALCOLM

What will you do? Let's not consort with them:
135 To show an unfelt sorrow is an office   App vs. Reality
Which the false man does easy. I'll to England.

DONALBAIN

To Ireland, I: our separated fortune
Shall keep us both the safer. Where we are,
There's daggers in men's smiles; the near in blood,
The nearer bloody.

139–40 *There's daggers … bloody:* Those who smile at us may be planning murder; the more closely people are related to us, the more likely they are to have designs on our lives.

140–1 *This murderous shaft … lighted:* The deadly arrow that has been fired has not yet finally hit its mark ('lighted'). Malcolm means that further bloodshed is inevitable.

MALCOLM

                    This murderous shaft that's shot
140 Hath not yet lighted, and our safest way
Is to avoid the aim: therefore, to horse;

And let us not be dainty of leave-taking,   143

But shift away: there's warrant in that theft

145 Which steals itself when there's no mercy left.

Exeunt.

143   *And let … leave-taking:* Let us not be too particular about saying courteous and polite farewells.

144   *shift:* steal

144–5   *there's warrant … mercy left:* One is justified in stealing oneself away from a place where no mercy is likely to be shown if one remains.

EXAMINATION-BASED QUESTIONS

- Mention the elements in the Porter's speech that are relevant to the main themes of the play.
- Why does the Porter imagine himself as 'porter of hell-gate' (1–2)?
- Does this scene give any hints of Macbeth's uneasiness?
- What is the significance of the reports of unnatural events on the night of Duncan's murder?
- Discuss Lady Macbeth's contribution to this scene.
- How do you think the other participants in this scene feel about Macbeth's explanation of the murder of the grooms? Consider especially Banquo's likely feelings.
- Is there any suggestion that Duncan's sons suspect Macbeth?

KEY THEMES AND IMPORTANT FACTS

- The Porter episode provides opportunities for a good comic actor, who must pretend that he is admitting a series of individuals through the gates of hell: a farmer who hanged himself, a treasonous man who swore a false oath and an English tailor who has cheated. The Porter can enliven the scene by acting the parts of these three in succession, using appropriate gestures, facial expressions and speech patterns.
- The first dramatic highlight of this scene occurs when Macduff reveals that he has discovered Duncan's body. The key passage is Macduff's call for the alarm bell to be rung and the stage business that must follow this (72–9). Macduff is calling on the sleepers in Macbeth's house to arise and witness an image of Judgement Day. Sleep is an image of death, and death is a prelude to final judgement. In a good performance, these verbal images will be matched by powerful visual ones.
- The sleepers of the house, clad in night-time attire, will come on the stage by every entrance, even using the trapdoor for greater effect. They will look like spirits rising from their graves on the Last Day. In this way, they will be eerily answering Macduff's command, 'As from your graves rise up, and walk like sprites' (78). Lady Macbeth's reference to the alarm bell as a 'hideous trumpet' reinforces the imagery of death and judgement.

Act Two

– Scene Four –

[Inverness. Outside Macbeth's Castle.]

*An information scene,
it include unnatural deeds
Macbeths coronation
and clothing imagery
(CF. Line 38)*

PLOT SUMMARY

It is day, but the sky is unnaturally dark. Ross and the Old Man discuss and interpret the strange omens that have accompanied Duncan's death. Macduff, unlike Ross, will not go to Scone for Macbeth's coronation.

This scene takes us outside the main action. The Old Man and Ross act as commentators on the unnatural events that have accompanied Macbeth's unnatural deed. The two participants in this commentary are a nicely contrasted pair. The Old Man is superstitious and relatively simple-minded. His language is natural and sincere. Ross speaks an artificial and affected language. The references by each to the upheavals in nature are intended to reflect the common belief that violent disorder in the world of man (the murder of a king, for example) was bound to be reflected in some parallel disorder in the natural world. It would be a mistake, however, to take such parallels too literally: Macbeth is not being compared to a mousing owl or Duncan to a falcon.

There is another example of contrast in characterisation here, this time between Ross and Macduff. Ross accepts the 'official' story that the princes have killed their father, which has made it possible for Macbeth to become king instead of Malcolm, Duncan's son and heir, who is now blocked from acceding to the throne. Ross goes off to attend Macbeth's coronation. Macduff has his reservations. He will go home to Fife, and his parting words to Ross indicate his fears for the future of Scotland under Macbeth's rule.

Enter ROSS and an OLD MAN

OLD MAN

Threescore and ten I can remember well,
Within the volume of which time I have seen
Hours dreadful and things strange; but this sore night
Hath trifled former knowings.

ROSS

                Ah, good father,
5 Thou seest, the heavens, as troubled with man's act,
Threatens his bloody stage: by the clock 'tis day,
And yet dark night strangles the travelling lamp.
Is't night's predominance, or the day's shame,
That darkness does the face of earth entomb,
10 When living light should kiss it?

3	*sore:* dreadful
4	*Hath trifled former knowings:* has made previous experience appear trivial
5	*as:* as if, as though
6	*his bloody stage:* the earth, here seen appropriately as the scene of bloody deeds
8–10	*Is't night's ... kiss it?:* Is it dark because night has acquired a dominant influence, or is day ashamed to appear because of the murder?

OLD MAN

The old man has got to the heart of the issue

'Tis unnatural,
Even like the deed that's done. On Tuesday last,
A falcon, towering in her pride of place,
Was by a mousing owl hawked at and killed.

ROSS

And Duncan's horses — a thing most strange and certain —
15 Beauteous and swift, the minions of their race,
Turned wild in nature, broke their stalls, flung out,
Contending 'gainst obedience, as they would
Make war with mankind.

OLD MAN

'Tis said they ate each other.

ROSS

They did so, to the amazement of mine eyes,
20 That looked upon't.

Enter MACDUFF

Here comes the good Macduff.
How goes the world, sir, now?

MACDUFF

Why, see you not?

ROSS

Is't known who did this more than bloody deed?

MACDUFF

Those that Macbeth hath slain.

ROSS

Alas, the day!
What good could they pretend?

MACDUFF

They were suborned.
25 Malcolm and Donalbain, the King's two sons,
Are stolen away and fled, which puts upon them
Suspicion of the deed.

ROSS

'Gainst nature still!
Thriftless ambition, that wilt ravin up
Thine own life's means! Then 'tis most like

12

13

towering … place: flying to the highest point before pouncing
a mousing owl: an owl whose normal prey is the mouse

15

16

17

the minions of their race: best specimens of their breed
Turned wild in nature: became like wild animals
Contending 'gainst obedience: The horses are rebelling against their natural master, man. This breakdown of order in the animal kingdom has its parallel in the disruptive forces at work in human society.

24

28–9

28

What … pretend?: What could they have hoped to gain by killing Duncan?
They were suborned: They were induced, prompted or bribed to do the deed by others.
Thriftless … means!: Wasteful or fruitless ambition that will swallow the very source of your life. (The image is of the sons destroying the father.)
ravin: devour

30   The sovereignty will fall upon Macbeth.

MACDUFF
He is already named, and gone to Scone
To be invested.

31   *named:* Appointed or elected
Scone: This was the palace
where Scottish kings were
crowned.

ROSS
                Where is Duncan's body?

MACDUFF
Carried to Colmekill,
The sacred storehouse of his predecessors
35   And guardian of their bones.

33   *Colmekill:* This is the island of
Iona which was known as the
island of Colm Cille after the
Irish saint who established a
monastic foundation there.

ROSS
                Will you to Scone?

MACDUFF
No, cousin, I'll to Fife.

36   *Fife:* Macduff is Thane of Fife.

ROSS
                Well, I will thither.

MACDUFF
Well, may you see things well done there: adieu!
Lest our old robes sit easier than our new!

Clothing imagery

ROSS
Farewell, father.

38   *Lest ... new!:* In case Duncan's
reign proves to have been a
happier one for all of us than
Macbeth's is likely to be.
Macduff is already sounding
an apprehensively critical note.
40–1   *God's benison ... foes!:* God's
blessing on all peacemakers!

OLD MAN
40   God's benison go with you; and with those
That would make good of bad, and friends of foes!

    Exeunt.

EXAMINATION-BASED QUESTIONS

- What are the main purposes of this scene?
- What is the relationship between this scene and the previous one?
- What do we learn about Ross from this scene?
- Is there anything to suggest that Macduff is unhappy with Macbeth's version of the events surrounding Duncan's murder or with Macbeth's accession to the throne? Contrast his attitude with that of Ross.
- At the end of the scene there is a hint of trouble to come. Explain.

Act Three
– Scene One –
[Forres. The Palace.]

PLOT SUMMARY

Banquo expresses his suspicions of Macbeth, but entertains his own hopes. Macbeth reminds him not to forget the feast, at which he will be the chief guest, and then discovers, by means of innocent-sounding questions, where and how far Banquo will ride. Macbeth sends for Banquo's murderers and motivates them.

Macbeth is given no time to enjoy the fruits of Duncan's murder. The first small threat to his security has already been hinted at in the previous scene. Macduff is not happy with the course of events. In the present scene Banquo voices *his* doubts about Macbeth in a soliloquy, suspecting that foul play has brought him to the throne. Banquo's own position appears somewhat ambiguous. He derives consolation, perhaps even guilty hope, from the thought that the witches have predicted good fortune for him too, even though he has earlier warned Macbeth about believing in the promises of the 'instruments of darkness' (1, 3, 124).

Macbeth's first words in this scene ('Here's our chief guest', 11) sound sinister in view of what has happened to his earlier chief guest, Duncan. This scene presents us with a Macbeth who is much changed from the conscience-stricken, terrified figure of Act 2, appalled by his own guilt and given over to outbursts of moral hysteria. Here we see him as a cunning hypocrite, coldly calculating and untroubled by conscience. He displays much deviousness in eliciting all the information he needs from his intended victim in order to arrange the details of Banquo's and Fleance's murder. The key questions ('Ride you this afternoon? ... Is't far you ride? ... Goes Fleance with you?', 19, 24, 36) are so innocuously placed that Banquo's suspicions are not aroused.

Banquo, too, wears a mask. He displays the outward marks of loyalty and respect for his new king, stressing the 'indissoluble tie' (17) between himself and his 'good lord' (37), Macbeth. The latter savours the irony of his direction to Banquo to 'Fail not our feast' (28). The irony of Banquo's reply, 'My lord, I will not' (29), will be fully realised in the tumult of the banquet scene (3, 4).

Macbeth's soliloquy on Banquo ('To be thus is nothing ... utterance!', 48–72) resembles his earlier one on Duncan ('If it were done, when 'tis done', 1, 7, 1). In each case, tribute is paid to the good and noble qualities of the victims: here we learn of Banquo's regal nature, his bravery and his wisdom. This time, however, Macbeth abandons logic. The witches have proved totally accurate in his own case: he has become Thane of Cawdor and king. But in this meditation he thinks he can prove the witches false by killing Banquo and Fleance. At the conclusion of the soliloquy he is challenging fate.

Macbeth's conference with the murderers marks a further degeneration of his character. His nobility and sensitivity give way to cunning, double-dealing and hypocrisy. He appeals to whatever self-esteem the murderers may have by implying that they are particularly well qualified to carry out this mission. He has learned a good deal from Lady Macbeth. In urging her husband to commit his first crime, she appealed above all to his sense of manliness, and her appeal proved decisive. Now he is appealing to the same quality in the murderers ('if you have a station in the file, / Not i'the worst rank of manhood, say it', 102–3).

Enter BANQUO SOLILIQUY

BANQUO

1	*it:* the crown
4	*stand in thy posterity:* pass to your descendants
8	*by the verities on thee made good:* the truths demonstrated in your case
9–10	*May they not … no more:* Banquo is here tempted by ambition: the last four words may mean that he is trying to shut it from his mind. *oracles:* prophets
10	*Sennet sounded:* This stage direction indicates an impressive flourish of trumpets announcing the stately entrance of the new king and queen.
11	*Here's our chief guest:* Duncan, the audience will readily recall, had been their chief guest not long ago. *If he had been forgotten.* There may be a double meaning here, as in the earlier determination that Duncan 'Must be provided for' (I, 5, 66).
13	*And all-thing unbecoming:* something completely inappropriate
14	*solemn:* formal
15	*request:* command, order
15–18	*Let your Highness … knit:* I will perform whatever your majesty commands. I am absolutely bound to your service by ties of duty and loyalty. Banquo's reply here is formal and artificial. He speaks like a courtier.

Thou hast it now: King, Cawdor, Glamis, all,
As the weird women promised; and I fear *Banquo is no fool*
Thou play'dst most foully for't; yet it was said *your children*
It should not stand in thy posterity,
5 But that myself should be the root and father
Of many kings. If there come truth from them —
As upon thee, Macbeth, their speeches shine —
Why, by the verities on thee made good,
May they not be my oracles as well,
10 And set me up in hope? But hush, no more.

He does not want to think about this anymore

Sennet sounded. Enter MACBETH, *as King;* LADY MACBETH *as Queen;* LENNOX, ROSS, *Lords, Ladies and Attendants*

MACBETH
Here's our chief guest.

LADY MACBETH
                        If he had been forgotten,
It had been as a gap in our great feast,
And all-thing unbecoming.

MACBETH
Tonight we hold a solemn supper, sir,
15 And I'll request your presence.

BANQUO
                        Let your Highness
Command upon me; to the which my duties
Are with a most indissoluble tie
For ever knit.

MACBETH
Ride you this afternoon?

BANQUO

20 Ay, my good lord.

MACBETH

We should have else desired your good advice —
Which still hath been both grave and prosperous —
In this day's council; but we'll take tomorrow.
Is't far you ride?

BANQUO

25 As far, my lord, as will fill up the time
'Twixt this and supper; go not my horse the better,
I must become a borrower of the night
For a dark hour or twain.

MACBETH

Fail not our feast.

BANQUO

My lord, I will not.

MACBETH

30 We hear our bloody cousins are bestowed
In England and in Ireland, not confessing
Their cruel parricide, filling their hearers
With strange invention; but of that tomorrow,
When therewithal we shall have cause of state
35 Craving us jointly. Hie you to horse; adieu,
Till you return at night. Goes Fleance with you?

BANQUO

Ay, my good lord: our time does call upon's.

MACBETH

I wish your horses swift and sure of foot;
And so I do commend you to their backs.
40 Farewell.

Exit BANQUO.

Let every man be master of his time
Till seven at night; to make society
The sweeter welcome, we will keep ourself
Till supper-time alone; while then, God be with you!

Exeunt all but MACBETH *and a* SERVANT.

19, 24, 36	*Ride you this afternoon? ... Is't far you ride? ... Goes Fleance with you?:* Macbeth places his vital questions skilfully, and apparently casually, at suitable intervals between insincere comments on other matters.
21–3	*we should ... council:* If you were not making a journey, I would have asked for the benefit of your advice at today's meeting of the Royal Council; I have always found your advice weighty and beneficial ('grave and prosperous').
23	*We'll take tomorrow:* We'll leave it until tomorrow.
26	*go not my horse the better:* if my horse does not go fast enough
28	*twain:* two
30	*bestowed:* lodged, settled
32	*parricide:* murder of their father
34–5	*When therewithal ... jointly:* when, in addition, we shall have state business needing our joint attention
37	*our time does call upon's:* It is time for us to go.
39	*I do commend you to their backs:* I entrust you to their backs.
41	*Let every man be master of his time:* Let everyone do as he pleases with his time.
42–4	*to make society ... alone:* I will remain alone till supper time so that I shall be all the more welcome to my courtiers and guests when I do appear.
44	*while then:* till then, meanwhile
45–6	*attend ... pleasure?:* Are the men I had arranged to see waiting for me? The men in question are the murderers.
48–9	*To be thus ... safely thus:* There is no point in being king unless one is secure in the title.
50	*Stick deep:* stick like thorns or daggers
51	*would:* should
52–4	*And, to that ... safety:* He combines a fearless temperament with the discretion that enables him to undertake dangerous exploits without undue risk to himself.
55–7	*under him ... Caesar:* Banquo's guardian spirit is able to domineer over mine. A man's 'genius' was the guardian spirit allotted to him at birth to guide him through life and shape his destiny.

Macbeth is saying that his guardian spirit is intimidated ('rebuked') by Banquo's, the implication being that Banquo seems destined to enjoy greater success than Macbeth. The fear that this may be the case is the origin of Macbeth's envy and insecurity. According to the Roman historian Plutarch, Mark Anthony felt the same kind of resentment for the successful Octavius Caesar as Macbeth does for Banquo.

57 *chid:* rebuked
61 *a fruitless crown:* a crown not to be inherited by children of mine
62 *gripe:* grip
63 *Thence ... unlineal hand:* The sceptre is to be snatched from my grip by somebody not descended from me.
65 *For Banquo's issue ... my mind:* I have defiled or sullied my mind for the sake of Banquo's descendants.
67 *Put rancours ... peace:* replace my peace and serenity of mind with bitterness and irritation
68-9 *and mine eternal jewel ... man:* I have given my soul over to the devil.
71-2 *Rather than so ... to the utterance!:* Rather than have that happen (the offspring of Banquo becoming kings), let fate confront me in a duel to the death.
list: arena. Shakespeare is using an image from a medieval tournament.
to the utterance: to the utmost limit, i.e. to the death (from the French à l'outrance).
76-9 *Have you considered ... innocent self?:* Have you thought about what I told you when we last spoke? I would like you to know that it was he (Banquo) who prevented you from getting your just desserts, not I, as you had thought.
80 *passed in probation:* spent my time supplying you with detailed proofs
81-4 *How you were borne ... 'Thus did Banquo':* how you were tricked and thwarted, what methods were used against you, who used these methods, and every other relevant detail that would convince even a feeble-minded person that Banquo was responsible.
82 *wrought with:* used

45 Sirrah, a word with you: attend those men
Our pleasure?

SERVANT (outside)
They are, my lord, without the palace gate.

MACBETH soliloquy
Bring them before us. *[Exit Servant.]* To be thus is nothing,
But to be safely thus. Our fears in Banquo
50 Stick deep, and in his royalty of nature (good)
Reigns that which would be feared: 'tis much he dares,
And, to that dauntless temper of his mind,
He hath a wisdom that doth guide his valour
To act in safety. There is none but he
55 Whose being I do fear; and under him
My genius is rebuked, as it is said → Classical reference
Mark Antony's was by Caesar. He chid the Sisters
When first they put the name of King upon me,
And bade them speak to him; then, prophet-like,
60 They hailed him father to a line of kings.
Upon my head they placed a fruitless crown,
And put a barren sceptre in my gripe,
Thence to be wrenched with an unlineal hand,
No son of mine succeeding. If't be so,
65 For Banquo's issue have I filed my mind;
For them the gracious Duncan have I murdered;
Put rancours in the vessel of my peace
Only for them, and mine eternal jewel
Given to the common enemy of man
70 To make them kings — the seed of Banquo kings!
Rather than so, come, Fate, into the list,
And champion me to the utterance! Who's there?

This soliloquy shows us the mind of a man that is beginning to become paranoid and deeply insecure

Re-enter SERVANT, *with two* MURDERERS

Now go to the door, and stay there till we call.

Exit SERVANT.

Was it not yesterday we spoke together?

FIRST MURDERER
75 It was, so please your Highness.

MACBETH
Well then, now
Have you considered of my speeches? — Know

That it was he in the times past which held you
So under fortune, which you thought had been
Our innocent self? This I made good to you
80 In our last conference; passed in probation with you,
How you were borne in hand, how crossed, the instruments,
Who wrought with them, and all things else that might
To half a soul and to a notion crazed
Say 'Thus did Banquo.'

FIRST MURDERER
           You made it known to us.

MACBETH
85 I did so; and went further, which is now
Our point of second meeting. Do you find
Your patience so predominant in your nature
That you can let this go? Are you so gospelled
To pray for this good man and for his issue,
90 Whose heavy hand hath bowed you to the grave
And beggared yours for ever?

FIRST MURDERER
              We are men, my liege.

MACBETH
Ay, in the catalogue ye go for men;
As hounds and greyhounds, mongrels, spaniels, curs,
Shoughs, water-rugs, and demi-wolves, are clept
95 All by the name of dogs: the valued file
Distinguishes the swift, the slow, the subtle,
The housekeeper, the hunter, every one
According to the gift which bounteous nature
Hath in him closed; whereby he does receive
100 Particular addition, from the bill
That writes them all alike: and so of men.
Now, if you have a station in the file,
Not i'the worst rank of manhood, say it;
And I will put that business in your bosoms
105 Whose execution takes your enemy off,
Grapples you to the heart and love of us,
Who wear our health but sickly in his life,
Which in his death were perfect. *a clothing & disease image in one*

SECOND MURDERER
            I am one, my liege,
Whom the vile blows and buffets of the world

88–91 *Are you so gospelled … for ever?:* Are you so influenced by the teaching of the Gospels that you are ready to pray for Banquo and his children, even though he has caused misery and poverty to you and yours?

91 *We are men, my liege:* We are not saints; we are only human, and therefore want revenge.

92–5 *Ay, in the catalogue … of dogs:* Macbeth is taunting the murderers, questioning their manliness (their ability to murder) just as Lady Macbeth questioned his. He is saying: In a general list of beings, you must be classified as men, for want of any other term, just as a varied assortment of canine creatures are all referred to as dogs.

94 *Shoughs:* shaggy dogs
water-rugs: rough, rugged water-dogs
demi-wolves: cross-breeds, part dog, part wolf
are clept: are called

95–101 *the valued file … so of men:* The 'catalogue' (lines 92–5) did not discriminate between one dog and another. The 'valued file' is a list designed to show the worth of each dog as this is reflected in its special talents and uses. One can think of men in much the same way: each has some quality to distinguish him from the rest.

100 *Particular addition:* some special mark of distinction

100–1 *the bill … all alike:* the list that describes all of them as dogs

102–3 *Now, if you have … say it:* If you can classify yourselves as human beings who do not belong to the lowest order of mankind (in manliness), tell me. They will have to show their manhood by killing Banquo.

104–5 *And I will put … your enemy off:* I will confide a proposal to you which, if you carry it out, will get rid of your enemy. Notice the double meaning of 'execution': the carrying out of a project and the killing of Banquo.

106 *Grapples:* binds

107–8 *Who wear … perfect:* whose (Macbeth's own) position is unstable and unhealthy while he (Banquo) is alive, but would be perfectly secure if he were dead

108–11 *I am one … spite the world:*

Having been the victim of so many terrible misfortunes, I am angry enough not to care what I do to avenge myself on mankind.

112–14 *So weary ... rid on't:* I am so tired of being knocked about by disaster and bad-luck, that I am prepared to stake ('set') my life on any opportunity to improve my fortunes or die in the attempt.

113 *set:* gamble

114 *on't:* of it

116–18 *and in such bloody distance ... near'st of life:* He hovers menacingly near me, so menacingly that his continued existence represents a continuous threat to my life. *in such bloody distance:* in such murderous proximity

118 *near'st of life:* vital parts

119 *bare-faced power:* naked force

120 *And bid my will avouch it:* defend or justify my action by saying that I destroyed him simply because I wanted to

120–3 *yet I must not ... struck down:* I must avoid killing him openly, for the sake of certain friends of his and mine whose affections I cannot afford to lose; I must therefore appear to lament the death of a man whom I myself have sent to his doom.

124 *That I to your assistance ... love:* I plead for your help.

125 *the common eye:* public view

127 *Though our lives — :* He was about to add: 'may be lost in the attempt'.

129 *plant:* hide

130 *Acquaint you with ... o'the time:* The meaning of this line is not clear. Some editors think it may refer to the Third Murderer, who turns up in Act 3, Scene 3. Other suggestions are: (a) the ideal time for carrying out the deed, (b) the ideal place of ambush. Against (a) is the fact that in the next line Macbeth refers to 'The moment on't' (of it). It has also been suggested that the words mean 'the ideal person to tell you the time for the deed'.

132 *something from the palace:* some distance from the palace

132–3 *always thought ... clearness:* always keeping in mind that I am to be kept free of suspicion

134 *To leave ... work:* Do not do an untidy, clumsy job.

110 Have so incensed that I am reckless what
I do to spite the world.

FIRST MURDERER

          And I another,
So weary with disasters, tugged with fortune,
That I would set my life on any chance,
To mend it or be rid on't.

MACBETH

          Both of you
115 Know Banquo was your enemy.

SECOND MURDERER

          True, my lord.

MACBETH

So is he mine; and in such bloody distance
That every minute of his being thrusts
Against my near'st of life: and though I could
With bare-faced power sweep him from my sight
120 And bid my will avouch it, yet I must not,
For certain friends that are both his and mine,
Whose loves I may not drop, but wail his fall
Whom I myself struck down. And thence it is
That I to your assistance do make love,
125 Masking the business from the common eye
For sundry weighty reasons.

[handwritten: Averting to the use of assassins represents the deterioration in his character]

[handwritten: Appearance vs. reality]

SECOND MURDERER

          We shall, my lord,
Perform what you command us.

FIRST MURDERER

          Though our lives —

MACBETH

Your spirits shine through you. Within this hour at most
I will advise you where to plant yourselves,
130 Acquaint you with the perfect spy o'the time,
The moment on't; for't must be done tonight,
And something from the palace; always thought
That I require a clearness: and with him —
To leave no rubs nor botches in the work —

135 Fleance his son, that keeps him company,
Whose absence is no less material to me
Than is his father's, must embrace the fate
Of that dark hour. Resolve yourselves apart;
I'll come to you anon.

SECOND MURDERER

We are resolved, my lord.

MACBETH

140 I'll call upon you straight: abide within.

Exeunt MURDERERS.

It is concluded: Banquo, thy soul's flight,
If it find heaven, must find it out tonight.

Exit.

136–8 *Whose absence … hour:* The death of Fleance is as important to me as that of Banquo; he must join his father in the darkness of death.

138 *Resolve yourselves apart:* Go aside and come to a decision.

140 *I'll call upon you straight:* I'll join you immediately.

141–2 *It is concluded … tonight:* See Act 2, Scene 1, 63–4.

EXAMINATION-BASED QUESTIONS

- Banquo's soliloquy throws light on his thinking at this point. Explain.
- Macbeth displays a new cunning in his dealings with Banquo. Give examples.
- Compare Macbeth's soliloquy on Banquo ('To be thus is nothing ...', 48 ff.) with his earlier soliloquy on Duncan ('If it were done ...', 1, 7, 1 ff.).
- Is Macbeth describing the prophecies of the witches correctly in his soliloquy on Banquo? Refer back to Act 1, Scene 3.
- There is evidence in Macbeth's interview with the murderers that his character has deteriorated. How does his present behaviour match Lady Macbeth's opinion of his character in Act 1, Scene 5, lines 14 ff. ('Glamis thou art ...')?
- Is there any evidence in this scene that the relationship between Macbeth and Lady Macbeth may be changing?

Act Three
– Scene Two –
[Forres. The Palace.]

PLOT SUMMARY

Lady Macbeth sends for her husband. She is weary and disillusioned. Macbeth is neither happy nor secure. He has murderous business in hand that he will not reveal to her until after it has been completed.

This domestic scene reveals the insecurity and unhappiness of Macbeth and his wife and marks a deterioration in the quality of their relationship. Her suffering and turmoil are evident from her pathetically brief soliloquy ('Nought's had, all's spent ...', 4 ff.). However, she will not let Macbeth know the full extent of her misery. She deflects attention from this by rebuking him for his gloomy mood (his 'sorriest fancies', 9) and advising him to accept the inevitable ('what's done is done', 12). Macbeth's speech ('We have scorched the snake ...', 13 ff.) is an unconscious echo of his wife's soliloquy; he, too, is suffering the torments of the damned ('terrible dreams', 'torture of the mind', 'restless ecstasy', 18, 21, 22). Like her, he envies the peaceful sleep of the dead.

What is most significant here is the change in the relationship between Macbeth and Lady Macbeth since Acts 1 and 2. It is she, not he, who must now ask, 'What's to be done?' (44). For the moment, she is more dependent on him than he is on her. He still needs her, if only because there is nobody else in whom he can confide his secret terrors ('O, full of scorpions is my mind, dear wife!', 36). He becomes protective; he wants to spare her the suffering he knows would accompany the knowledge of what he is about to do ('Be innocent of the knowledge, dearest chuck, / Till thou applaud the deed ...', 45–6). Macbeth is now the planner of dark deeds; Lady Macbeth is to play a passive role and await news of developments from him. She will, however, regain some of her initiative in the banquet scene (3, 4).

Enter LADY MACBETH *and a* SERVANT

LADY MACBETH
Is Banquo gone from court?

SERVANT
Ay, madam, but returns again tonight.

LADY MACBETH
Say to the king I would attend his leisure
For a few words.

Lady Macbeth has bomcke an appo mbment bo see Macbeth

SERVANT
Madam, I will.

Exit.

LADY MACBETH
            Nought's had, all's spent,
5 Where our desire is got without content:
'Tis safer to be that which we destroy
Than by destruction dwell in doubtful joy.

Enter MACBETH

How now, my lord! Why do you keep alone,
Of sorriest fancies your companions making,
10 Using those thoughts which should indeed have died
With them they think on? Things without all remedy
Should be without regard: what's done is done.

MACBETH   *Animal imagery*
We have scorched the snake, not killed it:
an echo of Macbeths earlier words. She doesnb fully understand
She'll close and be herself, whilst our poor malice
15 Remains in danger of her former tooth.
But let the frame of things disjoint, both the worlds suffer,
Ere we will eat our meal in fear, and sleep
In the affliction of these terrible dreams
That shake us nightly. Better be with the dead,
20 Whom we, to gain our peace, have sent to peace,
Than on the torture of the mind to lie
In restless ecstacy. Duncan is in his grave;
After life's fitful fever he sleeps well;
Treason has done his worst: nor steel, nor poison,
25 Malice domestic, foreign levy, nothing
Can touch him further.

---

3   *I would attend his leisure:* I am waiting until he is free to speak to me.

4–5 *Nought's had ... content:* We have sacrificed everything, and gained nothing in return, when we have achieved our aim but find that this achievement does not bring peace of mind.

6–7 *'Tis safer ... doubtful joy:* Those whom we destroy are more secure than we are, if by destroying them we have to live lives of fear, suspicion and apprehension.

8–9 *Why do you keep alone ... making:* Why do you shun human company and prefer to entertain your own miserable delusions?

10–11 *Using those thoughts ... on?:* Living on familiar terms with thoughts which should have ceased to trouble you once their objects (Duncan and, perhaps, others) had died.

11–12 *Things without ... regard:* We should ignore those things we can do nothing about.

13   *scorched:* slashed

14–15 *She'll close ... former tooth:* The threats to our security and welfare, which we have only partially dealt with, will re-assert themselves and prove as dangerous as they were before. Macbeth is referring to the belief that a wounded serpent, if not fully severed, can heal itself.

16   *But let ... suffer:* Let the universe disintegrate, and the heavens and the earth perish.

17–19 *and sleep ... nightly:* and endure the convulsive torment of nightmares each time we sleep

19–20 *Better ... peace:* It would be better to join the dead, whom we have sent to enjoy the peace of eternity, with a view to achieving our own kind of peace, the peace of fulfilled ambition.

21–2 *Than on the torture ... ecstasy:* Macbeth is picturing his bed as a rack on which he suffers fits of torment of mind, almost physical in its intensity.

22   *ecstasy:* madness, frenzy, delirium

24   *his worst:* its worst

25   *Malice domestic:* hostility directed against him from within the country
      foreign levy: armies raised abroad to fight against him

LADY MACBETH

Come on: App vs. Reality

Gentle my lord, <u>sleek o'er your rugged looks</u>;
Be bright and jovial among your guests tonight.

27 *sleek o'er your rugged looks:* Smooth over your distressed and worried appearance.

'Gentle my lord, sleek o'er your rugged looks; /
Be bright and jovial among your guests tonight.' (3, 2, 27–8)

MACBETH

So shall I, love; and so, I pray, be you.

30 Let your remembrance apply to Banquo;
Present him eminence, both with eye and tongue —
Unsafe the while, that we
Must lave our honours in these flattering streams,
And make our faces vizards to our hearts,

35 Disguising what they are.

30 *Let ... Banquo:* Be especially attentive to Banquo. Macbeth, excluding his wife from all knowledge of the murder he has planned, knows that she will never again need to attend to Banquo's needs. In the light of Banquo's later appearance, however, the words are profoundly ironic.

31 *Present him ... tongue:* Show him special honour both in your looks and in your speech.

32–3 *Unsafe the while ... streams:* We are so unsure of our position at the moment that we must try to compromise our honour and integrity by using flattery towards Banquo.

34 *vizards:* masks

38 *But in them nature's copy's not eterne:* Nature has not guaranteed them an eternal lease of life.

39 *assailable:* open to attack

40 *jocund:* joyful, cheerful

41 *cloistered flight:* flight in or near buildings

42 *shard-borne:* There are two possibilities here: (a) born in dung, (b) borne aloft on scaly wings.

43 *Hath ... peal:* Has sounded the signal for sleep. 'Night's yawning peal' can suggest the tolling of a bell heralding Banquo's death. In Shakespeare, death and sleep are intimately associated, while 'yawning' carries a hint of the grave as well as a suggestion of sleep.

LADY MACBETH

You must leave this.

MACBETH

O, full of scorpions is my mind, dear wife!
Thou know'st that Banquo and his Fleance lives.

LADY MACBETH

But in them nature's copy's not eterne.

MACBETH

There's comfort yet, they are assailable,

40 Then be thou jocund: ere the bat hath flown
His cloistered flight, ere to black Hecate's summons
The shard-borne beetle with his drowsy hums
Hath rung night's yawning peal, there shall be done
A deed of dreadful note.

LADY MACBETH
What's to be done?

MACBETH

45 Be innocent of the knowledge, dearest chuck,
Till thou applaud the deed … Come, seeling night,
Scarf up the tender eye of pitiful day,
And with thy bloody and invisible hand
Cancel and tear to pieces that great bond
50 Which keeps me pale! Light thickens, and the crow
Makes wing to the rooky wood;
Good things of day begin to droop and drowse,
Whiles night's black agents to their preys do rouse.
Thou marvell'st at my words: but hold thee still;
55 Things bad begun make strong themselves by ill:
So, prithee, go with me.

Exeunt.

(handwritten annotation: echo of LMB)

45–6 *Be innocent … deed:* Do not trouble your mind with knowledge of the deed until after it has been done, and then you will have an opportunity to admire it.

45 *chuck:* chicken; a term of endearment

46–7 *Come, seeling night … day:* Macbeth is asking night to conceal the deed from the light of day, just as the falconer blindfolded and sewed up the eyes of the hawk.

46 *seeling:* binding

49–50 *Cancel … pale!:* Destroy the bond by which Banquo and Fleance hold their lives. See the note on line 38 above. 'Pale' can mean 'confined' or 'fenced in'; it can also suggest fear or pity.

53 *Whiles night's black agents … rouse:* Murderous creatures who use night as a cloak for their deeds stir themselves as they prepare to stalk their prey.

54 *Thou marvell'st at my words:* Lady Macbeth appears startled by what he has been saying.

55 *Things bad begun … ill:* If a man sets out on an evil course, he needs to involve himself in further evil if he is to maintain his progress (see 3, 4, 136–8).

'Light thickens, and the crow / Makes wing to the rooky wood'
(3, 2, 50–1)

EXAMINATION-BASED QUESTIONS

- What is the significance of the dialogue between Macbeth and Lady Macbeth at the beginning of this scene?
- This scene marks a decisive change in the relationship between Macbeth and Lady Macbeth. Explain.
- Macbeth's state of mind is clearly exposed in this scene. How would you describe it?
- For many readers, Macbeth's final speech in this scene ('Be innocent of the knowledge …', 45 ff.) recalls one of Lady Macbeth's earlier speeches ('The raven himself is hoarse …' 1, 5, 37 ff.). Discuss the resemblances.

Act Three
‑ Scene Three ‑
[Forres. Near the Palace.]

PLOT SUMMARY

The assassination of Banquo is carried out in darkness by Macbeth's hirelings. Fleance escapes.

The key word in this scene is 'mistrust'. Macbeth cannot trust his two murderers and sends a third to make sure they do their work. The scene marks a significant change for the worse in Macbeth's position. He has failed to remove Fleance, who represents the main threat to his security and peace of mind, and at the same time has laid himself open to suspicion of involvement in Banquo's death. If Macbeth takes the prophecies of the witches seriously, his target should be Fleance rather than Banquo. Indeed, in his soliloquy in Act 3, Scene 1, he has been deeply disturbed by the thought that 'Banquo's issue' (3, 1, 65) may become kings. When the Second Murderer says that they have lost the 'Best half of our affair' (21), he is describing Macbeth's new position quite accurately: they have allowed Fleance, the ultimate long-term threat, to flourish and have eliminated Banquo, who, according to the witches, cannot endanger Macbeth's throne.

Enter three MURDERERS

FIRST MURDERER
But who did bid thee join with us?

THIRD MURDERER   He trusts no one anymore
                                    Macbeth.

SECOND MURDERER Macbeth has become paranoised
He needs not our mistrust, since he delivers
Our offices and what we have to do,
To the direction just.

FIRST MURDERER
                    Then stand with us.
5   The west yet glimmers with some streaks of day;
     Now spurs the lated traveller apace
     To gain the timely inn, and near approaches
     The subject of our watch.

2–4	*He needs not … direction just:* There is no need for us to be suspicious of him (the Third Murderer) since he is able to tell us our duties just as Macbeth laid them out for us.
6–7	*Now spurs … timely inn:* The traveller, overtaken by night, rushes towards the welcome shelter of the inn.

THIRD MURDERER

    Hark! I hear horses.

BANQUO

[Within] Give us a light there, ho!

a contrast to Macbeth's prayer for darkness?

SECOND MURDERER

     Then 'tis he: the rest   9–10   *the rest ... expectation:* the

10   That are within the note of expectation   other expected guests

  Already are i'the court.

FIRST MURDERER

    His horses go about.   11   *go about:* take the long way

THIRD MURDERER

Almost a mile; but he does usually —

So all men do — from hence to the palace gate

Make it their walk.

   Enter BANQUO *and* FLEANCE, *with a torch*

SECOND MURDERER

    A light, a light!

THIRD MURDERER

     'Tis he.

FIRST MURDERER   15   *Stand to't:* prepared for it

15   Stand to't.

BANQUO

It will be rain tonight.

FIRST MURDERER

    Let it come down.   16   *Let it come down:* let the rain

                  of blows come down

  The FIRST MURDERER *strikes out the torch, while the*

  others attack BANQUO.

BANQUO

O, treachery! Fly, good Fleance, fly, fly, fly!

Thou mayst revenge. O slave!   18   *Thou mayst revenge:* so that

                  you may get revenge on my

                  killers

  Dies. FLEANCE *escapes.*

THIRD MURDERER

Who did strike out the light?

FIRST MURDERER

Was't not the way?

THIRD MURDERER

20 There's but one down; the son is fled.

SECOND MURDERER

We have lost

Best half of our affair.

FIRST MURDERER

Well, let's away, and say how much is done.

Exeunt.

19   *Was't not the way?*: Wasn't that what we were supposed to do?

20–1   *We have lost ... affair*: By failing to kill Fleance, we have left the more important part of our task undone.

EXAMINATION-BASED QUESTIONS

- Comment on the significance of the Third Murderer.
- Things go badly here for Macbeth. Why is the outcome of this scene so unfortunate for him?

Act Three
– Scene Four –
[Forres. The Palace.]

PLOT SUMMARY

At the state banquet, **Macbeth and Lady Macbeth welcome their guests**. Having heard about Banquo's murder in gory detail from one of the assassins, Macbeth returns to join in the feast, only to find **Banquo's ghost** in his place. He betrays himself before his guests, who do not see the apparition, and loses control of his feelings. Lady Macbeth strives to save him from exposure, but fails, and the **banquet ends in total disorder**. At the close of the scene, when Lady Macbeth and her husband are alone together, she listens to his further plans with a weary indifference.

The lavish state banquet should, of course, be a triumphant celebration of Macbeth's rule, a way of winning the approval of society and making his kingship solidly respectable. Banquets in Shakespeare are symbols of friendship and social concord, of bodily health in the kingdom. The host and hostess show an almost exaggerated anxiety to make themselves agreeable to their guests ('at first and last, / The hearty welcome', 1–2; 'We will require her welcome', 6; 'they are welcome', 8; 'Be large in mirth', 11; 'good digestion wait on appetite', 38; 'love and health to all', 87; 'I drink to the general joy of the whole table', 89). But the false appearance of pleasant sociability cannot be maintained for long. **Macbeth and his wife are not allowed to enjoy the social fruits of their crimes**. Having violated order and hospitality by murdering the king who was their guest, they find their own kind of order violated in turn. The entry of the First Murderer with his bloody face is symbolic of the fact that **Macbeth cannot suppress his deeds or cover them with false pretence of order**: even 'The secret'st man of blood' (126), as Macbeth ruefully admits later, cannot escape detection.

The infinitely more ruinous entry of Banquo's ghost has a symbolic aspect as well as a functional one. The witches told Banquo that his children would be kings: he now sits in Macbeth's royal seat, which his children will one day inherit. It is this apparition that destroys the occasion and makes it end 'With most admired disorder' (110). For Macbeth, the **banquet scene** marks a turning point because it **involves his social ruin and total loss of face in his society**. It is a decisive stage in the quickening process of his isolation. In Act 3, Scene 6, we find Lennox, who has been present at the banquet, conspiring against him. Macbeth has tried to accommodate himself to his society and failed. When, towards the end of the play, we find him lamenting his loss of 'honour, love, obedience, troops of friends' (5, 3, 25), we inevitably think of the hasty exit of his guests in the banquet scene, and of Lady Macbeth and himself left alone on the stage amid the ruins of the feast. There is an ironic contrast between Macbeth's 'You know your own degrees, sit down' (1), at the beginning, and Lady Macbeth's 'Stand not upon the order of your going, / But go at once' (119–20) at the end. The irony deepens from banquet to banquet in *Macbeth*; the first (1, 7), from which Duncan retired 'In measureless content' (2, 1, 17) only to be murdered in his sleep, is a travesty of hospitality; at the second, Banquo's ghost refuses to allow Macbeth to enjoy the feasting and the hospitality he has desecrated by killing his 'chief guest'; the third is a parody of a banquet, where the witches prepare, not nourishing foods, but revolting recipes to cause 'toil and trouble' (4, 1, 10).

In the final part of the banquet scene, after the guests have gone, we find that **a distinctly new relationship has developed between Macbeth and his wife.** This new relationship can be dramatised by the behaviour of Lady Macbeth when the guests have gone. Her mood and feelings change. She should show sadness and extreme exhaustion. She should convey the impression of being as much in need of sleep as Macbeth. She should seem feeble, as if she were preparing for her final breakdown in Act 5. After she has spoken her goodnight to those at the banquet, she should appear shrunken in stature within her splendid robes. Her mind should appear to control her voice only through a great effort. Her few brief words while Macbeth plays out the scene are lifeless responses, spoken as if she had no further interest in Macbeth's doings. The acting at this point must make

it clear that **she now lacks the energy or the will to dominate Macbeth any longer.** All the initiative will be his from now on. The sleepwalking scene at the beginning of Act 5 will seem like the inevitable sequel to Lady Macbeth's performance at the close of Act 3, Scene 4. The strain of the events of the banquet scene, now intensified by a growing burden of guilt, has exhausted Lady Macbeth and broken her spirit, and it comes as no surprise that her next appearance is in the sleepwalking scene. The reply she makes to Macbeth's imperious question about Macduff is the strangely listless 'Did you send to him, sir?' (129). Her reaction to his terrible speech in reply is even more at odds with everything she has earlier seemed to represent: instead of being roused to excitement by his hints of further action, she wearily tells him that he needs sleep.

From now on, the initiative must be fully Macbeth's, since he can no longer expect help from his wife. But he no longer needs her help; he can now plan his crimes without anybody's assistance and without being afraid that his mind will be 'full of scorpions' (3, 2, 36). It is significant that he can now think of himself wading through a river of blood and then say 'Come, we'll to sleep' (142). This is a measure of the distance he has travelled since the earlier scenes, when it took all of his wife's vast powers of will to persuade him to murder Duncan. The changed relationship between the two has come about, paradoxically, through Lady Macbeth's very success in making a 'man' of her husband, as she would have it (1, 7, 49). He is soon able to outdo her in the arts of false seeming and cunning. As he learns to perfect the methods she has taught him, he keeps his precise intentions from her. After the crisis of the banquet scene, when he has faced and endured the worst that can afflict him, he is able to go on alone. **Their relationship collapses**.

A banquet prepared. Enter MACBETH, LADY
MACBETH, ROSS, LENNOX, *Lords, and Attendants*

MACBETH

You know your own degrees, sit down: at first and last,   1
The hearty welcome.

LORDS

                    Thanks to your majesty.   1–2

MACBETH

Ourself will mingle with society   3
And play the humble host.

5   Our hostess keeps her state, but in best time   5–6
We will require her welcome.

LADY MACBETH

Pronounce it for me, sir, to all our friends;   7
For my heart speaks they are welcome.

        Enter FIRST MURDERER, *to the door*

MACBETH

See, they encounter thee with their hearts' thanks;   9–10
10   Both sides are even: here I'll sit i'the midst:
Be large in mirth; anon, we'll drink a measure
The table round. *[Going to the door]*
                    There's blood upon thy face.

MURDERER

'Tis Banquo's then.   11–12

MACBETH

'Tis better thee without than he within.   14
15   Is he dispatched?   15

MURDERER

My lord, his throat is cut; that I did for him.

MACBETH

Thou art the best o'the cut-throats; yet he's good
That did the like for Fleance: if thou didst it,
Thou art the nonpareil.   19

MURDERER

                    Most royal sir,
20   Fleance is 'scaped.

[handwritten: the presence of assassins adds to the drama of this scene]

Glosses (right column):

You know your own degrees, sit down: You all know your own ranks; let each of you choose a place at table appropriate to his rank.
at first ... welcome: a hearty welcome from beginning to end (of the feast)

Ourself will mingle with society: I will move among the guests.

Our hostess ... welcome: Lady Macbeth remains seated on her throne, but when the proper time comes, I shall ask her to express her own welcome to you.
Pronounce it: make the speech of welcome

See ... midst: See, they reply to your welcome with hearty gratitude; this makes you and them even; now I will sit here among you. Many editors think that 'even' refers to the table, and that Macbeth is saying that both sides of the table are equally occupied.
Be large ... round: Enjoy yourselves. Presently I'll drink a toast to the whole company.
'Tis better ... within: It is better that the blood should be on your face than in Banquo's body.
dispatched: killed

the nonpareil: unparalleled, the best of the lot

21	*my fit:* my spasm of fear, emotional disturbance
	I had else been perfect: I would otherwise have been perfectly safe and secure
22	*Whole as the marble:* as solid as marble
	founded as the rock: as securely based as the rock
23	*As broad and general … air:* as free as the air around us
24	*cabined, cribbed:* imprisoned like the occupant of a miserable hovel
24–5	*bound in … fears:* the prisoner of insolent and nagging doubts and fears
25	*safe:* Safely dispatched, dealt with. Macbeth's hope that Banquo will no longer be a problem is an ironic one.
26	*bides:* waits
27	*trenched:* deep
28	*The least a death to nature:* The least of the wounds would be enough to kill a man.
29–30	*the worm … breed:* The serpent that has escaped (Fleance) will in time develop qualities that will prove dangerous.
31	*No teeth for the present:* not dangerous for the moment
32	*We'll hear, ourselves, again:* We'll talk to each other again.
33	*You do not give the cheer:* You are not encouraging your guests to enjoy your hospitality.
33–5	*The feast is sold … at home:* A feast is no better than a meal that one pays for unless the host often assures his guests that they are welcome; if a feast consisted merely of eating, it would be better to enjoy it at home.
34	*while 'tis a-making:* while the guests are making merry, while the feast is going on
36–7	*From thence … without it:* When one is eating away from home ('From thence'), it is the courteous entertainment offered by the host that gives the food its special quality. A feast would be a poor thing without the accompanying courtesies. Notice the pun on 'meeting' and 'meat'.
37	*remembrancer:* reminder to me of my duties
38–9	*Now good digestion … both!:* May good digestion accompany good appetite, and may both be conducive to good health!

MACBETH
Then comes my fit again: I had else been perfect;
Whole as the marble, founded as the rock,
As broad and general as the casing air:
But now I am cabined, cribbed, confined, bound in
25 To saucy doubts and fears. But Banquo's safe?

MURDERER
Ay, my good lord: safe in a ditch he bides,
With twenty trenched gashes on his head,
The least a death to nature.

MACBETH *a continuation of snake imagery*
↓   Thanks for that.
There the grown serpent lies; the worm that's fled
30 Hath nature that in time will venom breed,
No teeth for the present. Get thee gone; tomorrow
We'll hear, ourselves, again.

Exit MURDERER.

LADY MACBETH
                                    My royal lord,
You do not give the cheer. The feast is sold
That is not often vouched, while 'tis a-making,
35 'Tis given with welcome: to feed were best at home;
From thence, the sauce to meat is ceremony;
Meeting were bare without it.

MACBETH
                                    Sweet remembrancer!
Now good digestion wait on appetite,
And health on both!

LENNOX
                        May it please your Highness sit?

MACBETH
40 Here had we now our country's honour roofed,
Were the graced person of our Banquo present;

The ghost of BANQUO *enters, and sits in*
MACBETH's *place* more drama. The question is
whether this ghost is real or united
Who may I challenge for unkindness   App vs. real
Than pity for mischance!

ROSS

His absence, sir,
Lays blame upon his promise. Please't your Highness
45 To grace us with your royal company?

MACBETH
The table's full.

LENNOX

Here is a place reserved, sir.

MACBETH
Where?

LENNOX
Here, my good lord. What is't that moves your Highness?

MACBETH
Which of you have done this?

Lennox: *Here, my good lord. What is't that moves your Highness?*

Macbeth: *Which of you have done this? (3, 4, 48–9)*

LORDS

What, my good lord?

MACBETH
50 Thou canst not say I did it: never shake
Thy gory locks at me.

40–1 *Here had we now … Banquo present:* The assembly of our country's nobility would be complete if its chief glory, Banquo, were present. The nobles are here imagined as forming a building, with Banquo as its roof. It has also been suggested that the lines mean that all the nobility of Scotland would be under a single roof if Banquo were present.

42–3 *Who may I rather challenge … mischance!:* I hope I may have to rebuke Banquo for his lack of courtesy rather than pity him for some accident or other that may have befallen him (i.e. I hope his absence is due to his bad manners rather than to misadventure).

43–4 *His absence … promise:* His absence shows him guilty of promising something he could not fulfil.

48 *moves:* upsets, perturbs

49 *Which of you have done this?:* (a) played this trick by filling up the seat, (b) killed Banquo

ROSS

Gentlemen, rise; his Highness is not well.

'Thou canst not say I did it: never shake / Thy gory locks at me.'
(3, 4, 50–1)

LADY MACBETH

Sit, worthy friends: my lord is often thus,
And hath been from his youth: pray you, keep seat;

55	*upon a thought:* in a moment
56	*If much you note him:* if you continue to pay a lot of attention to him
57	*offend:* harm or injure (not annoy or vex)
	extend his passion: prolong his disorder, increase his agitation
59	*a bold one:* a brave one
60	*O proper stuff!:* What nonsense!
61	*This is the very painting of your fear:* this is fantasy inspired by your fear
62	*the air-drawn dagger:* the dagger sketched in the air
63	*flaws and starts:* sudden outbursts and fits of passion
64	*Imposters to true fear:* not inspired by real fear
64–6	*would well become ... grandam:* would be appropriate to an old wives' tale, told by one woman and vouched for by another — her grandmother

55 The fit is momentary; upon a thought
He will again be well. If much you note him,
You shall offend him and extend his passion:
Feed, and regard him not. *[Aside.]* Are you a man?

MACBETH

Ay, and a bold one that dare look on that
60 Which might appal the devil. diabolical imagery (makes
reference to devil)

LADY MACBETH

O proper stuff!
This is the very painting of your fear;
This is the air-drawn dagger which you said
Led you to Duncan. O, these flaws and starts —
Imposters to true fear — would well become
65 A woman's story at a winter's fire,
Authorised by her grandam. Shame itself!
Why do you make such faces? When all's done,
You look but on a stool.

MACBETH

Prithee, see there! Behold! Look! Lo! How say you?
70 Why, what care I! If thou canst nod, speak too.
If charnel-houses and our graves must send
Those that we bury back, our monuments
Shall be the maws of kites.

Exit GHOST.

LADY MACBETH

What! Quite unmanned in folly?

MACBETH

If I stand here, I saw him.

LADY MACBETH

Fie, for shame!

MACBETH

75 Blood hath been shed ere now, i'the olden time,
Ere human statute purged the gentle weal;
Ay, and since too, murders have been performed
Too terrible for the ear. The time has been
That when the brains were out the man would die,
80 And there an end; but now they rise again,
With twenty mortal murders on their crowns,
And push us from our stools. This is more strange
Than such a murder is.

LADY MACBETH

My worthy lord,
Your noble friends do lack you.

MACBETH

I do forget.
85 Do not muse at me, my worthy friends;
I have a strange infirmity, which is nothing
To those that know me. Come, love and health to all;
Then I'll sit down. Give me some wine, fill full.
I drink to the general joy of the whole table,
90 And to our dear friend Banquo, whom we miss;
Would he were here! *[Re-enter* GHOST.*]* To all, and him,
   we thirst,
And all to all.

70 *If thou … speak too:* Banquo's ghost has been shaking its head accusingly at him. He challenges it to accuse him in words.

71–3 *If charnel-houses … maws of kites:* If the dead insist on returning from their places of burial, then instead of burying them in tombs, we will have to let their bodies be devoured by kites, in which case they will not return.

71 *charnel-houses:* sepulchres
72 *monuments:* tombs
73 *maws:* stomachs
kites: birds of prey, of the falcon family
What! Quite unmanned in folly?: Has your foolishness destroyed your manhood?

74 *If I stand here:* as sure as I stand here

76 *Ere human statute … weal:* before human, and humane, laws mitigated the barbarism of society and made it more civilised and gentle

81 *twenty mortal murders:* twenty deadly wounds
82–3 *This is … murder is:* this apparition is more unnatural than even the murder (of Banquo)

84 *do lack you:* miss your company

85 *muse:* wonder

91 *Re-enter Ghost:* It is worth noting that Banquo's ghost appears each time Macbeth summons him.
92 *And all to all:* let us all drink to each other
Our duties, and the pledge: we give you our devotion, and honour the toast you have proposed

LORDS

> Our duties, and the pledge.

MACBETH

> Avaunt, and quit my sight, let the earth hide thee!
> Thy bones are marrowless, thy blood is cold;
95 Thou hast no speculation in those eyes
> Which thou dost glare with!

LADY MACBETH

> Think of this, good peers,
> But as a thing of custom: 'tis no other;
> Only it spoils the pleasure of the time.

MACBETH

> What man dare, I dare:
100 Approach thou like the rugged Russian bear,
> The armed rhinoceros, or the Hyrcan tiger;
> Take any shape but that, and my firm nerves
> Shall never tremble: or be alive again,
> And dare me to the desert with thy sword;
105 If trembling I inhabit then, protest me
> The baby of a girl. Hence, horrible shadow!
> Unreal mockery, hence!

A direct echo of earlier statements.

93 | *Avaunt …!:* Go away!

95 | *speculation:* understanding of what you see

97 | *a thing of custom:* something that happens quite often

100 | *like:* in the shape of
101 | *Hyrcan tiger:* These were tigers from Hyrcania, a province of the Persian empire. They were noted for their ferocity.
102 | *that:* the form of the murdered Banquo
104 | *dare me to the desert:* challenge me to single combat in a place where nobody else is present.
105–6 | *If trembling … a girl:* If cowardly thoughts then possess me, you may proclaim me a baby girl.

'Hence, horrible shadow! / Unreal mockery, hence!' (3, 4, 106–7)

Exit GHOST.

> Why, so; being gone,
> I am a man again. Pray you, sit still.

LADY MACBETH

You have displaced the mirth, broke the good meeting,
110 With most admired disorder.

MACBETH

Can such things be,
And overcome us like a summer's cloud,
Without our special wonder? You make me strange
Even to the disposition that I owe,
When now I think you can behold such sights
115 And keep the natural ruby of your cheeks,
When mine is blanched with fear.

ROSS

What sights, my lord?

LADY MACBETH

I pray you speak not; he grows worse and worse;
Question enrages him. At once, good night:
Stand not upon the order of your going,
120 But go at once.

LENNOX

Good night; and better health
Attend his Majesty!

LADY MACBETH

A kind good night to all!

Exeunt Lords and Attendants.

MACBETH

It will have blood; they say, blood will have blood:
Stones have been known to move and trees to speak;
Augurs and understood relations have _birds_
125 By maggot-pies and choughs and rooks brought forth
The secret'st man of blood. What is the night?

LADY MACBETH

Almost at odds with morning, which is which.

MACBETH

How say'st thou, that Macduff denies his person
At our great bidding?

LADY MACBETH

Did you send to him, sir?

---

109 *displaced the mirth:* shattered the happiness of the banquet

110 *admired disorder:* disorderly behaviour arousing astonishment in those who witness it

110–12 *Can such ... wonder?:* Can such dreadful events overtake us, like a dark cloud in summer, without causing us to register amazement?

112–16 *You make me ... with fear:* You make me feel like a stranger to my own nature, or amazed at my own nature. Macbeth has always thought himself brave; now that he sees his wife unmoved by what terrifies him, he wonders whether he is as brave as he thought he was.

113 *the disposition that I owe:* my distinctive personality

116 *When mine is blanched with fear:* when the natural red ('ruby') of my cheeks has turned white with fear

119–20 *Stand not ... go at once:* Do not bother to arrange your leave-taking according to rank, but all go together as fast as you can. This undignified instruction contrasts with Macbeth's formal injunction in the first line of the scene ('you know your own degrees').

122 *It:* the murder of Banquo
they say, blood will have blood. The idea comes from Genesis 4: 6: 'He who sheds man's blood will have his blood shed by men'.

123 *Stones ... to speak:* stones and trees have revealed the corpses of murdered people buried under them

124–6 *Augurs ... man of blood:* The proper study and interpretation of the omens associated with the behaviour of certain birds has brought the most cunning murderers to light.

124 *Augurs:* These are forecasts or guesses made by those who believe they can interpret the behaviour of birds and animals, in particular to throw light on the secrets of the past, present or future.
understood relations: Connections or relationships established between things which do not seem to be related. For example, the presence of four magpies was thought to herald death.

125 *maggot-pies:* magpies
choughs: red-legged crows

125–6	*brought forth ... blood:* exposed the guilt of even the most cunning murderer
127	*Almost at odds ... is which:* Dawn is breaking and it is impossible to say whether it is night or morning.
128–9	*How say'st thou ... bidding?:* What do you think of Macduff's refusal to come when I commanded him to do so?
130	*by the way:* indirectly *I will send:* I am determined to summon Macduff.
132	*a servant fee'd:* a paid spy
133	*betimes:* early, quickly
136	*All causes shall give way:* Every other consideration will take a lesser place.
136–8	*I am in blood ... go o'er:* Macbeth thinks of himself wading through a river of blood. He thinks it would be as weary a task to go back (and cease killing) as to continue with his murderous work (see 3, 2, 55).
139–40	*Strange things ... scanned:* I have some strange plans in mind which I must act upon before I examine them. The image, like many of the others in the play, is from the theatre. Macbeth finds his next role (as Macduff's antagonist) so pressing that he will have to perform it (play the part) without studying it properly.
141	*season:* preserver
142–4	*My strange ... in deed:* My odd delusions (at the sight of Banquo's ghost) are those of a beginner in crime who needs further practice to make him tough. As yet, I am merely a novice in bloody deeds.

MACBETH

130 I hear it by the way; but I will send:
There's not a one of them but in his house *He has resolved to*
I keep a servant fee'd. I will to-morrow — *using spies*
And betimes I will — to the Weird Sisters:
More shall they speak; for now I am bent to know,
135 By the worst means, the worst. For mine own good
All causes shall give way: I am in blood
Stepped in so far that, should I wade no more,
Returning were as tedious as go o'er. *In contrast to before*
Strange things I have in head that will to hand, *the murder of*
140 Which must be acted ere they may be scanned. *Duncan.*

He has no intention of using his conscience anymore

LADY MACBETH

You lack the season of all natures, sleep.

MACBETH

Come, we'll to sleep. My strange and self-abuse
Is the initiate fear that wants hard use:
We are yet but young in deed.

Exeunt.

'You lack the season of all natures, sleep' (3, 4, 141)

EXAMINATION-BASED QUESTIONS

- What do Macbeth and Lady Macbeth hope to achieve from the state banquet?
- The First Murderer supplies some graphic, gory details of Banquo's murder. Why are these details important?
- Macbeth's public reference to Banquo ('Here had we now our country's honour roofed ...', 40) is ironic. Explain.
- Lady Macbeth tells her husband (62) that his vision of Banquo is as much an illusion as 'the air-drawn dagger' of Act 2, Scene 1. Would you agree with her?
- What is the effect of Macbeth's behaviour on his principal subjects here?
- The appearance and reappearance of the ghost have something in common with its two disappearances. What is it?
- How would you describe Lady Macbeth's contribution to this scene? Mention some other episodes in the play where her intervention on Macbeth's behalf is also of critical importance.
- How would you account for the obvious change in Lady Macbeth's manner and attitude after the guests have gone and when she is alone with Macbeth?

KEY THEMES AND IMPORTANT FACTS

- This scene has all the elements of high drama: suspense, surprise, tension and powerful dialogue. It provides opportunities for great actors, particularly those playing Macbeth and Lady Macbeth. Macbeth's frenzy is reflected in his looks and actions, wild gestures and hysterical tone of voice.
- Lady Macbeth's task in the scene is to hide Macbeth's frenzy from the guests. In this, she has much scope to use a variety of facial expressions. For example, she can smile at one guest, whisper to another and distantly salute a third. She will cast angry looks at Macbeth, indicating both her vexation and uneasiness.
- The effort to control Macbeth finally proves too much for her. To show this, she will rise from her seat, seize Macbeth's arm and whisper 'Are you a man?' into his ear, assuming a look of anger and contempt.

Act Three
— Scene Five —
[A Heath.]

PLOT SUMMARY

Hecate, the spirit who rules over all witches, is angry that she has not been consulted up to now about Macbeth. She gives orders for a meeting with him on the morrow and foretells his downfall.

Most editors believe that this scene was not written by Shakespeare. We have not been prepared for the arrival of Hecate. The witches are not what they were in the earlier scenes. Originally they regarded Macbeth, like their other human contacts, as the victim of their plots; now they seem to think of him as one of their disciples ('a wayward son', 11). The last four lines of Hecate's speech, however, are worth attention, since they refer to an important theme in the tragedy: Macbeth's reckless confidence, which is to determine his conduct and attitude for the rest of the play.

Thunder. Enter the three WITCHES *meeting* HECATE

FIRST WITCH
Why, how now, Hecate, you look angerly.

HECATE
Have I not reason, beldams as you are,
Saucy and overbold? How did you dare
To trade and traffic with Macbeth
5 In riddles and affairs of death;
And I, the mistress of your charms,
The close contriver of all harms,
Was never called to bear my part,
Or show the glory of our art?
10 And, which is worse, all you have done
Hath been but for a wayward son,
Spiteful and wrathful; who, as others do,
Loves for his own ends, not for you.
But make amends now: get you gone,
15 And at the pit of Acheron
Meet me i'the morning: thither he
Will come to know his destiny.
Your vessels and your spells provide,
Your charms and everything beside.
20 I am for the air; this night I'll spend

---

2   *beldams:* old hags
3   *Saucy:* insolent, presumptuous
4   *To trade and traffic:* to have dealings with

7   *close contriver:* secret planner
8   *to bear my part:* to play my part

11   *a wayward son:* Macbeth, an unreliable and fickle follower of our cult
15   *the pit of Acheron:* The cavern used by the Witches. Acheron means hell.

18–19   *Your vessels ... beside:* bring your cauldrons, your magic formulae and everything else that is necessary

Unto a dismal and a fatal end.
Great business must be wrought ere noon:
Upon the corner of the moon
There hangs a vaporous drop profound;
25 I'll catch it ere it come to ground:
And that distilled by magic sleights
Shall raise such artificial sprites
As by the strength of their illusion
Shall draw him on to his confusion.
30 He shall spurn fate, scorn death, and bear
His hopes 'bove wisdom, grace, and fear;
And you all know security
Is mortals' chiefest enemy. *complacency*

    Music and a song within:

'Come away, come away, etc.'
Hark! I am called; my little spirit, see,
35 Sits in a foggy cloud, and stays for me.

    Exit.

FIRST WITCH
Come, let's make haste; she'll soon be back again.

    Exeunt.

21	*Unto a dismal and a fatal end:* with the purpose of bringing about a disastrous and fatal result
24	*a vaporous drop profound:* a drop of vapour with mysterious and powerful effects
26	*sleights:* arts
27	*artificial sprites:* the apparitions of Act 4, Scene 1
28	*their illusion:* their deceptive character
29	*confusion:* destruction
30–1	*He shall ... fear:* Macbeth will show contempt for fate and death and will entertain rash and foolish hopes which have no basis in common sense or religion, and which take no account of the fear a man should feel for the unknown.
31	*grace:* religion
32	*security:* over-confidence
34	*little spirit:* Her familiar spirit. A familiar spirit was a demon in animal form.

'And at the pit of Acheron / Meet me i' the morning: / thither he / Will come to know his destiny.' (3, 5, 15–17)

EXAMINATION-BASED QUESTIONS

- Does this scene suggest a new relationship between Macbeth and the witches?
- In the final lines of her speech ('He shall spurn fate ...', 30 ff.) what does Hecate have in store for Macbeth? How is this prophecy fulfilled?

Act Three

– Scene Six –

[Forres. The Palace.]

PLOT SUMMARY

Lennox knows the extent of Macbeth's guilt. We learn that Macduff has gone to the court of the King of England to join Malcolm.

The main purpose of this scene is to provide a commentary on the way Macbeth's subjects feel about his reign. With obvious irony, Lennox expresses the general suspicion that Macbeth has murdered Duncan and Banquo, and he sheds doubt on Macbeth's motives for killing the grooms. We are being prepared for Macbeth's move against Macduff's family and for the role the English will play in the liberation of Scotland from Macbeth's rule. Macbeth, although a murderer, is the lawfully crowned King of Scotland, and Shakespeare is careful to provide good reasons for a move against him. These reasons are given mainly by the anonymous lord, whose principal arguments are that Malcolm is the rightful heir to the throne and that Macbeth's reign is a tyranny. In Act 3, Scene 4, Macbeth announced his intention of sending for Macduff. Here we learn the result: Macduff has fled to England.

Enter LENNOX *and another* LORD

1–2	*My former speeches ... farther:* What I have said to you on other occasions has merely reflected your own ideas; you can draw your own conclusions.
2–3	*only I say ... borne:* All I can say is that the conduct of affairs (under Macbeth) has been very odd.
3–4	*The gracious Duncan ... dead:* Lennox is quoting Macbeth's own description of Duncan. He is saying ironically, 'Macbeth pitied Duncan, and of course Duncan died.' After Duncan's murder, Macbeth gave an impressive display of lamentation for his victim.
6	*Fleance killed:* This is Macbeth's explanation for Banquo's death.
8	*cannot want the thought:* cannot help thinking
10	*fact:* deed, act (in this case, crime)
12	*pious:* holy, devoted *delinquents:* men who neglected their duty
13	*thralls:* slaves or prisoners

LENNOX

My former speeches have but hit your thoughts,
Which can interpret farther: only I say
Things have been strangely borne. The gracious Duncan
Was pitied of Macbeth: marry, he was dead.
5   And the right-valiant Banquo walked too late;
Whom, you may say, if't please you, Fleance killed,
For Fleance fled: men must not walk too late.
Who cannot want the thought how monstrous
It was for Malcolm and for Donalbain
10   To kill their gracious father? Damned fact!
How it did grieve Macbeth! Did he not straight,
In pious rage, the two delinquents tear,
That were the slaves of drink and thralls of sleep?
Was not that nobly done? Ay, and wisely too;
15   For 'twould have angered any heart alive
To hear the men deny't. So that, I say,
He has borne all things well; and I do think
That had he Duncan's sons under his key —
As, an't please heaven, he shall not — they should find

[handwritten note: This links to Malcolm and Donalbain]

20 What 'twere to kill a father; so should Fleance. 17
But peace! For from broad words, and 'cause he failed
His presence at the tyrant's feast, I hear,
Macduff lives in disgrace. Sir, can you tell
Where he bestows himself?

LORD

The son of Duncan,
25 From whom this tyrant holds the due of birth, 19
Lives in the English court, and is received 19–20
Of the most pious Edward with such grace *sacred imagery*
That the malevolence of fortune nothing *used as was used*
Takes from his high respect. Thither Macduff *for Duncan*
30 Is gone to pray the holy king upon his aid
To wake Northumberland and war-like Siward, 21
That by the help of these (with Him above 24
To ratify the work) we may again 25
Give to our tables meat, sleep to our nights,
35 Free from our feasts and banquets bloody knives, 27
Do faithful homage and receive free honours:
All which we pine for now. And this report 28–9
Hath so exasperate the king that he
Prepares for some attempt of war.

LENNOX
Sent he to Macduff? 30

31
LORD 34
40 He did: and with an absolute 'Sir, not I!'
The cloudy messenger turns me his back
And hums, as who should say 'You'll rue the time
That clogs me with this answer.'

LENNOX 35
And that well might
Advise him to a caution to hold what distance 36
45 His wisdom can provide. Some holy angel *sacred images +*
Fly to the court of England and unfold *images of disease +*
His message ere he come, that a swift blessing *suffering* 37
May soon return to this our suffering country 37–8
Under a hand accursed!

LORD 40–3
I'll send my prayers with him.

Exeunt.

He has borne all things well:
There is irony here, as in most
of the references to Macbeth in
this speech. The surface
meaning is: 'Macbeth has
responded well to every
situation.' This is in total
contrast to the meaning
intended by Lennox: 'Macbeth
has arranged everything to his
own advantage.'
an't: if it
they should find … father:
They would discover what a
severe view Macbeth takes of
them because of the murder
of their father. This is heavy-
handed irony on the part
of Lennox.
broad words: loose,
careless talk
bestows himself: takes refuge,
or is in residence
holds the due of birth: prevents
him from having what is lawfully
his by birth (i.e. the throne)
Of the most pious … grace:
by Edward the Confessor with
such courtesy
*That the malevolence …
respect:* that his bad fortune in
having the throne usurped by
a tyrant does nothing to take
away the respect in which he
is rightly held as lawful king
upon his aid: for help, in his
support (i.e. Malcolm's)
To wake: to call to arms
*Give to our tables meat …
nights:* Be allowed to enjoy our
food and sleep. Notice the
parallel with Macbeth's 'Ere we
will eat our meal in fear, and
sleep/In the affliction of these
terrible dreams/That shake us
nightly' (3, 2, 17–19).
Free from … knives: remove
the threat of murder from our
feasts and banquets
*Do faithful homage …
honours:* honour the king
sincerely and have honours
conferred on merit, not for
dubious services
pine for: long for, desire
And this report … the king:
this news (of Malcolm's good
reception in England) has so
angered Macbeth
He did … with this answer':
When Macduff absolutely
refused to return to Scotland, the
scowling ('cloudy') messenger
turned back towards Macbeth,
muttering that Macduff would
regret having burdened him (the

messenger) with such an answer. The messenger knows that he is in for a hostile reception from Macbeth when he returns.

43   *clogs:* burdens. The messenger is thinking of Macduff's 'Sir, not I!' (line 40) as a burdensome piece of bad news to which Macbeth will respond violently.

43–5   *And that well might … provide:* That episode should make Macduff aware of the need to keep a sensible distance between Macbeth and himself.

45–7   *Some holy angel … ere he come:* Lennox is praying that an angel may get to the court of England even before Macduff arrives there and tell the king how urgently English help is needed. The idea is that the earlier the English know about Scotland's sufferings under Macbeth, the more quickly they will send help.

48–9   *our suffering country … accursed!:* our country suffering under evil rule

EXAMINATION-BASED QUESTIONS

- What is the tone of the opening speech of this scene?
- The scene as a whole serves some important purposes. What are they?
- The imagery of this scene is significant. In what ways?

Act Four

– Scene One –

[A Cave.]

PLOT SUMMARY

The witches prepare their spell, throwing revolting ingredients into a boiling cauldron. Macbeth arrives in the hope of discovering his destiny. The witches conjure up their apparitions, which offer him some consolation but which also confirm his fears and suspicions of Macduff. Lennox brings news that Macduff has fled to England and Macbeth decides on the slaughter of the fugitive's wife and children.

The ingredients of the witches' cauldron are, presumably, arranged to match Macbeth's developing wickedness. Macbeth here fulfils Hecate's earlier prophecy (3, 5). He is about to be ruined through over-confidence. His first greeting to the witches is frenzied; he is carried away by the force of his own inflated rhetoric.

The three apparitions are deceptive. The 'armed head' foretells Macbeth's decapitation by Macduff; Macbeth, however, takes it to represent Macduff, on whom his fears are now centred, and is thankful for the warning the apparitions seem to convey. The Second Apparition, the 'bloody child', is Macduff, 'from his mother's womb / Untimely ripped', as we will learn in the last act of the play (5, 8, 15–16). This apparition is 'More potent than the first' (76), because Macduff's strange birth will make him the means of Macbeth's destruction. The advice of this apparition is cruelly misleading to Macbeth; it urges him to remain utterly secure, since 'none of woman born' (80) can harm him. What Macbeth cannot know, however, is that the speaker represents somebody not 'of woman born', and therefore the agent of Macbeth's death. The Third Apparition is young Malcolm, coming to Dunsinane carrying a bough. Again, Macbeth is falsely reassured by the misleading prophecy about the moving of Birnam wood to Dunsinane.

Macbeth wants reassurance, and he is prepared to see the three apparitions as offering this. He takes everything they say and represent as a good omen. ('Sweet bodements! Good!', 96). The last part of the witches' tableau, however, can offer little comfort. The show of eight kings, representing the eventual succession of Banquo's descendants to the throne of Scotland, is a shattering experience for Macbeth, leading him to an outburst of helpless rage. He finds some relief in his determination to murder Macduff's family. This new plan marks an obvious deterioration in Macbeth's character. The murders of Duncan and Banquo had their own terrible logic, at least from Macbeth's point of view, but the planned killing of an innocent woman and her children can achieve no practical result; it is a piece of gratuitous villainy.

Thunder. Enter the three WITCHES

FIRST WITCH
Thrice the brinded cat hath mewed.

SECOND WITCH
Thrice and once the hedge-pig whined.

THIRD WITCH
Harpier cries; 'tis time, 'tis time.

FIRST WITCH
Round about the cauldron go;
5 In the poisoned entrails throw.
Toad, that under cold stone
Days and nights has thirty-one
Sweltered venom sleeping got,
Boil thou first i'the charmed pot.

ALL
10 Double, double toil and trouble;
Fire burn and cauldron bubble.

SECOND WITCH
Fillet of a fenny snake,
In the cauldron boil and bake;
Eye of newt, and toe of frog,
15 Wool of bat, and tongue of dog,
Adder's fork, and blind-worm's sting,
Lizard's leg, and howlet's wing —
For a charm of powerful trouble,
Like a hell-broth boil and bubble.

1   *the brinded cat:* the streaked cat, called Greymalkin in Act 1, Scene 1, 8

2   *hedge-pig:* hedgehog

3   *Harpier:* Shakespeare may have had in mind the harpy of Greek mythology, a creature half bird, half woman.

6–8   *Toad ... sleeping got:* The toad, lying a full month under the stone, has produced ('got') sweated poison.

12   *Fillet of a fenny snake:* a slice of snake from the marshes

14   *newt:* a lizardlike animal
16   *fork:* forked tongue
     blind-worm's sting: slow-worm's sting, once considered poisonous
17   *howlet's wing:* owlet's wing

'Fillet of a fenny snake / In the cauldron boil and bake' (4, 1, 12–13)

ALL

20 Double, double toil and trouble;
Fire burn and cauldron bubble.

THIRD WITCH

Scale of dragon, tooth of wolf,
Witch's mummy, maw and gulf
Of the ravined salt-sea shark,
25 Root of hemlock digged i'the dark,
Liver of blaspheming Jew,
Gall of goat, and slips of yew
Slivered in the moon's eclipse,
Nose of Turk, and Tartar's lips,
30 Finger of birth-strangled babe
Ditch-delivered by a drab —
Make the gruel thick and slab:
Add thereto a tiger's chaudron,
For the ingredients of our cauldron.

ALL

35 Double, double toil and trouble;
Fire burn and cauldron bubble.

SECOND WITCH

Cool it with a baboon's blood,
Then the charm is firm and good.

Enter HECATE

HECATE

O! Well done! I commend your pains,
40 And every one shall share i'the gains.
And now about the cauldron sing,
Like elves and fairies in a ring,
Enchanting all that you put in.

Music and a song, 'Black spirits,' etc.

Exit HECATE.

SECOND WITCH

By the pricking of my thumbs, *A true analysis*
45 Something wicked this way comes. *of Macbeth*
Open, locks,
Whoever knocks!

23 *Witch's mummy:* This can mean either human flesh mummified by a witch, or the mummified flesh of a witch. Such flesh was put to medicinal use.

23–4 *maw and gulf ... shark:* the stomach and gullet of a shark which has devoured his victim

24 *ravined:* sated, gorged

25 *Root ... dark:* Digging the root in the dark would ensure that it was at its most poisonous.

27–8 *slips of yew ... eclipse:* The yew, a common graveyard tree, was considered poisonous and also symbolises grief. These slips of yew were sliced off ('Slivered') during the lunar eclipse because this was a time of ill-omen.

29 *Turk, and Tartar:* These are in the spell, like the Jew, because of their paganism and their proverbial cruelty to Christians. *Tartars:* In Shakespeare's time, these were considered a barbarous race.

31 *Ditch-delivered by a drab:* the child of a harlot born in a ditch

32 *slab:* thick, sticky

33 *chaudron:* entrails

37 *Cool it with a baboon's blood:* The baboon's blood, being hot, won't cool it very much!

44 *By the pricking of my thumbs:* Such tingling sensations were supposed to herald evil.

Enter MACBETH

MACBETH

How now, you secret, black, and midnight hags!
What is't you do?

ALL

A deed without a name.

MACBETH

50 I conjure you, by that which you profess —
Howe'er you come to know it — answer me:
Though you untie the winds and let them fight
Against the churches; though the yesty waves
Confound and swallow navigation up;
55 Though bladed corn be lodged and trees blown down;
Though castles topple on their warders' heads;
Though palaces and pyramids do slope
Their heads to their foundations; though the treasure
Of Nature's germens tumble all together,
60 Even till destruction sicken — answer me
To what I ask you.

FIRST WITCH

Speak.

SECOND WITCH

Demand.

THIRD WITCH

We'll answer.

FIRST WITCH

Say if thou'dst rather hear it from our mouths,
Or from our masters?

MACBETH

Call 'em: let me see 'em.

FIRST WITCH

Pour in sow's blood, that hath eaten
65 Her nine farrow; grease that's sweaten
From the murderer's gibbet throw
Into the flame.

ALL

Come, high or low;
Thyself and office deftly show.

---

48 *secret, black, and midnight hags!:* occult, mysterious creatures of the night, devotees of black magic

50 *I conjure you … profess:* I call upon you, in the name of witchcraft.

51 *Howe'er you come to know it:* The 'it' here is witchcraft, and Macbeth knows that they derive their knowledge of this from evil spirits. The source does not trouble him.

52–60 *Though you untie … sicken:* even though you release forces which will cause the destruction of natural order, social order and even cosmic order

53 *yesty:* foamy

54 *Confound and swallow navigation up:* cause shipwrecks

55 *bladed corn be lodged:* Corn in the blade beaten down. The blade is the leaf of corn.

58–9 *the treasure … all together:* The patterns or seeds of all created things become utterly confused, with monstrous results.

59 *germens:* rudiments, basics

60 *Even till destruction sicken:* until disorder becomes sick of its own excesses

63 *our masters:* These are the Powers whom the Witches serve.

65 *Her nine farrow:* Nine was believed to be a magic number. The sow ate her nine piglets.
sweaten: sweated

66 *gibbet:* gallows

68 *Thyself … show:* be sharp about fulfilling your function

Thunder. FIRST APPARITION, *an armed head*

MACBETH

Tell me, thou unknown power —

FIRST WITCH

He knows thy thought:
70 Hear his speech, but say thou nought.

FIRST APPARITION

Macbeth! Macbeth! Macbeth! Beware Macduff;
Beware the Thane of Fife. Dismiss me. Enough.

Descends.

The tactic of beginning with a truth will trap Macbeth

MACBETH

Whate'er thou art, for thy good caution thanks;
Thou hast harped my fear aright. But one word more —

FIRST WITCH

75 He will not be commanded: here's another,
More potent than the first.

Thunder. SECOND APPARITION, *a bloody child*

SECOND APPARITION

Macbeth! Macbeth! Macbeth! —

MACBETH

Had I three ears, I'd hear thee.

SECOND APPARITION

Be bloody, bold, and resolute: laugh to scorn
80 The power of man, for none of woman born
Shall harm Macbeth.

Descends.

MACBETH

Then live, Macduff: what need I fear of thee?
But yet I'll make assurance double sure,
And take a bond of fate: thou shalt not live,
85 That I may tell pale-hearted fear it lies,
And sleep in spite of thunder.

Thunder. THIRD APPARITION, *a child crowned, with a tree in his hand.*

First Apparition, an armed head. The helmeted head probably represents Macbeth's head, which is to be cut off by Macduff and brought to Malcolm (Act 5, Scene 8).

74 *harped:* guessed

76 *More potent than the first:* A bloody child rises from the cauldron. The Second Apparition, the bloody child, is Macduff untimely ripped from his mother's womb. This apparition is more powerful than the first one because Macduff's strange birth will make him the means of Macbeth's destruction.

78 *three ears:* one for each greeting

83–4 *But yet I'll make ... bond of fate:* Macbeth will make certain that fate will keep the promise just given by killing Macduff anyway.

85 *That I may ... lies:* so that I will be able to dismiss my fears as baseless

86 *And sleep in spite of thunder:* and enjoy such sound sleep that nothing will disturb it (because he thinks he will at last enjoy peace of mind)
Third Apparition ... hand: This is the royal child Malcolm. The tree he is carrying is like the boughs he will order his men to cut down in Birnam wood.

What is this,
That rises like the issue of a king,
And wears upon his baby brow the round
And top of sovereignty?

ALL
                              Listen, but speak not to't.

THIRD APPARITION
90   Be lion-mettled, proud, and take no care
Who chafes, who frets, or where conspirers are:
Macbeth shall never vanquished be until
Great Birnam wood to high Dunsinane hill
Shall come against him.

        Descends.

MACBETH
              That will never be:
95   Who can impress the forest, bid the tree
Unfix his earth-bound root? Sweet bodements! Good!
Rebellious dead, rise never till the wood
Of Birnam rise, and our high-placed Macbeth
Shall live the lease of nature, pay his breath
100 To time and mortal custom. Yet my heart
Throbs to know one thing: tell me (if your art
Can tell so much) shall Banquo's issue ever
Reign in this kingdom?

ALL
                              Seek to know no more.

MACBETH
I will be satisfied: deny me this,
105 And an eternal curse fall on you! Let me know.

        Hautboys.

Why sinks that cauldron? And what noise is this?

FIRST WITCH
Show!

SECOND WITCH
Show!

THIRD WITCH
Show!

88–9   *round … sovereignty:* the crown, the supreme symbol of kingship

90   *lion-mettled:* lion-hearted
91   *chafes:* is angry

94–101   *That will never be … if your art:* It is worth noting that Macbeth, like the Apparitions, speaks in rhyme. This suggests that he feels an identity with the lying spirits who make him feel falsely secure. The tone and content of his prophetic utterance match those of the supernatural voices.
95   *impress:* conscript
96   *bodements:* prophecies
97   *Rebellious dead:* Macbeth fears that the dead will rise and be avenged on him, as Banquo has done.
99   *the lease of nature:* a normal life span
99–100   *pay … custom:* Macbeth shall give up his life only to old age and natural causes of death.
103   *Reign in this kingdom?:* Macbeth may be hoping that Banquo's descendants were destined to rule some other kingdom.
104   *I will be satisfied:* I insist on being satisfied.
105   *Hautboys:* oboes (woodwind musical instruments), from the French hautbois, 'high wood'

ALL

110 Show his eyes, and grieve his heart;
Come like shadows, so depart.

A show of eight kings, and BANQUO *last; the last king
with a glass in his hand*

MACBETH

Thou art too like the spirit of Banquo; down!
Thy crown does sear mine eyeballs. And thy hair,
Thou other gold-bound brow, is like the first.
115 A third is like the former. Filthy hags!
Why do you show me this? A fourth? Start, eyes!
What, will the line stretch out to the crack of doom?
Another yet? A seventh? I'll see no more:
And yet the eighth appears, who bears a glass
120 Which shows me many more; and some I see
That two-fold balls and treble sceptres carry.
Horrible sight! Now I see 'tis true,
For the blood-boltered Banquo smiles upon me,
And points at them for his.

The show vanishes.

What! Is this so?

FIRST WITCH

125 Ay, sir, all this is so. But why
Stands Macbeth thus amazedly?
Come, sisters, cheer we up his sprites,
And show the best of our delights.
I'll charm the air to give a sound,
130 While you perform your antic round,
That this great king may kindly say
Our duties did his welcome pay.

Music. The WITCHES *dance, and vanish.*

MACBETH

Where are they? Gone? Let this pernicious hour
Stand aye accursed in the calendar!
Come in, without there!

Enter LENNOX

LENNOX

135   What's your Grace's will?

A show of eight kings: These are the eight Stuart kings; the eighth with the glass is James the First, Shakespeare's sovereign, whom the play politely flatters. Some editors suggest that the eighth figure represents Mary Queen of Scots, the eighth Stuart monarch, and that the glass was used to reflect the figure of James who was a spectator at the first performance of the play.

113 *sear:* burn

113–14 *And thy hair ... brow:* Macbeth sees a second crowned king appearing.

116 *Start, eyes!:* May my eyes start from their sockets!

117 *the crack of doom:* the sound of the trumpet that will herald the Day of Judgment

119 *a glass:* a magic glass that reveals the future

121 *two-fold balls and treble sceptres:* the two orbs used in the coronation of the British monarch, and the three sceptres used for the same purpose

123 *blood-boltered:* his hair matted with blood

124 *And points at them for his:* claims them as his own

130 *antic round:* fantastic dance

133 *this pernicious hour:* this evil hour

134 *aye:* ever, always

MACBETH
Saw you the Weird Sisters?

LENNOX

No, my lord.

MACBETH
Came they not by you?

LENNOX

No indeed, my lord.

MACBETH _an image of disease_

Infected by the air whereon they ride,
And damned all those that trust them! I did hear
140 The galloping of horse: who was't came by?

LENNOX
'Tis two or three, my lord, that bring you word
Macduff is fled to England.

MACBETH

Fled to England!

LENNOX
Ay, my good lord.

MACBETH _soliloquy_

[_Aside._] Time, thou anticipat'st my dread exploits;
145 The flighty purpose never is o'ertook
Unless the deed go with it. From this moment
The very firstlings of my heart shall be _contrast to MacB_
The firstlings of my hand. And even now, _at start of play_
To crown my thoughts with acts, be it thought and done:
150 The castle of Macduff I will surprise,
Seize upon Fife, give to the edge of the sword
His wife, his babes, and all unfortunate souls
That trace him in his line. No boasting like a fool:
This deed I'll do before this purpose cool.
155 But no more sights! [_Aloud._] Where are these gentlemen?
Come, bring me where they are.

Exeunt.

138   _Infected:_ contaminated by plague
139   _And damned all those that trust them!:_ Macbeth is damning himself

144   _Time ... exploits:_ Time has forestalled the terrible things I had in mind for Macduff.
145–6 _The flighty purpose ... with it:_ Our fleeting plans never come to anything unless we act upon them as soon as we make the decision.
147–8 _The very firstlings ... hand:_ I shall convert my very first thoughts into immediate action.
149   _crown:_ complete
152–3 _all unfortunate souls ... his line:_ all his descendants

155   _no more sights!:_ no more apparitions!
       these gentlemen: the ones who brought word about Macduff's flight to England

EXAMINATION-BASED QUESTIONS

- What impression of the witches do we get from this scene?
- What does Macbeth's speech ('I conjure you ...', 50 ff.) reveal about his state of mind?
- Comment on Macbeth's understanding of what the apparitions stand for.
- What do the three apparitions represent?
- 'From this moment / The very firstlings of my heart shall be / The firstlings of my hand' (146–8). What does this mean? Is it a new resolution on Macbeth's part?

KEY THEMES AND IMPORTANT FACTS

- The characterisation of the witches is interesting. Their speech and behaviour in this scene shows them as cheap, vulgar fortune-tellers, not serious embodiments of evil. The real evil in the play is not represented in the absurd antics of the witches, but in the human heart. There is a comic element in the list of ingredients for the witches' brew and the story of the sailor's wife and her chestnuts.

Act Four

– Scene Two –

[Fife. Macduff's castle.]

PLOT SUMMARY

The location is Macduff's castle. Ross tells Lady Macduff and her son that Macduff has fled to England. She is angry and confused at Macduff's apparent desertion of her and her family. A messenger comes to warn her of immediate danger. It is too late. The murderers sent by Macbeth arrive, kill her son and go in pursuit of Lady Macduff herself.

Here a harmless, innocent, vulnerable family awaits execution. The inoffensiveness of Lady Macduff is emphasised ('I have done no harm', 72). Many readers and spectators have found her clever, precocious son rather difficult to like. The exchanges between mother and son tend to detract from rather than enhance the pathos of the scene as a whole.

The killing of young Macduff in full view of the audience is the most harrowing moment of the play. At this point, sympathy for Macbeth and all he stands for reaches its lowest ebb. It should be noted, however, that Macbeth does not do the deed himself, and it is possible to feel that he would not have been able to do it. The nervous anxiety of the messenger underlines the effects of Macbeth's tyranny on his subjects; secrecy and intrigue have become conditions of survival.

Enter LADY MACDUFF, *her* SON, *and* ROSS

LADY MACDUFF
What had he done to make him fly the land?

ROSS
You must have patience, madam.

LADY MACDUFF
He had none;
His flight was madness. When our actions do not,
Our fears do make us traitors.

ROSS
You know not
5   Whether it was his wisdom or his fear.

---

2   *patience:* in this context, it means self-discipline

3–4   *When our actions … traitors:* Macduff's actions did not justify his being called a traitor, but his fear caused him to fly and his flight will be considered evidence enough by Macbeth of his treason. The same applied to Malcolm, Donalbain and Fleance.

LADY MACDUFF

Wisdom! To leave his wife, to leave his babes,

His mansion and his titles, in a place

From whence himself does fly? He loves us not;

He wants the natural touch; for the poor wren,

10   The most diminutive of birds, will fight —

Her young ones in her nest — against the owl.

All is the fear and nothing is the love;

As little is the wisdom, where the flight

So runs against all reason.

the nature theme again

ROSS

             My dearest coz,

15   I pray you, school yourself: but, for your husband,

He is noble, wise, judicious, and best knows

The fits o'the season. I dare not speak much further:

But cruel are the times, when we are traitors

And do not know ourselves; when we hold rumour

20   From what we fear, yet know not what we fear,

But float upon a wild and violent sea

Each way, and move — I take my leave of you:

Shall not be long but I'll be here again.

Things at the worst will cease, or else climb upward

25   To what they were before. My pretty cousin,

Blessing upon you!

LADY MACDUFF

             Fathered he is, and yet he's fatherless.

ROSS

I am so much a fool, should I stay longer,

It would be my disgrace and your discomfort:

30   I take my leave at once.

Exit.

LADY MACDUFF

             Sirrah, your father's dead:

And what will you do now? How will you live?

SON

As birds do, mother.

LADY MACDUFF

             What, with worms and flies?

SON

With what I get, I mean; and so do they.

---

7   *titles:* all his property

9   *He wants the natural touch:* He lacks the natural affection a father should feel for his family.

11   *Her young:* when her young

12   *All is ... the love:* Fear for his own safety dominates him; he has no love for us.

13   *As little is the wisdom:* He is lacking in wisdom as much as he is lacking in love.

13–14   *where the flight ... reason:* when his flight is such a totally irrational act

14–15   *My dearest coz ... husband:* My dearest cousin, please control yourself, but as for your husband ...

17   *The fits o'the season:* the disturbed times we live in

18–19   *when we ... ourselves:* when we are deemed to be traitors without knowing that we are traitors

19–22   *when we ... move:* When our fears cause us to believe rumours, even though the fears are vague; people who fear fear itself are subject to constantly threatening anxieties. Some editors read 'none' for 'move', but however they are read, the lines are unclear.

24   *Things at the worst ... upward:* When things are at their worst, they must either come to an end or else get better.

25   *My pretty cousin:* Ross is talking to Lady Macduff's son.

28–9   *I am so much a fool ... discomfort:* Ross means that if he stayed longer he would weep and so disgrace himself and embarrass Lady Macduff.

30   *Sirrah:* Here it is used as a term of affection.

32   *As birds do:* He is probably thinking of the reference in the Gospel of St Matthew to the birds of the air being fed by the heavenly father.

LADY MACDUFF

Poor Bird! Thou'dst never fear the net nor lime,

35 The pitfall nor the gin.

SON

Why should I, mother? Poor birds they are not set for.
My father is not dead, for all your saying.

LADY MACDUFF

Yes, he is dead: how wilt thou do for a father?

SON

Nay, how will you do for a husband?

LADY MACDUFF

40 Why, I can buy me twenty at any market.

SON

Then you'll buy 'em to sell again.

LADY MACDUFF

Thou speak'st with all thy wit; and yet, i' faith,
With wit enough for thee.

SON

Was my father a traitor, mother?

LADY MACDUFF

45 Ay, that he was.

SON

What is a traitor?

LADY MACDUFF

Why, one that swears and lies.

SON

And be all traitors that do so?

LADY MACDUFF

Every one that does so is a traitor, and must
be hanged.

SON

50 And must they all be hanged that swear and lie?

LADY MACDUFF

Every one.

34–5 *Thou'dst never fear ... gin:* You would never be afraid of the traps set to catch birds: the net, bird-lime, the snare or the trap.

42–3 *Thou speak'st ... for thee:* Your last remark has stretched your small intelligence to its limit; still, you are reasonably intelligent for your age.

45 *Ay, that he was:* As far as she is concerned, he is a traitor to his family, and perhaps a traitor to his king and country.

47 *one that swears and lies:* One who takes an oath and breaks it, the reference applying equally to a false husband and to a betrayer of his country.

SON
Who must hang them?

LADY MACDUFF
Why, the honest men.

SON
Then the liars and swearers are fools; for there are liars
55 and swearers enow to beat the honest men and hang up
them.

55 *enow*: enough

LADY MACDUFF
Now God help thee, poor monkey!
But how wilt thou do for a father?

56 *monkey*: Here it is used affectionately.

SON
If he were dead, you'd weep for him: if you would not,
60 it were a good sign that I should quickly have a new
father.

59–61 *If he were dead ... father:*
If he were really dead, you
would be weeping; if you
were not weeping, this would
indicate that you had a second
husband in mind.

LADY MACDUFF
Poor prattler, how thou talk'st!

62 *prattler*: chatterbox

Enter a MESSENGER

MESSENGER
Bless you, fair dame! I am not to you known,
Though in your state of honour I am perfect.
65 I doubt some danger does approach you nearly.
If you will take a homely man's advice,
Be not found here; hence, with your little ones.
To fright you thus, methinks, I am too savage;
To do worse to you were fell cruelty,
70 Which is too nigh your person. Heaven preserve you!
I dare abide no longer.

64 *Though in your state of honour
I am perfect:* though I am fully
acquainted with your
honourable condition

65 *doubt:* fear
66 *homely:* simple, humble
68–70 *To fright you ... your person:*
It seems a barbarous thing on
my part to frighten you like this
(by telling you to leave), but I
could do worse (by not
alerting you in time), thus
allowing the cruel enemies
who are close to you to carry
out their murderous work.

Exit.

LADY MACDUFF
                    Whither should I fly?
I have done no harm. But I remember now
I am in this earthly world, where to do harm
Is often laudable, to do good sometime
75 Accounted dangerous folly: why then, alas!
Do I put up that womanly defence,
To say I have done no harm?

a perfect description of Scotland at the time

73 *earthly:* imperfect
74 *sometime:* sometimes

Enter MURDERERS

What are these faces?

77   *faces:* probably masks

MURDERER
Where is your husband?

LADY MACDUFF
I hope in no place so unsanctified

79   *unsanctified:* unholy

80   Where such as thou mayst find him.

MURDERER
                                    He's a traitor.

SON
Thou liest, thou shag-haired villain.

81   *shag-haired villain:* A villain
whose ears had been cropped.
Mutilation of the ears was a
punishment inflicted on criminals
in Shakespeare's time

MURDERER
                                    What, you egg!

Stabbing him.

Young fry of treachery!

82   *Young fry of treachery!:*
child of a traitor

SON
                        He has killed me, mother:
Run away, I pray you!

Dies

Exeunt, LADY MACDUFF *crying 'Murder!'*

EXAMINATION-BASED QUESTIONS

- In the opening lines of the scene, Lacy Macduff raises doubts about her husband's motives for leaving Scotland and his family. Do these doubts affect your view of Macduff's character?
- Does Ross appear to have changed his attitude to Macbeth?
- What impression is conveyed by the exchanges between Lady Macduff and her son?
- Some commentators feel that the son's talk detracts from the dignity and seriousness of this grim scene. Would you agree?
- How do the events of this scene affect our view of Macbeth?

This is a scene about kingship - what makes a good king [handwritten annotation]

Act Four
– Scene Three –
[England. Before King Edward's Palace.]

PLOT SUMMARY

Macduff and Malcolm are together at the English court. Malcolm tests Macduff's loyalty by pretending to be a reckless libertine, totally unfit to replace Macbeth as king. As Macduff turns away in despair, Malcolm reveals that he is really a virtuous young man and now accepts Macduff's loyalty without question. **Ross comes with news of opposition to Macbeth in Scotland** and is finally forced to reveal that **Macduff's wife and family have been slain**.

The scene falls naturally into three divisions: (a) Malcolm's testing of Macduff (1–139)/ (b) the Doctor's account of Edward the Confessor (140–59)/ (c) the news of the murders of all the members of Macduff's family and of unrest in Scotland (160–239).

This scene has attracted much unfavourable comment for its supposed lack of dramatic power, for an element of tediousness in the long exchange between Malcolm and Macduff at the beginning, and because, for all its length, **it does comparatively little to advance the action**. But each of the three sections outlined above can be defended on a variety of grounds. From them we learn more fully than we do elsewhere the damage Macbeth has done to Scotland; the scene as a whole functions as a choric commentary in this respect. It illustrates the deviousness to which even men like Malcolm must resort in times of political tyranny, when spies are everywhere. Macduff's interview with Malcolm and its outcome help to bring matters to a head. At this point, too, the characters of both Malcolm and Macduff need development if the two are to appear convincing and sympathetic as Macbeth's conquerors and as champions of the new order in Scotland. The scene fulfils this function.

Malcolm's elaborate testing of Macduff is best seen in conjunction with his father's fatal error of judgement in relation to both Thanes of Cawdor. Malcolm has experienced the sad consequences of trusting even those who appear – as Macduff does – most sympathetic and helpful. He has learned early in his life that 'To show an unfelt sorrow is an office / Which the false man does easy' (2, 3, 135–6). His anxiety not to be trapped as his father was is reflected in his tortuous probing of Macduff's character and motives. Macduff's integrity is confirmed in Malcolm's eyes by Macduff's outburst of feeling (102–14) and by the news that Ross brings.

Another function of the scene is to **establish an important set of contrasts between opposing kinds of kingship** and between opposing attitudes and reactions to similar events. One example of the latter is Macduff's response to the news of his wife's death, a response that is in marked contrast to Macbeth's reception of similar news. Malcolm is, of course, pretending to be an utterly unfit candidate for monarchy, but what he is really describing in his unflattering 'self-portrait' is Macbeth's conduct as king.

Against this, we have three presentations of **virtuous kingship**. The first lists the 'king-becoming graces', i.e. the qualities a king should have (91–4). The second reminds us that Duncan was a 'most sainted king' (109). The third embodies a more palpable contrast to Macbeth's rule. Edward the Confessor is the ideal monarch. His activities are invested with religious associations ('sanctity'; 'heaven'; 'miraculous work'; 'healing benediction'; 'sundry blessings'; 'full of grace', 144–59), while Macbeth's proceedings are almost invariably characterised, both by himself and by others, in terms of images of hell, disease and damnation. **Edward heals his subjects, Macbeth murders his**. Edward prays, Macbeth curses and is damned, both in his own estimation and in that of others. At the court of Edward, holy arts are practised, but in the witches' cavern, Macbeth's place of resort, evil charms are concocted. Edward spreads benedictions, whereas the air around the witches is infected. The disease imagery used by the Doctor in this scene should be contrasted with that used by the other Doctor in Act 5, Scene 1 and by Macbeth himself in Act 5, Scene 3 ('Throw physic to the dogs', 47).

3	*Hold fast the mortal sword:* grasp the deadly sword firmly *mortal:* deadly
4	*Bestride our down-fall'n birthdom:* The birthdom is their native land. Macduff is picturing Scotland as a fallen warrior, guarded and defended by Malcolm and himself.
5–8	*new sorrows ... dolour:* New sorrows rise from the earth so that heaven re-echoes the cries of distress and utters the same kind of sorrowful sound, as if it felt the misery Scotland feels.
8	*Like:* Here it is used as an adjective, meaning similar. *What I believe, I'll wail:* I will mourn only on account of things I am sure have happened.
9	*What know, believe:* I will believe only what I have evidence of.
9–10	*and what I can ... I will:* I will remedy whatever I can when I get a favourable opportunity.
11	*perchance:* perhaps
12	*sole:* mere
14–17	*I am young ... an angry god:* I am young (and therefore not significant), but you may be able to earn a reward by betraying me, and it would be a good policy for you to sacrifice a weak, innocent victim like myself in order to satisfy the demands of Macbeth.

Enter MALCOLM *and* MACDUFF

MALCOLM

Let us seek out some desolate shade, and there
Weep our sad bosoms empty.

MACDUFF

             Let us rather
Hold fast the mortal sword, and like good men
Bestride our down-fall'n birthdom. Each new morn
5 New widows howl, new orphans cry; new sorrows
Strike heaven on the face, that it resounds
As if it felt with Scotland and yelled out
Like syllable of dolour.

MALCOLM

             What I believe, I'll wail;
What know, believe; and what I can redress,
10 As I shall find the time to friend, I will.
What you have spoke, it may be so perchance.
This tyrant, whose sole name blisters our tongues,
Was once thought honest; you have loved him well;
He hath not touched you yet. I am young; but something
15 You may deserve of him through me; and wisdom
To offer up a weak, poor, innocent lamb
To appease an angry god.

MACDUFF

I am not treacherous.

MALCOLM

                But Macbeth is.

A good and virtuous nature may recoil

20 In an imperial charge. But I shall crave your pardon;

That which you are, my thoughts cannot transpose;

Sacred imagery → Angels are bright still, though the brightest fell.

Though all things foul would wear the brows of grace,

Yet grace must still look so. *App vs. Reality*

MACDUFF

                I have lost my hopes.

MALCOLM

25 Perchance even there where I did find my doubts.

Why in that rawness left you wife and child —

Those precious motives, those strong knots of love —

Without leave-taking? I pray you,

Let not my jealousies be your dishonours,

30 But mine own safeties: you may be rightly just,

Whatever I shall think.

MACDUFF

            Bleed, bleed, poor country!

Great tyranny, lay thou thy basis sure,

For goodness dare not check thee: wear thou thy wrongs,

The title is affeered! Fare thee well, lord:

35 I would not be the villain that thou think'st

For the whole space that's in the tyrant's grasp,

And the rich East to boot.

MALCOLM

           Be not offended!

I speak not as in absolute fear of you.

I think our country sinks beneath the yoke;

40 It weeps, it bleeds, and each new day a gash *more images of blood & wounds*

Is added to her wounds. I think withal

There would be hands uplifted in my right;

And here from gracious England have I offer

Of goodly thousands. But, for all this,

45 When I shall tread upon the tyrant's head,

Or wear it on my sword, yet my poor country

Shall have more vices than it had before,

More suffer, and more sundry ways than ever,

By him that shall succeed.

19–20 *A good and virtuous nature ... charge:* Even a good and upright man may turn to evil under pressure from someone in high authority.

20 *But I shall crave your pardon:* I shall ask you to forgive me if I have slandered you.

21 *That which ... transpose:* What I think of you cannot change your nature.

22 *Angels ... fell:* Although Lucifer, the brightest of all the angels, turned to evil, there are still good angels. There is a clear hint here at Macbeth's fall from glory and grace.

23–4 *Though all things foul ... look so:* Although evil men can counterfeit a virtuous appearance, this does not mean that a virtuous appearance is always deceptive.

24 *I have lost my hopes:* Macduff's hopes are based on raising a force led by Malcolm and himself against Macbeth; now that Malcolm does not trust him, these hopes have faded.

25 *Perchance ... doubts:* Macduff has fled to England with the hope of saving Scotland from Macbeth, but the haste with which he abandoned his family only serves to make Malcolm suspect his motives.

26 *rawness:* unprotected state

27 *motives:* incentives to stay *knots of love:* bonds of affection

29–30 *Let not my jealousies ... safeties:* Look upon my suspicions of you not as reasons for feeling dishonoured, but as ways of protecting myself.

32 *lay thou thy basis sure:* Macbeth will have a secure foundation for his tyrannical rule.

33 *For goodness dare not check thee:* Malcolm's goodness will not be able to curb Macbeth's tyranny.

wear thou ... affeered!: Let Macbeth continue to possess his ill-gotten gains; his title to them is legally confirmed and secure.

33–4 *to boot:* in addition

37 *I speak not as in absolute fear of you:* This line probably means: 'My fear of you is not the only reason why I am speaking as I am.' An alternative is: 'I cannot be absolutely certain that you are to be feared.'

39	*sinks beneath the yoke:* labours under the burden of Macbeth's rule
41	*withal:* furthermore, in addition
43	*gracious England:* the King of England
44	*thousands:* thousands of men
48	*More suffer ... than ever:* suffer more, and in more varied ways than before
49	*By him:* because of him
	What should he be?: To whom are you referring?
51	*All the particulars of vice so grafted:* each individual vice, so much a part of myself
52	*opened:* revealed, arrive at full maturity, come to fruition
55	*confineless:* unlimited, boundless
57	*top:* surpass, outdo
58	*Luxurious:* Lustful. There is no evidence elsewhere in the play that Macbeth is lustful. Malcolm is here attributing to Macbeth a vice conventionally associated with tyrants. One need not take the charge too seriously.
	avaricious: Greedy. Macbeth's avarice, like his supposed lustfulness, is nowhere evident.
59	*Sudden:* violent
61	*voluptuousness:* lust
64–5	*All continent impediments ... my will:* would overpower all restraining influences that might oppose my lustful desires
67	*nature:* Here it refers to human nature.
67–9	*it hath been ... many kings:* Excess has been the reason why many happy and prosperous reigns have ended before their due time.
70–2	*you may ... hoodwink:* You may secretly and stealthily manage your pleasures in a lavish way and yet seem chaste because you may deceive those around you.
73–6	*We have willing ... inclined:* There are plenty of women in Scotland prepared to yield their virtue to please a king; your lustful appetites cannot be so extreme that you will not find enough satisfaction in those women who will gladly place themselves at the disposal of someone of your importance if they find you so inclined.
76	*With this:* in addition to this
77	*In my most ill-composed affection:* in my most unbalanced and evil temperament

MACDUFF

What should he be?

MALCOLM

50 It is myself I mean; in whom I know
All the particulars of vice so grafted
That, when they shall be opened, black Macbeth
Will seem as pure as snow, and the poor state
Esteem him as a lamb, being compared
With my confineless harms.

MACDUFF

Not in the legions
55 Of horrid hell can come a devil more damned
In evils to top Macbeth.   *diabolical imagery*

MALCOLM

I grant him bloody,
Luxurious, avaricious, false, deceitful,
Sudden, malicious, smacking of every sin
60 That has a name: but there's no bottom, none,
In my voluptuousness. Your wives, your daughters,
Your matrons and your maids, could not fill up
The cistern of my lust, and my desire
All continent impediments would o'erbear
65 That did oppose my will. Better Macbeth
Than such a one to reign.

MACDUFF

Boundless intemperance
In nature is a tyranny; it hath been
Th'untimely emptying of the happy throne
And fall of many kings. But fear not yet
70 To take upon you what is yours: you may
Convey your pleasures in a spacious plenty,
And yet seem cold, the time you may so hoodwink.
We have willing dames enough; there cannot be
That vulture in you, to devour so many
75 As will to greatness dedicate themselves,
Finding it so inclined.

MALCOLM

With this there grows
In my most ill-composed affection such
A stanchless avarice that, were I king,
I should cut off the nobles for their lands,

80   Desire his jewels and this other's house;
       And my more-having would be as a sauce
       To make me hunger more, that I should forge
       Quarrels unjust against the good and loyal,
       Destroying them for wealth.

MACDUFF
                   This avarice
85   Sticks deeper, grows with more pernicious root
       Than summer-seeming lust; and it hath been
       The sword of our slain kings: yet do not fear;
       Scotland hath foisons to fill up your will,
       Of your mere own. All these are portable,
90   With other graces weighed.

MALCOLM
       But I have none. The king-becoming graces, *[honesty self-control]*
       As justice, verity, temperance, stableness, *Shakespeare's own*
       Bounty, perseverance, mercy, lowliness, *[generosity] theory of what a king*
       Devotion, patience, courage, fortitude, *[strength] should be*
95   I have no relish of them, but abound
       In the division of each several crime,
       Acting in many ways. Nay, had I power, I should
       Pour the sweet milk of concord into hell,
       Uproar the universal peace, confound
       All unity on earth.

MACDUFF
100   O Scotland, Scotland!

MALCOLM
       If such a one be fit to govern, speak:
       I am as I have spoken.

MACDUFF
             Fit to govern!
       No, not to live. O nation miserable,
       With an untitled tyrant bloody-sceptred, *disease*
105   When shalt thou see thy <u>wholesome</u> days again,
       Since that the truest issue of thy throne
       By his own interdiction stands accused,
       And does blaspheme his breed? Thy royal father
       Was a most sainted king; the queen that bore thee,
110   Oft'ner upon her knees than on her feet,
       Died every day she lived. Fare thee well!
       These evils thou repeat'st upon thyself

---

78   *stanchless avarice:* unquenchable greed

80   *Desire his ... house:* covet one man's jewels and another man's house

81–2   *And my more-having ... more:* The more I have, the more I would want.

84–6   *This avarice ... lust:* Avarice is more deeply rooted than lust, which passes like the summer heat.

86–7   *and it hath been ... slain kings:* It was the cause of our slain kings' downfall.

88   *Scotland ... will:* Scotland has plentiful supplies ('foisons') to satisfy your wants.

89   *Of your mere own:* belonging entirely to you, being royal property

89–90   *All these ... weighed:* All these vices you have attributed to yourself are endurable, provided they are compensated for by virtuous qualities.

91   *The king-becoming graces:* the virtues proper to a king

95   *relish:* trace

95–7   *but abound ... many ways:* I commit every kind of crime in all its variations and sub-divisions.

98   *concord:* harmony

99   *Uproar:* cause uproar and confusion in
      confound: overthrow

104   *an untitled tyrant:* a tyrant without legal right to his throne
      bloody-sceptred: His reign is a bloody one.

106–8   *Since that ... breed:* Since the rightful heir accuses himself of crimes so revolting that he is a disgrace to his parents and to his entire royal house.

111   *Died every day she lived:* She spent her life with the thought of her death always in her mind. Her life reflected the Christian motto: 'Remember thy last end, and thou shalt never sin.'

112–13   *These evils ... Scotland:* The evils you accuse yourself of are the very ones that have caused me to leave Scotland (since Macbeth also exemplified them).

Hath banished me from Scotland. O my breast,
Thy hope ends here!

MALCOLM

Macduff, this noble passion,
115 Child of integrity, hath from my soul
Wiped the black scruples, reconciled my thoughts
To thy good truth and honour. Devilish Macbeth
By many of these trains hath sought to win me
Into his power, and modest wisdom plucks me
120 From over-credulous haste: but God above
Deal between thee and me! For even now
I put myself to thy direction, and
Unspeak mine own detraction, here abjure
The taints and blames I laid upon myself
125 For strangers to my nature. I am yet
Unknown to woman, never was forsworn,
Scarcely have coveted what was mine own,
At no time broke my faith, would not betray
The devil to his fellow, and delight
130 No less in truth than life: my first false speaking
Was this upon myself. What I am truly
Is thine and my poor country's to command:
Whither indeed, before thy here-approach,
Old Siward, with ten thousand warlike men
135 Already at a point, was setting forth.
Now we'll together, and the chance of goodness
Be like our warranted quarrel! Why are you silent?

MACDUFF

Such welcome and unwelcome things at once
'Tis hard to reconcile.

Enter a DOCTOR

MALCOLM

140 Well, more anon. Comes the King forth, I pray you?

DOCTOR

Ay, sir; there are a crew of wretched souls
That stay his cure. Their malady convinces
The great assay of art; but at his touch,
Such sanctity hath heaven given his hand,
145 They presently amend.

---

113 *breast:* heart
114–15 *Macduff ... Child of integrity:*
This noble outburst of emotion
is an expression of your
upright and honest nature.
116 *Wiped the black scruples:*
removed the dark suspicions
and doubts
118 *trains:* plots, devices
119–20 *modest wisdom ... haste:*
Good sense restrains me from
placing rash trust in anybody.
120–1 *but God ... and me!:* May
God direct all dealings
between us!
123 *Unspeak mine own detraction:*
withdraw the accusations I
have made against myself
abjure: renounce
125 *For strangers to my nature:* as
foreign to my nature
126 *forsworn:* guilty of perjury
127 *coveted:* desired
128–9 *would not betray ... fellow:*
I would not even betray one
devil to another.

131 *upon myself:* against myself

135 *at a point:* ready for action
136–7 *the chance of goodness ...
quarrel!:* May the likelihood
that right will triumph be as
soundly based as the justice of
our cause.

140 *the King:* Edward the Confessor

142 *stay:* wait for
142–3 *Their malady ... art:* Their
illness defies the best efforts of
medical science.
145 *presently:* immediately
amend: get better

MALCOLM

I thank you, doctor.

Exit DOCTOR.

MACDUFF

What's the disease he means?

MALCOLM

'Tis called the evil:
A most miraculous work in this good king,
Which often, since my here-remain in England,
I have seen him do. How he solicits heaven,
150 Himself best knows; but strangely-visited people,
All swoln and ulcerous, pitiful to the eye,
The mere despair of surgery, he cures,
Hanging a golden stamp about their necks,
Put on what holy prayers; and 'tis spoken,
155 To the succeeding royalty he leaves
The healing benediction. With this strange virtue
He hath a heavenly gift of prophecy,
And sundry blessings hang about his throne
That speak him full of grace.

Enter ROSS

MACDUFF

See, who comes here?

MALCOLM

160 My countryman; but yet I know him not.

MACDUFF

My ever-gentle cousin, welcome hither.

MALCOLM

I know him now. Good God, betimes remove
The means that makes us strangers!

ROSS

Sir, amen.

MACDUFF

Stands Scotland where it did?

ROSS

Alas, poor country,

---

146   *the evil:* This is scrofula, tuberculosis of the bones and the lymphatic glands.

148   *since my here-remain in England:* during my stay here in England

149   *solicits heaven:* appeals to heaven for help

150   *strangely-visited people:* people with unusual afflictions

152   *The mere despair of surgery:* people whom surgeons have completely despaired of healing

153   *a golden stamp:* This was a special coin bearing the figure of St Michael.

154   *'tis spoken:* it is said

156   *The healing benediction:* the blessed power of healing
With this strange virtue: along with this unusual power

157   *He hath a heavenly gift of prophecy:* This contrasts with the hellish gift of prophecy possessed by the witches.

158–9   *And sundry … grace:* The various blessed gifts associated with this monarch are a mark of his extreme virtue.

160   *My countryman … not:* Malcolm knows by Ross's dress that he is a Scot, but either doesn't know his identity or pretends not to until he learns more about the purpose of Ross's arrival.

162   *betimes:* quickly
163   *means:* circumstances

165 Almost afraid to know itself! It cannot
Be called our mother, but our grave; where nothing,
But who knows nothing, is once seen to smile;
Where sighs and groans and shrieks that rend the air
Are made, not marked; where violent sorrow seems
170 A modern ecstasy; the dead man's knell
Is there scarce asked for who; and good men's lives
Expire before the flowers in their caps,
Dying or ere they sicken.

MACDUFF

O, relation
Too nice, and yet too true!

MALCOLM

What's the newest grief?

ROSS

175 That of an hour's age doth hiss the speaker;
Each minute teems a new one.

MACDUFF

How does my wife?

ROSS
Why, well.

MACDUFF
And all my children?

ROSS

Well too.

MACDUFF
The tyrant has not battered at their peace?

ROSS
No; they were well at peace when I did leave 'em.

MACDUFF
180 Be not a niggard of your speech: how goes't?

ROSS
When I came hither to transport the tidings
Which I have heavily borne, there ran a rumour
Of many worthy fellows that were out;
Which was to my belief witnessed the rather

166–7 *where nothing ... smile:* The only people who are cheerful are those entirely ignorant of the situation.
168–9 *Where sighs ... not marked:* Signs of misery and woe go unnoticed because they are commonplace.
170 *A modern ecstasy:* an everyday emotion
170–1 *the dead man's knell ... who:* Hardly anybody bothers to enquire for whom the funeral bell tolls.
171–3 *and good men's lives ... sicken:* Good men die before the flowers in their caps wither; they do not die in old age through illness because they are slaughtered before that.
173–4 *O, relation ... true!:* An elaborate account, and yet how accurate it is!
175 *That of an hour's age doth hiss the speaker:* If someone reports news that is only one hour old, he will be hissed by his audience, who knows that subsequent horrible events have made even that news stale. Horrors, as the next line points out, are being perpetrated by the minute.

178 *battered at their peace:* shattered the peace of their household

179 *well at peace:* Ross takes refuge in puns because he can't face telling what happened.
180 *niggard:* miser
183 *out:* in arms
184–5 *Which ... power afoot:* Rumour turned to belief when I saw Macbeth's army on the move.

precise

185   For that I saw the tyrant's power afoot.
Now is the time of help; your eye in Scotland
Would create soldiers, make our women fight,
To doff their dire distresses.

MALCOLM

Be't their comfort
We are coming thither. Gracious England hath
190   Lent us good Siward and ten thousand men;
An older and a better soldier none
That Christendom gives out.

ROSS

Would I could answer
This comfort with the like! But I have words
That would be howled out in the desert air,
195   Where hearing should not latch them.

MACDUFF

What concern they?
The general cause? Or is it a fee-grief
Due to some single breast?

ROSS

No mind that's honest
But in it shares some woe, though the main part
Pertains to you alone.

MACDUFF

If it be mine,
200   Keep it not from me; quickly let me have it.

ROSS

Let not your ears despise my tongue for ever,
Which shall possess them with the heaviest sound
That ever yet they heard.

MACDUFF

Humh! I guess at it.

ROSS

Your castle is surprised; your wife and babes
205   Savagely slaughtered. To relate the manner,
Were, on the quarry of these murdered deer,
To add the death of you.

186–7	*your eye ... soldiers:* Your mere presence in Scotland would prompt men to rally to our cause.
188	*doff:* cast off
189	*Gracious England:* King Edward the Confessor
191–2	*An older ... gives out:* The Christian world can show no example of a better or more experienced soldier.
192–3	*Would I could ... the like!:* I wish I could match this good news with similar good news.
194	*would be:* should be
195	*latch:* catch
195–7	*What concern ... single breast?:* What is the subject of your news? Does it concern matters of public interest, or is it a purely private and personal sorrow concerning one individual?
197–8	*No mind ... woe:* There can be no decent or honourable man who will not feel grief at the news I have.
202	*possess:* inform
205–7	*To relate the manner ... of you:* To describe the manner in which they were killed would only add your death to theirs, your body to the pile which resembles a heap ('quarry') of slaughtered deer. There is an emotive pun on 'deer/dear'.

208   *Ne'er ... brows:* Malcolm is asking Macduff not to indulge in this silent gesture of mourning.

209–10   *Give sorrow ... break:* It is best to express your sorrow in words. If you suppress your grief, it will overload your heart and break it.

MALCOLM

         Merciful heaven!
What, man! Ne'er pull your hat upon your brows;
Give sorrow words. The grief that does not speak
210   Whispers the o'erfraught heart and bids it break.

MACDUFF
My children too?

ROSS

            Wife, children, servants, all
That could be found.

MACDUFF

          And I must be from thence!
My wife killed too?

ROSS

        I have said.

212   *And I must be from thence!:* And I had to be away!

214–15   *Let's make us ... grief:* Let us use revenge as a means of driving out the grief caused by these murders.

216   *He has no children:* 'He' is a crux here. Macduff may be referring to Macbeth, whose crime cannot be properly punished because he has no children of his own. With Macbeth in mind again Macduff may be saying that he would not have killed his children if he had children of his own. There is also the possibility that he is referring to Malcolm, who in the innocence of youth thinks revenge is a cure for bereavement, an attitude he would not entertain if he had children of his own.

MALCOLM

            Be comforted:
Let's make us medicines of our great revenge   *medicinal imagery*
215   To cure this deadly grief.

MACDUFF
He has no children. All my pretty ones?   *It is unclear who he means*
Did you say all? O hell-kite! All?
What, all my pretty chickens and their dam   *diabolical imagery*
At one fell swoop?   *birds*

MALCOLM

        Dispute it like a man.

217–19   *O hell-kite! ... swoop?:* Macbeth is seen as a devilish bird of prey descending on a hen-roost and taking all the occupants in one cruel ('fell') swoop.

218   *dam:* mother
219   *Dispute:* fight against
223–4   *Sinful Macduff ... thee!:* Macduff thinks that his family was wiped out because of his sins.

224   *Naught:* sinful, wicked, evil
225–6   *Not for their own ... souls:* They were slaughtered not for any wrong on their part, but because of my sins.

227–8   *let grief ... enrage it:* Change from grief to anger; do not become passive and insensible, but let rage be your motive. Malcolm is thinking of anger as a means of overcoming the effects of grief.

MACDUFF

        I shall do so;   *The theme of masculinity*
220   But I must also feel it as a man: *Macduff has a more mature understanding of manhood*
I cannot but remember such things were
That were most precious to me. Did heaven look on,
And would not take their part? Sinful Macduff,
They were all struck for thee! Naught that I am,
225   Not for their own demerits, but for mine,
Fell slaughter on their souls. Heaven rest them now!

MALCOLM
Be this the whetstone of your sword: let grief
Convert to anger; blunt not the heart, enrage it.

MACDUFF

O, I could play the woman with mine eyes

230 And braggart with my tongue. But, gentle heavens,

Cut short all intermission; front to front

Bring thou this fiend of Scotland and myself;

Within my sword's length set him; if he 'scape,

Heaven forgive him too!

MALCOLM

This tune goes manly.

235 Come, go we to the King, our power is ready,

Our lack is nothing but our leave. Macbeth

Is ripe for shaking, and the powers above

Put on their instruments. Receive what cheer you may;

The night is long that never finds the day.

Exeunt.

229–30 *O, I could play … tongue:* Macduff is torn between a desire to weep for his family and to utter threats against Macbeth.

231 *Cut short all intermission:* Shorten the interval between now and our confrontation with Macbeth!
front to front: face to face

232 *fiend:* devil

233–4 *if he 'scape … too!:* If he escapes me, may his crimes be pardoned, something that I would regard as a punishment on myself.

234 *This tune goes manly:* This is a manly way of speaking.

235 *our power:* our army

236 *Our lack is nothing but our leave:* All that is left for us to do is to take our leave of the king.

237 *ripe for shaking:* Macbeth is ready for shaking, like a fruit tree in autumn. His reign is coming to an end.
powers: angels responsible for opposing the influence of Satan and, by association, of Macbeth

238 *Put on their instruments:* arm themselves

EXAMINATION-BASED QUESTIONS

- One critic has argued that the lengthy exchange between Malcolm and Macduff in this scene 'serves to emphasise the mistrust that has spread from the central evil of the play'. Elaborate on this idea.
- What are Malcolm's motives in behaving as he does here? What does he hope to achieve?
- What do Macduff's responses tell us about his character?
- This scene serves as a commentary on the condition of Macbeth's Scotland. What does it tell us?
- Malcolm attributes many vices to Macbeth. Is there evidence elsewhere in the play that he is as bad as he is presented here?
- This scene presents various views on kingship, both good and bad. Discuss these.
- What is the significance of the short discussion of the English king (140–59)?
- This scene marks a major turning point in Macbeth's fortunes, although he does not appear in it. Explain.

'Did heaven look on, / And would not take their part?' (4, 3, 222–3)

Act Five

– Scene One –

[Dunsinane. Macbeth's Castle.]

PLOT SUMMARY

In Dunsinane castle, a deranged Lady Macbeth is sleepwalking. She relives the guilt and terror associated with the crimes committed by her husband and herself.

Lady Macbeth's last appearance was at the end of Act 3, Scene 4, where her tremendous effort to save appearances for Macbeth taxed her resources and resulted in the almost total collapse of her will power. At that point she had become a mere shadow of her former self, reacting passively to her dominant husband.

In this scene we find the process of Lady Macbeth's disintegration carried a step further. There was a time when she felt able to dismiss the guilty fears of her husband with contempt, since she did not share them: her mind and her imagination were free of all the haunting terrors that pursued him and destroyed his peace. Now it is her turn to be harried by guilt-ridden fancies. She was once able to reduce the supernatural and the mysterious to the level of commonplace, everyday experiences ('The sleeping and dead / Are but as pictures', 2, 2, 54–5). Now in this scene we find that her very reason has broken down and that she is in the grip of terrifying, unknown fears. The sleepwalking scene, a soliloquy unheard even by its speaker, is a brilliantly successful means of revealing her subconscious acknowledgement of the forces she has so long denied. The womanly nature she has violated in a frightening display of 'manliness' now takes its revenge and demands its payment. The price she must pay is a frightful one: the loss of her reason. Macbeth has known all along that whoever dares to do more than is proper to a human being will forfeit humanity. Lady Macbeth is now learning this lesson, painfully and too late.

What is happening in this scene illustrates the essential difference between the two main characters. Throughout the first half of the play, she displays savage energy and determination in pursuit of an ambition. However, she is unable to maintain her momentum as her mental faculties disintegrate under the weight of her guilt. Macbeth, on the other hand, is initially more reluctant to engage with evil, but once he does, he overcomes his early sense of guilt and maintains his evil course to the end, even when he knows that all is lost.

Lady Macbeth's disjointed talk in the sleepwalking scene has one controlling theme: guilty recollection of past deeds. She relives the circumstances of Duncan's murder ('who would / have thought the old man to have had so much blood in / him?', 34–6). The blood she could once wash so easily from her hands will not now go away ('Here's the smell of the blood still', 44). The memory of the killing of Macduff's family is pathetically evoked ('The Thane of Fife had a wife: where is she now?', 38). These reminiscences are shot through with a tender and moving concern for her dream husband, as she imagines herself trying to strengthen and support him in his actions ('none can call our power to account ... you mar all with this starting ... Wash your hands, put on your nightgown ... Banquo's buried ... What's done / cannot be undone', 34, 40, 54, 55, 59–60). The scene ends on a note of irony. Lady Macbeth is deluded into feeling close to her husband ('come, / come, come, come, give me your hand', 58–9) at the very time when their relationship has collapsed, certainly in Macbeth's eyes. We are soon to learn that she no longer occupies any place in Macbeth's world: her death will come to him as an annoying irrelevance ('She should have died hereafter', 5, 5, 17).

The sleep theme is present in this scene

Enter a DOCTOR *of Physic and a* WAITING-GENTLEWOMAN

DOCTOR

I have two nights watched with you, but can perceive no truth in your report. When was it she last walked?

1   *watched:* stayed awake

LADY-IN-WAITING

Since his Majesty went into the field, I have seen her rise from her bed, throw her nightgown upon her,
5   unlock her closet, take forth paper, fold it, write upon it, read it, afterwards seal it, and again return to bed; yet all this while in a most fast sleep.   *The sleep theme*

3   *into the field:* To do battle against the Scots rebels mentioned in Act 4, Scene 3, 182–3.
4   *nightgown:* dressing-gown
5   *closet:* chest or cabinet for valuables

DOCTOR

A great perturbation in nature, to receive at once the benefit of sleep and do the effects of watching! In this
10   slumbery agitation, besides her walking and other actual performances, what, at any time, have you heard her say?

8   *A great perturbation in nature:* a violent upheaval in her constitution
9   *do the effects of watching!:* behave as if she were awake
10   *slumbery agitation:* physical activity during sleep
11   *actual performances:* things she does

LADY-IN-WAITING

That, sir, which I will not report after her.

13   *after her:* in her actual words

DOCTOR

You may to me, and 'tis most meet you should.

14   *meet:* proper, appropriate

LADY-IN-WAITING

15   Neither to you nor any one, having no witness to confirm my speech.

Enter LADY MACBETH, *with a taper*

Lo you, here she comes! This is her very guise; and, upon my life, fast asleep. Observe her, stand close.

17   *This is her very guise:* This is precisely the way she behaves.
18   *stand close:* stay concealed

19	*How came she by that light?:* How did she get that candle?
23	*their sense are shut:* She sees nothing. 'Sense' here means 'powers' or 'faculties'.
28–60	*Yet here's a spot ... to bed:* In this passage, Lady Macbeth relives in painful detail the crucial incidents of her murderous past. The revelation of her tortured soul in its unrelieved anguish is powerfully affecting, as is her pathetic show of devotion to Macbeth. The whole nightmarish, hallucinatory sequence is one of the high points of the play. It is filled with echoes from earlier scenes.
28	*Yet here's a spot:* This recalls the misplaced confidence of 'A little water clears us of this deed:/How easy is it then!' (2, 2 68–9).
29	*set down:* write down
31–2	*One, two ... time to do't:* This is a reminder of 'Go bid thy mistress, when my drink is ready/She strike upon the bell' (2, 1, 31–2).
32	*Hell is murky:* She wanted darkness above all to abet the murder of Duncan: 'Come, thick night,/And pall thee in the dunnest smoke of hell; (1, 5, 49–50). Now she dreads the dark; it is the most terrifying feature of hell for her.
32–3	*A soldier,/and afeard?:* She is remembering, with whatever degree of remorse, her taunting challenges before Duncan's death: 'Art thou afeared/To be the same in thine own act and valour/As thou art in desire? (1, 7, 39–41), and 'When you durst do it, then you were a man' (1, 7, 49).
34	*none can call our power to account?:* This recalls: 'Who dares receive it other,/As we shall make our griefs and clamour roar/Upon his death?' (1, 7, 77–9).
34–6	*Yet who would/ have thought ... him?:* This reminds us of 'My hands are of your colour' (2, 2, 65).
38	*The Thane ... now?:* Where is Macduff's wife now?
39	*will these hands ne'er be clean?:* Here is another re- collection of 'A little water clears us of this deed:' (2, 2, 68).
40	*you mar all with this starting:* This harks back to her rebuke

DOCTOR

How came she by that light?

This is ironic as she has prayed for darkness (Act 1 Sc 5 Line 50)

LADY-IN-WAITING

20 Why, it stood by her: she has light by her continually, 'tis her command.

DOCTOR

You see her eyes are open.

LADY-IN-WAITING

Ay, but their sense are shut.

DOCTOR

What is it she does now? Look how she rubs her hands.

LADY-IN-WAITING

25 It is an accustomed action with her, to seem thus washing her hands: I have known her to continue in this a quarter of an hour.

LADY MACBETH

Yet here's a spot.

DOCTOR

Hark, she speaks! I will set down what comes from her,
30 to satisfy my remembrance the more strongly.

LADY MACBETH

Out, damned spot! Out, I say! One, two: why, then 'tis
time to do't. Hell is murky. Fie, my lord, fie! A soldier,
and afeard? What need we fear who knows it, when
none can call our power to account? Yet who would
35 have thought the old man to have had so much blood in
him?

DOCTOR

Do you mark that?

LADY MACBETH

The Thane of Fife had a wife: where is she now? What,
will these hands ne'er be clean? No more o' that, my
40 lord, no more o' that: you mar all with this starting.

DOCTOR

Go to, go to: you have known what you should not.

LADY-IN-WAITING
She has spoke what she should not, I am sure of that:
Heaven knows what she has known.

LADY MACBETH
Here's the smell of the blood still: all the perfumes of
45 Arabia will not sweeten this little hand. Oh! oh! oh!

IRONIC

DOCTOR
What a sigh is there! The heart is sorely charged.

LADY-IN-WAITING
I would not have such a heart in my bosom for the
dignity of the whole body.

DOCTOR
Well, well, well.

LADY-IN-WAITING
50 Pray God it be, sir.

DOCTOR
This disease is beyond my practice: yet I have known
those which have walked in their sleep who have died
holily in their beds.

LADY MACBETH
Wash your hands, put on your nightgown, look not so
55 pale: I tell you yet again, Banquo's buried; he cannot
come out on's grave.

DOCTOR
Even so?

LADY MACBETH
To bed, to bed: there's knocking at the gate: come,
come, come, come, give me your hand. What's done
60 cannot be undone. To bed, to bed, to bed.

Exit.

DOCTOR
Will she go now to bed?

LADY-IN-WAITING
Directly.

44–5   *all the perfumes … this little hand:* This is her version of Macbeth's 'Will all great Neptune's ocean wash this blood/Clean from my hand?' (2, 2, 61–2).

46   *The heart is sorely charged:* She is overwhelmed by a heavy burden of grief.

47–8   *I would not have … body:* She would prefer to be a humble gentlewoman with an easy conscience than to be a queen with Lady Macbeth's guilt-burdened feelings.
the dignity of the whole body: the status enjoyed by Lady Macbeth as queen.

51–3   *This disease … beds:* I do not have a remedy for this disorder. Still, I have known victims of sleepwalking who had holy deaths.

54–5   *Wash your hands … pale:* This echoes her comments before and after Duncan's murder.

57   *Even so?:* Is that so? The Doctor is expressing amazement.

58   *To bed, to bed:* This recalls: 'Come, we'll to sleep' (3, 4, 142).
there's knocking at the gate: She remembers: 'Hark! More knocking' (2,2, 70).

59–60   *What's done/cannot be undone:* Here we have an ironic echo of 'what's done is done' (3, 2, 12).

at the banquet: 'O, these flaws and starts' (3, 4, 63).

63	*Foul whisperings are abroad:* Evil rumours are everywhere.
63–4	*Unnatural deeds ... troubles:* Crimes such as the killing of a king inevitably lead to chaos in the kingdom and even in the mind. When monarchs behave as Macbeth has done, disorder in the kingdom is inevitable.
64–5	*infected minds ... secrets:* People cannot keep their guilty secrets to themselves. They must express them, if only to their pillows during sleep.
66	*More needs she the divine than the physician:* She needs the priest rather than the doctor. Her real ailment is a spiritual one.
68	*Remove ... annoyance:* The doctor knows that in her present state she may be tempted to commit suicide.
70	*mated:* confounded, perplexed

DOCTOR

Foul whisperings are abroad. Unnatural deeds

Do breed unnatural troubles; infected minds

To their deaf pillows will discharge their secrets.

More needs she the divine than the physician.

God, God forgive us all! Look after her;

Remove from her the means of all annoyance,

And still keep eyes upon her. So, good-night:

My mind she has mated, and amazed my sight.

I think, but dare not speak.

LADY-IN-WAITING

Good-night, good doctor.

Exeunt.

65

70

EXAMINATION-BASED QUESTIONS

- Comment on the symbolism in this scene.
- Many of Lady Macbeth's comments refer to earlier episodes in the play. Identify these.
- How do you respond to Lady Macbeth in this scene?
- There is irony in the breakdown of Lady Macbeth's reason. Explain.
- Comment on the significance of the Doctor's view that 'Unnatural deeds / Do breed unnatural troubles' (63–4). Is there any evidence to support this view here or elsewhere in the play?

KEY THEMES AND IMPORTANT FACTS

- This scene is the final and most convincing expression of the theme of guilt.

Act Five
– Scene Two –

[The Countryside near Dunsinane.]

> ## PLOT SUMMARY
>
> Those of his own countrymen who have turned against Macbeth are preparing for the arrival of the English forces near Birnam wood. Reports suggest that Macbeth's support is declining as growing numbers desert his cause.
>
> All the significant things in this scene concern Macbeth. The descriptions of his enemies gathering to overthrow him are relatively uninteresting and uninspiring. The really vivid images are reserved for him. Angus's comment about a giant's robe hanging on a dwarfish thief, if taken too seriously as an account of Macbeth's situation, can mislead. Some commentators think that Shakespeare wants us to regard Macbeth, personifying evil, as having shrunk to insignificance in the face of advancing forces of good. This view is certainly not borne out by Macbeth's subsequent appearances; he is never dwarfish, either in a physical or in a moral sense. If he were, the ending of the play would simply be a bore, which it certainly is not.
>
> At this point, the real interest is not in the outward action, what happens to Macbeth or to his opponents in battle, but in what is going on in his mind. This is where the focus of attention is increasingly directed. The most memorable things in the final scene are the soliloquies in which he records his world-weariness and radical disillusionment, the emptiness of a life without significance or hope.

Enter, with drum and colours, MENTEITH,
CAITHNESS, ANGUS, LENNOX *and Soldiers*

MENTEITH

The English power is near, led on by Malcolm,   1
His uncle Siward, and the good Macduff.   3
Revenges burn in them; for their dear causes
Would to the bleeding and the grim alarm   3–5
5   Excite the mortified man.

ANGUS

        Near Birnam wood   5
Shall we well meet them; that way are they coming.   5–6

CAITHNESS

Who knows if Donalbain be with his brother?

LENNOX

For certain, sir, he is not: I have a file   8
Of all the gentry: there is Siward's son,

power: army
Revenges burn in them: They have a passionate desire for revenge.
for their dear … mortified man: Such is the justice of their cause that it should rouse even the dead to answer the bloody call to battle.
mortified: dead
Near Birnam wood … meet them: We are likely to meet them near Birnam wood.

file: list

10–11	*And many ... manhood:* And many beardless youths who now, for the first time, declare that they are men. Lennox is implying that even very young men wish to support Malcolm's worthy cause.	
14	*valiant fury:* Savage courage (a brave display of savagery). Compare 1, 2, 15–23.	
15–16	*He cannot buckle ... rule:* There is probably a double reference here: (a) Macbeth cannot maintain control over his disordered kingdom; (b) Macbeth cannot control his diseased mind.	
17	*sticking:* like blood	
18	*Now minutely ... faith-breach:* The revolts against his authority, which are happening every minute, rebuke him for his own rebellion against royal authority.	
19–20	*Those he commands ... love:* Macbeth's soldiers act only under orders, not out of any sense of love or loyalty to him.	
20–2	*now does he feel ... thief:* Angus sees Macbeth's kingship as a garment that is both ill-fitting and stolen.	
22–3	*Who then ... start:* Who can blame his shattered nerves for causing him to take fright in sudden fits of frenzy.	
24–5	*When all ... there:* When his whole being is revolted at the contemplation of its own degeneracy.	
28–30	*Meet we ... of us:* Let us meet Malcolm, the physician who will heal our sick country, and let us be ready to sacrifice every drop of our blood to cleanse Scotland of its disease.	
30–1	*Or so much ... weeds:* Or let us shed as much blood as is needed to nurture the flower of good kingship and to kill the weeds of tyranny (i.e. to make Malcolm's cause a success and to defeat Macbeth).	

10 And many unrough youths that even now
Protest their first of manhood.

MENTEITH
                                   What does the tyrant?

CAITHNESS
Great Dunsinane he strongly fortifies.
Some say he's mad; others, that lesser hate him,
Do call it valiant fury; but for certain
15 He cannot buckle his distempered cause
Within the belt of rule.   *disease imagery*

ANGUS
                    Now does he feel
His secret murders sticking on his hands;
Now minutely revolts upbraid his faith-breach;
Those he commands move only in command,
20 Nothing in love: now does he feel his title
Hang loose about him, like a giant's robe
Upon a dwarfish thief. *This clothing image tells us he was never fit to be king*

MENTEITH
                    Who then shall blame
His pestered senses to recoil and start,
When all that is within him does condemn
25 Itself for being there?

CAITHNESS
Well, march we on,
To give obedience where 'tis truly owed:
Meet we the medicine of the sickly weal, *images of disease*
And with him pour we, in our country's purge,
30 Each drop of us. *imagery of disease*

LENNOX
                    Or so much as it needs
To dew the sovereign flower and drown the weeds.
Make we our march towards Birnam.

Exeunt, marching.

EXAMINATION-BASED QUESTIONS

- How close to the truth is the picture of Macbeth given by his enemies in this scene?
- What are the implications of the various strands of imagery in this scene?

Act Five
– Scene Three –
[Dunsinane. Macbeth's Castle.]

PLOT SUMMARY

Macbeth is at bay in Dunsinane castle. He violently rebukes all bringers of bad news as cowards. He derives no consolation from the Doctor's unhelpful account of Lady Macbeth's illness and looks to him for a remedy to cure the maladies afflicting the country.

In the previous scene, Menteith has given a clue to Macbeth's behaviour. In this one, Macbeth is showing signs of strain; his 'pestered senses' are his overwrought nerves, which 'recoil' (5, 2, 23) or give way as further troubles come. His behaviour now is certainly volatile. He is given to sudden changes of mood. His first speech is marked by a false sense of security: he still trusts the 'spirits that know / All mortal consequence' (4–5). He momentarily loses control at the news of the approach of the English army, treating the unfortunate messenger with cruel contempt. Then he lapses suddenly into a pitiful, despairing, extremely moving reflection on his desolate life, a life that he finds increasingly intolerable. This mood is succeeded by one of determination to face all the odds bravely ('I'll fight, till from my bones my flesh be hacked', 32). Again, he becomes reflective and philosophical as he broods on the power of medicine to eradicate the troubles of the brain and extends his meditation to developing an analogy between the troubles of the human body and those of the commonwealth. At the end, he resumes his blustering, daredevil attitude ('I will not be afraid of death and bane', 59).

Enter MACBETH, DOCTOR, *and* ATTENDANTS

MACBETH

Bring me no more reports; let them fly all:
Till Birnam wood remove to Dunsinane
I cannot taint with fear. What's the boy Malcolm?   1
Was he not born of woman? The spirits that know   3
5   All mortal consequence have pronounced me thus: 4
'Fear not, Macbeth; no man that's born of woman
Shall e'er have power upon thee.' Then fly, false Thanes,   4–5
And mingle with the English epicures: *soft*
The mind I sway by and the heart I bear
10   Shall never sag with doubt, nor shake with fear.   8

Enter a SERVANT

diabolical imagery

The devil damn thee black, thou cream-faced loon!   9
Where gott'st thou that goose look?

let them fly all: let all the thanes desert me
taint: become weak
The spirits: This reference is to the 'masters' who appeared as the apparitions in Act 4, Scene 1.
The spirits that know … consequence: the spirits who can foresee the course of human history
the English epicures: An epicure is a self-indulgent person. Macbeth is expressing a hardy Scotsman's contempt for the reputed softness and luxurious living of the English enemy.
sway by: govern myself, or rule myself by

SERVANT
There is ten thousand —

MACBETH

Geese, villain?

SERVANT

Soldiers, sir.

MACBETH
Go prick thy face, and over-red thy fear,
Thou lily-livered boy. What soldiers, patch?
Death of thy soul! Those linen cheeks of thine
Are counsellors to fear. What soldiers, whey-face?

SERVANT
The English force, so please you.

MACBETH
Take thy face hence.

Exit SERVANT.

Seyton! — I am sick at heart
When I behold — Seyton, I say! — This push
Will cheer me ever, or disseat me now.
I have lived long enough: my way of life
Is fall'n into the sere, the yellow leaf;
And that which should accompany old age,
As honour, love, obedience, troops of friends,
I must not look to have; but, in their stead,
Curses, not loud but deep, mouth-honour, breath,
Which the poor heart would fain deny, and dare not.
Seyton!

Enter SEYTON

SEYTON
What's your gracious pleasure?

MACBETH

What news more?

SEYTON
All is confirmed, my lord, which was reported.

MACBETH
I'll fight, till from my bones my flesh be hacked.

A glimpse of the old macbeth.

11	*loon:* fool or rogue
14	*Go prick thy face ... fear:* The servant is white-faced with fear at Macbeth's probable response to his message. Macbeth is telling him to pinch his face and restore it to a healthy red colour.
15	*lily-livered:* cowardly
	patch: clown
16	*linen:* pale
17	*Are counsellors to fear:* prompt other people to be afraid
	whey-face: pale face
20	*push:* military offensive or advance
21	*Will cheer me ever, or disseat me now:* This offensive will hearten and encourage me for ever, or else dethrone me now. Some editors print 'chair' for 'cheer'. The former would fit in better with 'disseat' (enthrone and dethrone).
22–6	*my way of life ... have:* I am coming into the autumn of my life and I cannot look forward to the benefits and blessings which should be part of old age — honour, love, obedience and multitudes of friends.
27	*mouth-honour, breath:* lip-service, empty words
28	*Which the poor heart ... not:* Those wretches who honour me only with their insincere words would like to withhold even that tribute, but are afraid to do so.

Give me my armour.   *This clothing detail means Macbeth wants to resume his identity as a warrior*

SEYTON

       'Tis not needed yet.

MACBETH

I'll put it on.

35 Send out more horses, skirr the country round;

Hang those that talk of fear. Give me mine armour. —

How does your patient, doctor?

DOCTOR

            Not so sick, my lord,

As she is troubled with thick-coming fancies

That keep her from her rest.

MACBETH

           Cure her of that:

40 Canst thou not minister to a mind diseased,

Pluck from the memory a rooted sorrow,

Raze out the written troubles of the brain,

And with some sweet oblivious antidote

Cleanse the stuffed bosom of that perilous stuff

45 Which weighs upon the heart?

DOCTOR

           Therein the patient

Must minister to himself.

MACBETH

Throw physic to the dogs, I'll none of it. —

Come, put mine armour on; give me my staff.

Seyton, send out. — Doctor, the thanes fly from me. —

50 Come sir, dispatch. If thou couldst, doctor, cast

The water of my land, find her disease,   *medical*

And purge it to a sound and pristine health,   *imagery.*

I would applaud thee to the very echo,

That should applaud again. — Pull't off, I say. —

55 What rhubarb, senna, or what purgative drug

Would scour these English hence? Hear'st thou of them?

DOCTOR

Ay, my good lord; your royal preparation

Makes us hear something.

MACBETH

          Bring it after me. —

I will not be afraid of death and bane

35	*skirr:* scour
37	*your patient:* Macbeth's use of the word 'your' may indicate that he is making a distinction between Lady Macbeth, the doctor's patient, and Scotland, which he regards as his own patient needing to be restored to sound health (see lines 50–6 below).
38	*thick-coming fancies:* fantasies following quickly upon each other
40	*minister to:* prescribe a cure for
41	*a rooted sorrow:* a strongly entrenched grief
42	*Raze … brain:* erase the troubles engraved on the mind
43	*oblivious:* causing forgetfulness
44–5	*Cleanse … heart:* rid the mind of the hazardous burden that encumbers it
47	*physic:* medicine
48	*staff:* baton carried by the commander
50	*dispatch:* hurry
50–1	*cast … disease:* discover the country's disease by analysing its urine
52	*purge … health:* treat it so that it may return to its original good health
54	*Pull't off, I say:* He is referring to a part of his armour.
55	*senna:* Tea made from the dried leaves of the senna plant may be used as a purgative.
56	*scour:* purge
57–8	*your royal preparation … something:* The Doctor's answer is a diplomatic one; he does not want to commit himself by suggesting that he knows too much. He is saying: 'Your military preparations make us aware that some kind of invasion is imminent.'
58	*Bring it:* The piece of armour. Macbeth's behaviour here betrays his nervous agitation.
59	*bane:* destruction

60   Till Birnam forest come to Dunsinane.

Exeunt all but DOCTOR.

DOCTOR
Were I from Dunsinane away and clear,
Profit again should hardly draw me here.

Exit.

Act Five

– Scene Four –

[Before Birnam Wood.]

PLOT SUMMARY

Malcolm orders the assembled soldiers to cut boughs from Birnam wood in order to mislead Macbeth regarding their numbers. They make their way towards Macbeth's stronghold.

The arrangements ordered by Malcolm in this scene ('Let every soldier hew him down a bough', 5) prepare us for the unfortunate confirmation of one prophecy for Macbeth. We now know that Birnam wood is about to 'move' to Dunsinane, and that the confidence Macbeth has just expressed at the end of Act 5, Scene 3 is not soundly based. If he knew the whole truth, he would have every reason to be afraid of 'death and bane' (5, 3, 59).

Enter, with drum and colours, MALCOLM,
OLD SIWARD *and his Son,* MACDUFF, MENTEITH,
CAITHNESS, ANGUS, LENNOX, ROSS
and Soldiers, marching

MALCOLM
Cousins, I hope the days are near at hand
That chambers will be safe.

MENTEITH
                                    We doubt it nothing.

OLD SIWARD
What wood is this before us?

MENTEITH
                        The wood of Birnam.

MALCOLM
5   Let every soldier hew him down a bough
And bear't before him: thereby shall we shadow
The numbers of our host, and make discovery
Err in report of us.

SOLDIERS
                        It shall be done.

1–2	*I hope … safe:* I hope we will soon see the time when it will be safe for us to sleep without fear of being murdered in our beds, as Duncan was.
2	*We doubt it nothing:* We have no doubt that your hopes will be realised.
6	*shadow:* conceal
7–8	*and make discovery … us:* and cause Macbeth's scouts to give an inaccurate report

[handwritten annotation:] Use of camoflage – Appearance vs. Reality

10–11	*and will endure ... before't:* and is prepared to stand firm against our siege of it
11	*setting down before't:* besieging it
12–13	*For where ... revolt:* Wherever the opportunity has arisen, people of high and low rank have deserted his cause. *to be given:* to be gained
14	*constrained things:* unfortunates who are compelled to serve
15–16	*Let ... event:* We cannot pass an accurate judgement until we see how events turn out.
16–17	*put we on ... soldiership:* Let us prepare diligently for battle.
17–19	*The time ... owe:* We shall soon discover, as the outcome of the battle becomes clear, what we really possess as distinct from what we say we possess. *owe:* own
20–1	*Thoughts ... arbitrate:* Old Siward is adding his voice to Macduff's, urging caution on Malcolm. There is little point in speculating about the outcome, since speculation is always uncertain. Only fighting can decide the result.

OLD SIWARD
We learn no other but the confident tyrant
10 Keeps still in Dunsinane, and will endure
Our setting down before't.

MALCOLM
           'Tis his main hope;
For where there is advantage to be given,
Both more and less have given him the revolt,
And none serve with him but constrained things
15 Whose hearts are absent too.

MACDUFF
           Let our just censures
Attend the true event, and put we on *clothing image*
Industrious soldiership.

OLD SIWARD
           The time approaches
That will with due decision make us know
What we shall say we have and what we owe.
20 Thoughts speculative their unsure hopes relate,
But certain issue strokes must arbitrate:
Towards which advance the war.

Exeunt, marching.

'What wood is this before us? / The Wood of Burnam' (5, 4, 4)

EXAMINATION-BASED QUESTIONS

- Malcolm's order to the soldiers to cut down the boughs of Birnam wood has major significance. Explain.
- Malcolm and Macduff have different approaches to coming events. Explain.

Act Five
– Scene Five –
[Dunsinane. Macbeth's Castle.]

PLOT SUMMARY

Macbeth prepares to offer stiff resistance to his enemy; just then he hears of his wife's death. His response is to comment on the futility of human life and its transitory nature. A messenger brings news that Birnam wood is moving towards Dunsinane. Macbeth, although he now senses that his cause is lost, is determined to die fighting.

The focal point of this scene is Macbeth's troubling response to the news of his wife's death (17–28). By this time, his existence has been drained of all significance; he sees one day creeping after another in the same trivial ('petty', 20) way, until life ends. In lines 22–3 we have the image of poor, foolish, deluded human beings having only enough light to find their way to the darkness of death. The idea of death as 'dusty' derives from the image of 'dust to dust'. Life is like a candle flame, extinguished all too quickly; it is a 'walking shadow'(24). Here Shakespeare wants us to picture the doomed fools finding their way to their dusty deaths with the aid of candles, casting shadows as they walk along. The miserable chronicle of all those yesterdays is a reminder of the futility of human effort. 'Shadow' refers back to the candle and forward to the 'poor player' (24), since the acting he does is only a shadow of reality. The human actor is 'poor' because he is to be pitied: he is soon to be silenced by death; he is also poor because he plays his part without proper dignity, straining for effort ('struts and frets', 25). In lines 26–8, life is no longer seen in terms of the human action represented by fools walking to death or the poor actor strutting on the stage. It becomes even more unreal; it is merely a meaningless story told by an 'idiot' speaker.

The messenger who interrupts Macbeth's meditation is another speaker, a frightened man looking almost idiotic, who has to tell his strange, incomprehensible story, the story of a wood that moves.

Macbeth's most famous speech ends with a view of man as a pawn or puppet 'activated by an uncomprehending and mad creator', as one critic describes it. Another critic sees the speech as a reflection of 'the nothingness that life becomes to him before it is taken from him'. It should be noted that Shakespeare makes use of allusions to the Bible throughout the speech. The candle and shadow images are found in the Book of Job (18: 6 and 8: 9) and the Psalms (18: 28 and 39: 7), while the idea of life as a tale is found in Psalm 90: 'We spend our years as a tale that is told'.

The speech as a whole, but particularly the player image, is a point of convergence for several lines of imagery developed throughout the play: the interlocked images of desire and act, appearance and reality, clothes that fit another and cannot be borrowed, daggers breeched with gore and painted faces – all relate to acting. In an earlier speech, Lady Macbeth reminded her husband that the sleeping and the dead were no more real than pictures (2, 2, 54–5). Macbeth has now come to regard everything, even life itself, as unreal. He has, for the moment, cut himself adrift from all that has bound him to solid reality and entered a world of illusions.

The full power of the speech can be realised only in performance. For some of the lines to take on their full meaning, it is necessary for them to be spoken out loud. As he speaks the fourth line, for example ('Creeps in this petty pace', 20) and the ninth ('That struts and frets his hour upon the stage', 25), he is pacing the stage, enacting his meaning. Again, gesture and movement lend an added significance to lines 22–3. 'And all our yesterdays' is accompanied by a sweeping movement of the hand, which points limply to the ground at 'dusty death'.

The play does not end on the despairing note sounded at the end of this speech. In his final moments, Macbeth emerges from his vision of a totally meaningless world. He again faces life in a way that suggests his recognition that at least some things retain significance for him. His display of courage and determination and his refusal to yield to a future of mockery and humiliation are not meaningless gestures.

Enter, with drum and colours, MACBETH, SEYTON *and Soldiers*

MACBETH
Hang out our banners on the outward walls;
The cry is still 'They come'. Our castle's strength
Will laugh a siege to scorn. Here let them lie
Till famine and the ague eat them up. *— hardly the archuncle of Bellanc's Bridegroom*
Were they not forced with those that should be ours,   5
We might have met them dareful, beard to beard,
And beat them backward home.

A cry of women within.

What is that noise?

SEYTON
It is the cry of women, my good lord.

Exit.

MACBETH
I have almost forgot the taste of fears.
The time has been my senses would have cooled   10
To hear a night-shriek, and my fell of hair
Would at a dismal treatise rouse and stir
As life were in't. I have supped full with horrors;
Direness, familiar to my slaughterous thoughts,

2–3   *Our castle's strength ... scorn:*
The strength of our defences will make a mockery of the efforts of the besiegers to penetrate them.
4   *the ague:* fever
5–6   *Were they not ... beard:*
If they were not reinforced with some of our men, we would have been able to meet them defiantly face to face.

10   *cooled:* chilled or frozen
11   *a night-shriek:* a cry in the night
fell of hair: hair on the skin
12   *a dismal treatise:* a grim or sinister story
13   *As life were in't:* as if it had a life of its own
I have supped full with horrors: I have had my fill of horrors.

15   Cannot once start me.

Enter SEYTON

             Wherefore was that cry?

SEYTON
The Queen, my lord, is dead.

MACBETH
She should have died hereafter;
There would have been a time for such a word.
Tomorrow, and tomorrow, and tomorrow,
20   Creeps in this petty pace from day to day,
To the last syllable of recorded time;
And all our yesterdays have lighted fools
The way to dusty death. Out, out, brief candle!
Life's but a walking shadow, a poor player *actor*
25   That struts and frets his hour upon the stage
And then is heard no more. It is a tale
Told by an idiot, full of sound and fury,
Signifying nothing. *He is totally nihilistic by now*

Enter a MESSENGER

Thou comest to use thy tongue; thy story quickly.

MESSENGER
30   Gracious my lord,
I should report that which I say I saw,
But know not how to do't.

MACBETH
             Well, say, sir.

MESSENGER
As I did stand my watch upon the hill,
I looked toward Birnam, and anon methought
35   The wood began to move.

MACBETH
             Liar and slave!

MESSENGER
Let me endure your wrath if't be not so.
Within this three mile may you see it coming;
I say, a moving grove.

14–15 *Direness ... start me:* My murderous thoughts are so accustomed to horror that it can no longer startle me.

17–18 *She should ... a word:* She would have died sometime; if news of her death ('such a word') had not come now, the time for such news would most certainly have come some day. Macbeth's second statement here is merely a reinforcement of the first. He is underlining an idea common in Shakespeare: since everyone must endure death, it does not matter very much when it comes.

20 *Creeps ... day:* One day follows another in a trivial, tedious manner. The actor playing Macbeth can enact the meaning here by slowly pacing the stage.

21 *To the last ... time:* Until the last syllable of the book of life has been written, and time is no more.

22–3 *And all ... death:* Every day we have lived has marked the passage of some poor fools to their dusty graves. There is an echo here of the 'dust to dust' of the burial service.

23 *Out, out, brief candle!:* Life is a candle flame quickly snuffed out.

24 *walking shadow:* This image is prompted by 'lighted' and 'candle' above. It suggests the shadow cast by a person carrying a candle, something unreal and insubstantial.

24–6 *a poor player ... more:* The player is suggested by 'shadow'. The player's short and inglorious hour upon the stage, like the life of man, peters out into silence.

25 *struts and frets:* walks with an affected air of dignity and importance and, at the same time, worries about his performance. Compare Shakespeare's Sonnet 23: 'As an imperfect actor on the stage,/Who with his fear is put beside his part'.

31 *I should:* I am obliged

37 *Within this ... see it coming:* The moving wood can be seen within three miles of the castle.

MACBETH

               If thou speak'st false,

	Upon the next tree shalt thou hang alive
40	Till famine cling thee. If thy speech be sooth,
	I care not if thou dost for me as much.
	I pull in resolution, and begin *It's beginning to dawn on him now tract*
	To doubt th' equivocation of the fiend,
	That lies like truth: 'Fear not, till Birnam wood
45	Do come to Dunsinane'; and now a wood
	Comes toward Dunsinane. Arm, arm, and out!
	If this which he avouches does appear,
	There is nor flying hence, nor tarrying here.
	I 'gin to be aweary of the sun,
50	And wish th' estate o' the world were now undone.
	Ring the alarum bell! Blow wind, come wrack!
	At least we'll die with harness on our back.

The old macbeth is back

Exeunt.

Side glosses (left column):

40   *cling:* shrink, wither
      sooth: truth

42   *I pull in resolution:* I suddenly feel less assured and less determined.

43   *To doubt … fiend:* I suspect that the evil spirits have made dishonest, double-meaning promises.

47   *avouches:* affirms, states as a fact

49   *I 'gin to be aweary of the sun:* Macbeth longs for darkness. Light and darkness have a potent symbolic force in the play. See particularly Act 2, Scene 1 and Act 5, Scene 1.

50   *And wish … undone:* I wish the order of the universe were destroyed. Macbeth wants everything and everybody to share in his destruction.

51   *wrack:* wreck

52   *harness:* Armour. Here we get a glimpse of the old warlike Macbeth.

'Tomorrow, and tomorrow, and tomorrow, / Creeps in this petty pace from day to day, / To the last syllable of recorded time; / And all our yesterdays have lighted fools / The way to dusty death.'
(5, 5, 19–23)

EXAMINATION-BASED QUESTIONS

- In this scene, Macbeth is the dominant figure, the focus of intense interest. How is this interest created?
- What is the tone of Macbeth's first speech here?
- Consider Macbeth's second speech ('I have almost forgot the taste of fears …', 9 ff.) as a commentary on his career.
- What does the speech beginning 'She should have died hereafter …' (17 ff.) reveal about the state of Macbeth's mind at this point?
- As in the previous scene, Macbeth goes through significant changes of mood. Explain.

KEY THEMES AND IMPORTANT FACTS

- The finest speech in this act is 'She should have died hereafter' (17–28). The speech offers a splendid opportunity to the actor. When he comes to line 19 ('Tomorrow, and tomorrow, and tomorrow'), he gradually lowers his pitch and gradually lowers his arm as he does so. At the end of the line his limp arm points to the ground on which the 'petty pace of time creeps' (20). The gesture accompanying 'all our yesterdays' ends with the limp arm pointing to the ground of 'dusty death' (23). At this point the actor's head is bowed.
- The actor, his shadow reflected on the floor of the stage by candlelight, is acting the part of the 'poor player' (24) he is describing, the image of life 'That struts and frets his hour upon the stage' (25). The actor, too, struts and frets.

Act Five

– Scene Six –

[Dunsinane. Before the Castle.]

PLOT SUMMARY

Macbeth's enemies, led by Malcolm and Macduff, besiege the castle of Dunsinane, Macbeth's last stronghold. The 'leafy screens' (1) fulfil the prophecy made by the Third Apparition in Act 4, Scene 1. They are also symbols of the kind of life that is in store for Scotland following Macbeth's fall.

Enter, with drum and colours, MALCOLM, SIWARD, MACDUFF, *and their Army, with boughs*

MALCOLM
Now near enough; your leafy screens throw down, *the need for pretence (pretending) is no longer there*
And show like those you are. You, worthy uncle,   2   *And show like those you are:* and reveal yourselves as soldiers
Shall with my cousin, your right noble son,
Lead our first battle. Worthy Macduff and we   4   *first battle:* the main army
5   Shall take upon's what else remains to do,   *we:* Malcolm is using the royal plural
According to our order.   6   *According to our order:* in accordance with our battle plan

SIWARD
             Fare you well.
Do we but find the tyrant's power tonight,   7   *Do we but find:* if only we can find
Let us be beaten, if we cannot fight.   *the tyrant's power:* Macbeth's army

MACDUFF
Make all our trumpets speak; give them all breath,
10   Those clamorous harbingers of blood and death.   10   *clamorous harbingers:* noisy heralds

Exeunt. Alarums.

EXAMINATION-BASED QUESTIONS

- What does this scene suggest about Malcolm's position?
- Does this scene give the impression that Malcolm, Macduff and Siward are confident about the outcome?

Act Five

– Scene Seven –

[Another part of the Field.]

PLOT SUMMARY

The opening of Scene 7 shows Macbeth possessed by a rugged determination to face a situation that he now knows is desperate. His enemies have closed in on him and escape is impossible, hence his image of himself as a bear tied to a stake at the mercy of savage dogs. However, he still clutches at the witches' promise that only a man not born of woman can kill him.

There are three other brief episodes in this scene. Young Siward hopes to achieve a heroic reputation by killing Macbeth, but fails. Macbeth's success here renews his confidence in his safety ('Thou wast born of woman', 11). Macduff stresses his strong personal motives for confronting Macbeth: the ghosts of his wife and children will always haunt him if he fails to avenge them personally. The third episode, featuring the arrival of Malcolm and Old Siward, deals with the larger political theme. The final collapse of Macbeth's cause is suggested in Malcolm's ambiguous 'We have met with foes / That strike beside us' (28–9); this may mean either that Macbeth's soldiers have joined his enemies or that they are deliberately not fighting very hard.

Alarums. Enter MACBETH

MACBETH

1–2   *They have tied ... course:* The image is from bear-baiting, a popular sport in Shakespeare's day. The bear was chained to a stake and baited by mastiffs. The 'course' is a single round.

2   *What's he:* What kind of man can he be?

They have tied me to a stake; I cannot fly,
But bear-like I must fight the course. What's he
That was not born of woman? Such a one
Am I to fear, or none.

Enter YOUNG SIWARD

YOUNG SIWARD
5   What is thy name?

MACBETH
                  Thou'lt be afraid to hear it.

YOUNG SIWARD

6–9   *No; though thou ... ear:* Diabolic imagery is often used to define Macbeth. Note the words 'hotter', 'hell', 'devil'.

No; though thou call'st thyself a hotter name
Than any is in hell.

MACBETH

My name's Macbeth.

YOUNG SIWARD

The devil himself could not pronounce a title [*more diabolical imagery.*]
More hateful to mine ear.

MACBETH

No, nor more fearful.

YOUNG SIWARD

10   Thou liest, abhorred tyrant; with my sword
I'll prove the lie thou speak'st.

They fight and YOUNG SIWARD *is slain.*

MACBETH

                  Thou wast born of woman.
But swords I smile at, weapons laugh to scorn,
Brandished by man that's of a woman born.

Exit.

Alarums. Enter MACDUFF

MACDUFF

That way the noise is. Tyrant, show thy face!
15   If thou beest slain and with no stroke of mine,
My wife and children's ghosts will haunt me still.
I cannot strike at wretched kerns, whose arms
Are hired to bear their staves: either thou, Macbeth,
Or else my sword with an unbattered edge
20   I sheathe again undeeded.

Alarums.

                There thou shouldst be;
By this great clatter, one of greatest note
Seems bruited. Let me find him, Fortune!
And more I beg not.

Exit. Alarums.

Enter MALCOLM *and* OLD SIWARD

OLD SIWARD

This way, my lord; the castle's gently rendered:

16	*still:* for ever
17	*kerns:* Irish mercenaries. Macbeth is forced to hire soldiers, as were the rebels he defeated earlier.
18	*staves:* spear shafts
20	*undeeded:* unused *There thou shouldst be:* There you are likely to be.
21–2	*By this great clatter … bruited:* To judge by the loud din, someone of the highest distinction seems to be indicated.
24	*gently rendered:* surrendered without much of a struggle

25 The tyrant's people on both sides do fight,
The noble thanes do bravely in the war,
The day almost itself professes yours,
And little is to do.

27 *The day ... yours:* You have
almost completed your victory.

28–9 *foes ... beside us:* This
probably means 'enemies who
are fighting on our side now',
although some editors have
suggested that the enemies in
question are deliberately trying
to miss.

MALCOLM

We have met with foes
That strike beside us.

OLD SIWARD

30 Enter, sir, the castle.

Exeunt. Alarums.

EXAMINATION-BASED QUESTIONS

- Give your response to Macbeth's short speech at the beginning of Scene 7.
- What is the tone of Macbeth's comment on Young Siward: 'Thou wast born of woman' (11)?
- What is Macbeth's mood after he has killed Young Siward?
- Explain the motivation behind Macduff's speech beginning 'That way the noise is ...' (14 ff.).

Act Five

– Scene Eight –

[Another part of the Field.]

PLOT SUMMARY

Macbeth and Macduff face each other. Macbeth boasts that he is invulnerable to any man born of woman, but Macduff shatters his confidence by revealing the strange circumstances surrounding his own birth. Macbeth dies fighting fiercely for the life he has not long before described as meaningless.

Enter MACBETH

MACBETH
Why should I play the Roman fool, and die   1
On mine own sword? Whiles I see lives, the gashes
Do better upon them.
                                                        2

Enter MACDUFF

MACDUFF
Turn, hell-hound, turn! *Diabolical & animal image.*

MACBETH
Of all men else I have avoided thee: 4
5 But get thee back, my soul is too much charged
With blood of thine already.

MACDUFF
                    I have no words —   5
My voice is in my sword, thou bloodier villain   8
Than terms can give thee out!

They fight.

MACBETH
                    Thou losest labour,   8–10
As easy may'st thou the intrenchant air
10 With thy keen sword impress as make me bleed:
Let fall thy blade on vulnerable crests,   11
I bear a charmed life, which must not yield   12
To one of woman born.

the Roman fool: The Roman tradition was for the defeated warrior to kill himself rather than be captured.
lives: living enemies

Of all men else I have avoided thee: I have avoided you more than any other man. The main reason is that he was warned by the apparitions to 'Beware Macduff' (4, 1, 71–2). The next two lines may suggest a further reason.
charged: burdened
terms: words

Thou losest labour ... bleed: You are wasting your energy. You can as easily wound the invulnerable air as make me bleed.
crests: helmets
must not: cannot

MACDUFF

13   *Despair thy charm:* Abandon your faith in your good fortune!

14   *And let ... served:* and let the devil whom you have always served

16   *Untimely ripped:* born prematurely

18   *my better part of man:* my spirit

19   *juggling fiends:* cheating devils

20   *That palter ... sense:* who trifle with us and trick us with words that can be interpreted in two different ways

21–2   *That keep ... hope:* They tell us things that turn out to be true in a sense we did not anticipate, but untrue in the sense we did anticipate. Our hopes are consequently shattered.

24   *the show and gaze o'the time:* a popular national spectacle *the time:* the country, the nation

25–6   *We'll have thee ... underwrit:* Macbeth, as if he were a freak on show in a fairground, will have his portrait painted on a banner fastened to a pole, the banner bearing the inscription 'Here may you see the tyrant'

29   *baited:* tormented

30–2   *Though Birnam wood ... the last:* The promises made by the witches have proved deceptive: Birnam wood has now come to Dunsinane and Macbeth has been confronted ('opposed') by a man not born of woman. Thus his faith in a happy destiny for himself has been shattered. In spite of this, he is prepared to fight to the bitter end ('try the last').

33   *Lay on:* Fight on!

                            Despair thy charm;
And let the angel whom thou still hast served
15 Tell thee, Macduff was from his mother's womb
Untimely ripped.

MACBETH

Accursed be that tongue that tells me so,
For it hath cowed my better part of man!
And be these juggling fiends no more believed,
20 That palter with us in a double sense,
That keep the word of promise to our ear,
And break it to our hope. I'll not fight with thee.

MACDUFF

Then yield thee, coward,
And live to be the show and gaze o'the time.
25 We'll have thee, as our rarer monsters are,
Painted upon a pole, and underwrit,
'Here may you see the tyrant.'

MACBETH

                  I will not yield,
To kiss the ground before young Malcolm's feet,
And to be baited with the rabble's curse.
30 Though Birnam wood be come to Dunsinane,
And thou opposed, being of no woman born,
Yet I will try the last. Before my body
I throw my war-like shield. Lay on, Macduff,
And damned be him that first cries 'Hold, enough!'

Exeunt, fighting. Alarums.   This is the MacBeth we
                               met at the start

Re-enter, fighting, and MACBETH *is slain.*

Exit MACDUFF.

'Lay on, Macduff, / And damned be him that first cries 'Hold, enough!' (5, 8, 33–4)

EXAMINATION-BASED QUESTIONS

- Describe Macbeth's varying moods in this scene.
- How does Shakespeare want us to see Macbeth as his death approaches?
- What fate awaits Macbeth if he is taken alive?
- How are Macbeth's false hopes in the promises of the witches shattered?
- Is there any way in which the Macbeth we encounter at the end of the scene resembles the Macbeth we met at the beginning of the play?

Act Five

– Scene Nine –

[Inside Macbeth's Castle.]

PLOT SUMMARY

The victors congratulate themselves on their success and Macduff enters with Macbeth's head. Malcolm, the new king, pledges that he will restore order and harmony to Scotland and repeats the rumour that Lady Macbeth has died by her own hand.

It is difficult to be enthusiastic about this final scene. The play ends on a falling note. After the tempestuous earlier scenes involving Macbeth, the congratulations and rejoicing of his enemies are a tame affair. Good has triumphed and the forces of evil have been overcome, but in the process, all that gave the play its life and excitement has been banished. Set against Macbeth's terrible and heart-rending utterances during his final hours, the sentiments expressed by his conquerors seem pallid and uninspiring.

Retreat and flourish. Enter, with drum and colours,
MALCOLM, SIWARD, ROSS, *Thanes, and Soldiers*

MALCOLM
I would the friends we miss were safe arrived.   1   *we miss:* we are missing

SIWARD
Some must go off; and yet, by these I see,   2   *go off:* die
So great a day as this is cheaply bought.   *by these I see:* to judge by the survivors I see

MALCOLM
Macduff is missing, and your noble son.

ROSS
5   Your son, my lord, has paid a soldier's debt.
He only lived but till he was a man,
The which no sooner had his prowess confirmed   7–8   *The which ... fought:* no sooner had his brave conduct confirmed that he was a man in the post where he fought so fearlessly
In the unshrinking station where he fought,
But like a man he died.

SIWARD
                    Then he is dead?

ROSS
10   Ay, and brought off the field. Your cause of sorrow   10–12   *Your cause ... no end:* He was such an excellent young man that if you proportioned your grief to his worth, your mourning would never cease.
Must not be measured by his worth, for then
It hath no end.

SIWARD
> Had he his hurts before?

ROSS
Ay, on the front.

SIWARD
> Why then, God's soldier be he.
Had I as many sons as I have hairs,
15 I would not wish them to a fairer death.
And so his knell is knolled.

MALCOLM
> He's worth more sorrow,
And that I'll spend for him.

SIWARD
> He's worth no more.
They say he parted well and paid his score;
And so God be with him! Here comes newer comfort.

Enter MACDUFF, with MACBETH's head

MACDUFF
20 Hail, King! for so thou art. Behold, where stands
Th' usurper's cursèd head. The time is free.
I see thee compassed with thy kingdom's pearl,
That speak my salutation in their minds;
Whose voices I desire aloud with mine:
25 Hail, King of Scotland!

ALL
> Hail, King of Scotland!

Flourish.

MALCOLM
We shall not spend a large expense of time
Before we reckon with your several loves,
And make us even with you. My thanes and kinsmen,
Henceforth be earls, the first that ever Scotland
30 In such an honour named. What's more to do,
Which would be planted newly with the time —
As calling home our exiled friends abroad
That fled the snares of watchful tyranny,
Producing forth the cruel ministers

---

12   *Had he his hurts before?:* Did he sustain his wounds on the front of his body? Did he die facing the enemy?

14   *hairs:* If there is a pun on 'heirs', Siward is taking his son's death with remarkable detachment.
16   *his knell is knolled:* The funeral bell is tolled for him, and no other mark of mourning is called for in his case.

18   *paid his score:* paid his debt as a warrior by doing his duty

20   *where stands:* Macbeth's head is on a pole
21   *The time is free:* the country is liberated
22   *I see thee ... pearl:* I see you surrounded by the nobility of Scotland.
23–4   *That speak ... mine:* who echo my greeting inwardly, and whom I ask to say aloud with me "Hail, King of Scotland!"

27–8   *Before ... you:* before I properly reward the love each of you has shown me and repay my debt to you
30–1   *What's more to do ... time:* We must deal with the other things that remain to be done, new things best done at the beginning of a new age.
34–5   *Producing forth ... fiend-like queen:* bringing to trial the cruel subordinates of Macbeth and his wife

35 Of this dead butcher and his fiend-like queen,
Who, as 'tis thought, by self and violent hands   36   *by self:* by her own
Took off her life — that, and what needful else
That calls upon us, by the grace of Grace,
We will perform in measure, time, and place.   39   *in measure:* in proper
40 So thanks to all at once, and to each one,   proportion
Whom we invite to see us crowned at Scone.

Flourish. Exeunt.

EXAMINATION-BASED QUESTIONS

- Malcolm talks about Macbeth and Lady Macbeth as 'this dead butcher and his fiend-like queen' (35). Is this a fair and reasonable summary of their characters as we have known them from the beginning?
- Discuss the implications of 'fiend-like' as applied to Lady Macbeth.

Notes for further study

MACBETH IN HISTORICAL CONTEXT

It is generally accepted that *Macbeth* was written in 1606 for a special performance before James I and his brother-in-law, Christian IV of Denmark. It was first staged at a private court performance. James I of England was also James VI of Scotland, and on his accession to the throne of England in 1603 he had united the thrones of the two countries. *Macbeth*, a play about a medieval king of Scotland, was certain to appeal to James, particularly as it included many of his ancestors. The House of Stuart, to which he belonged, had eight successive monarchs who could trace their royalty in an unbroken line to a marriage between a supposed descendant of Banquo and a woman descended from King Duncan. The celebration of this royal line in the pageant of eight kings in Act 4, Scene 1 ('What, will the line stretch out to the crack of doom?', 117) was bound to gratify James, since he was the eighth king in the procession. The pageant incorporated a further element of flattery. Shakespeare represents the eighth king carrying a mirror showing many more future descendants of James as kings of England and Scotland, thus assuring James that his royal line would long remain supreme.

The contemporary historical context helps to explain why Shakespeare felt the need to provide such assurance to James. The year before the play was first performed saw a major conspiracy by a group of Catholics against the king. In 1605, these Catholic conspirators, driven to desperation by the government's active discrimination against their religion, attempted to overthrow the Protestant administration of James by blowing up the Houses of Parliament at a time when the king and the members of the Houses of Lords and Commons were all in the building. Government propagandists falsely alleged that the Gunpowder Plot was inspired by some Jesuit priests, who were imprisoned, tortured and hanged. The plot was undertaken by a group of Catholic laymen led by Guy Fawkes. The date was fixed for 5 November and the explosives were all laid, but the plot was betrayed and Fawkes was arrested on the threshold of the cellar of the Houses of Parliament on 4 November.

The events surrounding the conspiracy provoked widespread popular horror and resentment, which find obvious echoes in *Macbeth*. In the temptation scene (1, 5) Lady Macbeth encourages her husband to 'look like the innocent flower, / But be the serpent under't' (64–5), an image which would instantly remind any contemporary audience of the medal recently struck to commemorate the detection of the Gunpowder Plot and which depicted a Catholic serpent lurking beneath flowers.

The Porter scene (2, 3) is particularly rich in reference to alleged Jesuit involvement in the plot. The farmer who 'hanged / himself on the expectation of plenty' (4–5) is Father Garnet, who was hanged in 1606 for his supposed part in the affair and who went under the name Farmer. The Porter refers derisively to the 'equivocator, that could swear in both the scales against / either scale; who committed treason enough for God's / sake, yet could not equivocate to heaven' (9–11). To equivocate is to tell misleading half-truths. At his trial in March 1606, Father Garnet had claimed that his evidence had been equivocal, and therefore justified as an effort to save his life. Such demeaning references to conspirators against King James were calculated both to reassure and to flatter that monarch.

Shakespeare's various accounts of monarchs and monarchy in *Macbeth* are strong affirmations of the sacredness of kingship and of the divine sanction it was thought to enjoy, contemporary monarchs being pleased to see themselves as owing their position to God. This was a theory of kingship propagated by King James and his apologists, popularly formulated as 'the divine right of kings'. In *Macbeth*, Shakespeare makes this theory a fundamental feature of his presentation of legitimate monarchs. Thus, Duncan, the lawful king, is a sacred person. His body is 'The Lord's anointed temple' and its violation through murder is supremely 'sacrilegious' (2, 3, 66–7). To attack the king is to attack God through his earthly representative.

The English king, Edward the Confessor, is associated even more emphatically with divinity. He is the 'holy king' (3, 6, 30) with the miraculous power to heal his sick subjects: 'sundry blessings hang about his throne / That speak him full of grace' (4, 3, 158–9). Contemporaries would have recognised the implied association here between the medieval monarch Edward and his successor, James. Edward is presented as curing scrofula, or 'the King's Evil'. By 1606, James had begun to perform this hereditary cure on his subjects.

It should be noted that *Macbeth* is a play full of second, or coded, meanings. For example, the lines describing the murder of Duncan ('Most sacrilegious murder hath broke ope / The Lord's anointed temple, and stole thence / The life o'the building' (2, 3, 66–8) have overtones of the destruction of the Catholic religion during the Protestant Reformation, in particular the removal of the Real Presence from the altars and churches and monasteries, thus depriving English religion of its life and soul. Shakespeare's family background was staunchly Catholic, while many of those with whom he associated still professed the Catholic faith.

MACBETH AND SHAKESPEARE'S WORLD VIEW

Shakespearean drama reflects a distinctive world view, whose main outlines are strongly influenced by a conservative view of life, a respect for inherited traditions and values and an acceptance of monarchy as the ideal form of government. Shakespeare and most of his contemporaries saw the maintenance of order as an essential foundation for a civilised way of life. The collapse of order represented ultimate disaster.

In *Macbeth*, Shakespeare suggests a symbolic correspondence between three kinds of order: order within the universe, order within the commonwealth and order within the human being. The violation of good order in the kingdom, a consequence of the murder of Duncan, is paralleled by the disruption of nature represented by the storm and the other portents on the night of the murder, as well as by the apparitions conjured up by the witches and of Banquo's ghost. It has a further parallel in Lady Macbeth's mental disintegration. The imagery of the play enforces the idea that Macbeth's revolt against lawful authority involves much more than the murder of a king and the usurpation of his throne. The initial crime is a huge *symbolic* gesture, releasing forces of universal disorder. Macbeth's career gradually becomes one of revolt against everything in the world.

Once the first evil step has been taken there is no turning back: men and nature are caught up in a process that causes havoc everywhere until the evil forces have played themselves out. Images of disease and unnatural happenings give concrete expression to the significance of Macbeth's violation of natural order. Even as he contemplates killing Duncan, his heart knocks at his ribs 'Against the use of nature' (1, 3, 137). Lady Macbeth's sleepwalking is described as a 'great perturbation in nature' (5, 1, 8).

The murder of Duncan ('The Lord's anointed temple', 2, 3, 67) is repeatedly presented as a monstrous violation of the natural order; it is committed when 'Nature seems dead' (2, 1, 50). In preparation for it, Lady Macbeth invokes the aid of those murdering ministers who 'wait on nature's mischief' (1, 5, 49), that is, assist the malignant forces in nature and accompanying natural disasters. The association between Macbeth's crime and disruption in nature is further enforced in the comment on the violent behaviour of the elements following Duncan's murder: ''Tis unnatural, / Even like the deed that's done' (2, 4, 10–11). The same kind of association between evil deeds and disorder within the individuals is implied in the Doctor's comment on Lady Macbeth's sickness: 'Unnatural deeds / Do breed unnatural troubles' (5, 1, 63–4).

The effects of Macbeth's identification with evil, which reaches an apocalyptic climax in Act 5, when he wants everything and everybody to share in his destruction, wishing that 'th' estate o' the world were now undone' (5, 5, 50), is suggested in a series of disease images that appear with particular frequency in the final act. The point made by these images is that Scotland is sick and that the cause of her disease is Macbeth's criminal career. Health and disease are symbolically related to moral good and evil. Macbeth's speech to the Doctor is an extended disease metaphor:

> ... If thou couldst, doctor, cast
> The water of my land, find her disease,
> And purge it to a sound and pristine health ...
> What rhubarb, senna, or what purgative drug
> Would scour these English hence?
>
> (5, 3, 50–6)

It is in relation to this kind of speech that the description of the King's Evil (4, 3, 141–59) takes on its true importance. At the hands of the good English king, diseased souls 'presently amend' (4, 3, 145). At Macbeth's hands, 'good men's lives / Expire before the flowers in their caps, / Dying or ere they sicken' (4, 3, 171–3). The English King Edward, upholder of good order and a healthy commonwealth, heals his subjects, while Macbeth, violator of order, kills his. Macbeth's cause is 'distemper'd' or diseased; Malcolm is to be the physician who will heal Scotland:

> Caithness: Meet we the medicine of the
> sickly weal,
> And with him pour we, in our
> country's purge,
> Each drop of us.
> Lennox: Or so much as it needs
> To dew the sovereign flower and
> drown the weeds.
>
> (5, 2, 28–31)

The medicine is Malcolm, while 'sovereign' means both 'royal' and 'powerfully medicinal'.

The play depicts the restoration of order as well as its violation. A whole society is disordered and sickly. Macbeth's famous catalogue of dogs (3, 1, 92) emphasises the idea of a proper order among animals as well as men; it is a fine stroke of irony on Shakespeare's part to make the prime enemy of order concede its propriety. In the third movement of the play (which belongs to Malcolm and Macduff in the way that the first did to Duncan and the second to Banquo), we see violated nature preparing itself to put an end to the unnatural disintegration set in train by Macbeth's acts. As Macbeth's power begins to wane, supernatural aid is invoked on behalf of those who would restore the beneficent order of nature ('the powers above / Put on their instruments', 4, 3, 237–8). Shakespeare uses visual imagery to suggest the restoration of the natural order in Act 5, Scene 4. The movement of Birnam wood towards Dunsinane is a tableau of nature overturning anti-nature as the play moves to its climax.

WITCHCRAFT IN SHAKESPEARE'S TIME

In the early seventeenth century, there was much debate in England and throughout Europe as to whether or not witches existed. Witch trials were commonplace; those deemed to be witches were generally hanged or burned to death. King James, whom Shakespeare had in mind when he wrote *Macbeth*, was fascinated by the subject. In 1597 he wrote a celebrated treatise on witchcraft, published in 1603 under the title *Daemonologie*. This was the king's answer to those who denied the existence of witches. He felt that he could call on his own experience to support his faith in the active role of witches in human affairs and in their capacity to do the kinds of harm Shakespeare shows them capable of in *Macbeth*. James had been appalled to learn that a coven of Scottish witches had cast spells in an effort to prevent his safe return by sea from Denmark after his marriage to Anne of Denmark, sister of Christian IV. The offending witches were put on trial and acknowledged their guilt. Their confession, published in 1591, provided a detailed account of how they had gone about their work. Their rituals had included collecting venom from a toad, christening a cat and sailing out to sea in a sieve. They also cast a dismembered corpse into the water. James was interested in their trial, partly because it facilitated his research into the activities of

witches, and partly because his ship had been delayed by unexplained winds.

Shakespeare included many of the details of James's experience at the hands of the witches in his account of the activities of the Weird Sisters in *Macbeth*, as if to affirm the soundness of the monarch's views on witchcraft:

> *Though his bark cannot be lost,*
> *Yet it shall be tempest-tost.*
>
> (1, 3, 24–5)

> *Toad, that under cold stone*
> *Days and nights has thirty-one*
> *Sweltered venom sleeping got,*
> *Boil thou first i'the charmed pot.*
>
> (4, 1, 6–9)

James believed that the great majority of witches were women, but women with a difference. Their features were unnaturally masculine, with a profusion of facial hair, remarked upon by Banquo ('you should be women, / And yet your beards forbid me to interpret / That you are so', 1, 3, 45–7). They were in league with the devil, and they travelled in the company of familiar spirits in the form of cats and toads. Graymalkin is a grey cat and Paddock is a toad (1, 1). They were able to conjure up images of people, the apparitions in Act 4, Scene 1, for example, and cause disease in animals as well as in people. These latter activities are suggested in such lines as 'Where hast thou been, sister?' with the answer 'Killing swine' (1, 3, 1–2) and 'I'll drain him dry as hay' (1, 3, 18). The reference to draining a man dry as hay is a reminder that witches were in the habit of sending spirits called *succubi* to deprive men of their vital powers.

In the first printed edition of *Macbeth*, the sinister women are called 'the Weyard Sisters'; the word 'weyward' may have been intended to suggest their prophetic power as well as their waywardness. Some contemporaries thought of them as fairies, and Shakespeare may have wanted them to resemble sibyls, prophetic woman found in classical literature. Some scholars believe that the witch scene in Act 4, Scene 1 was not written by Shakespeare, but added to the play by a contemporary dramatist, Thomas Middleton, who had written a play called *The Witch*. It is worth noting that on 27 August 1605 the students of St John's College, Oxford, greeted King James dressed up as three sibyls and saluted him as a descendant of Banquo.

MACBETH, A TRAGEDY
TRAGIC DRAMA

Macbeth is a tragedy. In tragic drama we have a ritual enactment of man's sense of the ultimate threat to individual and social well-being from **the random operation of external forces (fate, chance, accident) and human weakness (vice, folly, error, blindness, stupidity)**. In tragedy, we normally see a protagonist (the tragic hero) moving **from positive purpose through intense suffering**, which is an inescapable part of the tragic situation, **and through questioning to awareness and perception**. The direction of the protagonist's movement is from **prosperity to adversity**. Macbeth begins his tragic career as a universally admired hero and ends it as an object of hatred and derision, deserted by his former friends and allies.

The sequence of actions accompanying **the passage of the hero from good to bad fortune** is generally seen as the product of some initial and fundamental 'error' for example, false step, miscalculation, defect of character on his part. The 'error' in question does not always involve a moral failing. Indeed, in one of the greatest of all tragedies, *Oedipus Rex* by Sophocles, the hero is eventually doomed as a result of his efforts to avoid committing an offence against the moral law. **Macbeth's initial fault, on the other hand, the source of all that is to happen to him, is fundamentally a moral one**. It lies in the failure of his will to control the incitements to evil which so powerfully affect his imagination. His terrified question, 'why do I yield to that suggestion / Whose horrid image doth unfix my hair' (1 ,3, 134–5), makes the point. The 'suggestion' here is the temptation to murder Duncan. It remains true, however, that Macbeth's 'error' is committed in ignorance of its *full* consequences for himself.

Writers of tragedies are not concerned with preserving a sense of proportion between the initial tragic act of the hero and its consequences. In the case of *Macbeth*, however, act and consequence are more closely related than is the case in *King Lear*. Lear's tragic error is foolish rather than wicked, but its ultimate result is social and moral chaos, a state of affairs where men and women become predatory monsters. Macbeth, on the other hand, **sins greatly against the social and moral order of his world and opens the way for the entrance of appalling and universal forces of destruction**. Macbeth's deeply ironic comment on the 'gashed stabs' he has inflicted on Duncan, which 'looked like a breach in nature / For ruin's wasteful entrance' (2, 3, 113–14), is powerfully expressive of the unpredictable consequences of the original tragic act. The breach or gap in nature (man's social and moral order) opened up by the tragic hero may be comparatively great (as in Macbeth's case) or comparatively small (as in Lear's), but once the gap is opened, the destruction wrought by the evil forces which enter through the breach can be boundless.

Status in the protagonist is an important tragic requirement. The essential features here are moral stature and greatness of personality. In Shakespearean tragedy, such qualities are invariably associated with eminent people engaged in great events.

A useful way to appreciate the status of tragic heroes like Macbeth is to imagine them as the highest points on their human landscape by far, dominating everything around them. Yet like giant trees, they are more likely to be struck by lightning than smaller features are. Shakespeare does not explore the tragic implications of the lives of humble, mundane people like Arthur Miller's Willy Loman, whose very name indicates his status. Shakespeare's contemporaries would have regarded such figures as proper subjects of comedy, not of tragedy. In the Shakespearean tragic scene, it is essential that the hero be a man who can command our earnest good will, whose fortunes are of active and compelling interest and concern to us. He is not necessarily virtuous or free from profound guilt: Macbeth, for example, is neither. His ethical standing is less important than his purpose.

THE TRAGIC HERO

The presentation of the tragic hero must be such that we can identify with him in his sufferings. He must be a man who reminds us strongly of our humanity, who we can accept as in some way standing for us. He must be vulnerable to extreme suffering, as Macbeth clearly is, a fact which his wife recognises long before the end:

How now, my lord! Why do you keep alone,
Of sorriest fancies your companions making
(3, 2, 8–9)

By the close of the play, his life has become meaningless to him:

... It is a tale
Told by an idiot, full of sound and fury,
Signifying nothing.
(5, 5, 26–8)

In Shakespearean tragedy, the protagonist meets with final and impressive disaster resulting from an unrealised or unforeseen failure. The false step which sets the tragic process in motion is *consciously* undertaken, but with no intention on the hero's part of bringing about the evil result which must inevitably follow for him. The notion of blindness is appropriate to his condition at this stage, just as the notion of rediscovered sight is appropriate to his later recognition of what he has done, and how he has acted subsequently. A further aspect of the protagonist's tragic error is that once he commits it, its consequences cannot be undone. When he decides to murder Duncan and usurp the throne, Macbeth deprives himself of his freedom: his life follows a determined and inescapable pattern after the initial fateful act.

TRAGIC REVERSAL

Central to the tragic plot is the process known as reversal, which is what happens when the protagonist's actions are found to have consequences that are the direct opposite to what he meant or expected. The idea of acts recoiling on those who perform them is clearly expressed in *Macbeth*: 'that we but teach / Bloody instructions, which being taught return / To plague the inventor' (1, 7, 8–10). In their blindness, both Macbeth and his wife believe that if they usurp Duncan's throne they will be happy in the satisfaction of their highest ambitions; what they actually achieve is almost total misery culminating in ruin. The Captain's 'So from that spring whence comfort seemed to come / Discomfort swells' (1, 2, 27–8) is an appropriate motto for this aspect of tragedy.

To further explore the idea of reversal in tragedy, it is necessary to take account of two closely related features associated with the process. The tragic reversal is commonly the result of human failing, sometimes allied with the working-out of fate. It invariably involves tragic irony.

This arises when a character acts in a manner inappropriate to his actual circumstances, expects the opposite of what fate holds in store for him or says something that anticipates the actual outcome, but not at all in the way that he meant it. The most profound tragedy is that which makes free use of this tragic irony or irony of fate, where the hero's destruction is the work of his own unwitting hands or of somebody who wished him well, where the reversal is a working in blindness to self-defeat. *Macbeth* is such a tragedy. The main irony for Macbeth is the ambiguous nature of the witches' prophecies on which he so confidently relies for so long. He discovers their deceptiveness too late: 'And be these juggling fiends no more believed, / That palter with us in a double sense' (5, 8, 19–20). A major irony is found in the scene where he goes to the witches for reassurance: what he gets instead, without realising it, is an exact forecast of the manner of his defeat and death (4, 1).

The problem of the relative importance of fate and human responsibility in bringing about the reversal in tragedy is an extremely complex one. Discussion often tends to result in the formulation of maddening paradoxes. **In Shakespearean tragedy it is difficult to escape the impression that fatal circumstances are working against the hero from the beginning, that whatever he may do he is in some sense a doomed man.** The influence of reason, order and justice is extremely limited. In his book *Shakespearean Tragedy*, A.C. Bradley expressed this idea admirably when he argued that we fail to receive an essential part of the tragic effect unless we feel at times that the tragic hero and others 'drift struggling to destruction like helpless creatures borne on an irresistible flood towards a cataract; that faulty as they may be, their fault is far from being the sole or sufficient cause of all they suffer; and that the power from which they cannot escape is relentless and unmovable'.

TRAGIC INEVITABILITY AND FREE WILL

A useful way to grasp the notion of tragic inevitability is to see it in terms of the kind of world in which Shakespeare places his hero and in which the latter must face his tragic situation. It is the tragic dramatist's task to create this world and to oppose this situation in such a way that there is no chance of a happy outcome. Most tragedies begin with foreboding; the earliest expectation aroused is one of misfortune, and all accidents are unfortunate ones. **If we could seriously feel that, in light of all the data supplied by the drama, a more hopeful ending was quite possible and artistically acceptable, then we would not be dealing with genuine tragedy**.

To accept all this as applying to Macbeth is not inconsistent with the notion that Shakespeare allows his hero at least a minimal and initial free will, even though his first tragic act sets off a train of events leading to disaster, and what follows from this act is made to appear beyond human control. However strong the sense of inevitability, human action is a central fact of Macbeth's tragedy. It would be absurd to argue that Shakespeare makes us see Macbeth's lapse into crime as primarily the effect of witchcraft, or that he wants us to believe that only the limitless influence the witches exert over his mind could make him act in a way totally contrary to his natural disposition. He is not *shown* as being powerless to resist the various incitements to murder, nor does the play give us a sense of his initial action being forced upon him by some unseen power.

Thus, inevitability is the fundamental condition of all tragedy. A work can be defined as tragic if it meets the following conditions:

- The protagonist (tragic hero) must command our good will and possess qualities that can inspire our serious interest.

- He undertakes a significant action or is impelled by a significant purpose.

- The world in which the tragedy is set is such that by pursuing his purpose or action, the tragic hero inevitably meets with grave spiritual or physical suffering, often both.

- The laws of the tragic world are such that the hero's purposes are inseparable from disaster.

The most that one can say about the witches' influence is that it is considerable; there is no suggestion that Macbeth is not free to reject it, as Banquo appears to do. They beckon him towards a course of action that he has probably already contemplated, however vaguely (see 1, 3, 134–42). **The thought of murder originates with him, not with them.** They do not suggest that he should hasten to fulfil their prophecies by having recourse to action, evil or otherwise. The idea is his own, and he is never in a position to shift responsibility for his acts entirely to their shoulders. It is significant that the witches do not advise any course of action until long after he has already committed himself to evil. Only after he has had Banquo murdered does the Second Apparition tell him to be 'bloody, bold, and resolute' (4, 1, 79).

In the case of *Macbeth*, then, the formula that tragedy exhibits the omnipotence of an external fate will not work. However limited we find the power of human effort against whatever forces impel men to make their unfortunate choices, it remains true that in the play, as in many other tragedies, fate becomes external to the hero only after the tragic process has been set in motion. It appears that the best one can advance by way of a formula to describe the process of reversal in tragedy is to say that a combination of error of judgement and fate (in whatever proportions) is involved. The tragedies of Macbeth, Hamlet, Lear and Othello flow from placing particular kinds of men in particular sets of circumstances. Their human limitations and a fateful conjunction of events work against them to their destruction.

TRAGIC RECOGNITION

Plot reversal (the hero's fall from prosperity) is an essential formal element in tragedy, but discovery or recognition is often regarded as the essential tragic experience. **Recognition comes to the hero through physical and mental suffering.** His tragic purpose or action necessarily entails the process through which he comes to know the truth about himself and becomes aware of the part he has played in bringing about his doom. Suffering alone, without recognition, is not fully tragic. Suffering and recognition in tragedy must be considered together. The degree of tragic experience involved in suffering depends on the degree of knowledge it yields. **The more the tragic hero (who is the principal focus of tragic suffering) understands his own character and situation, the greater will be his suffering.**

A summary of what happens in *Macbeth* could make the play look like an exciting crime story, but it is what happens *within* the hero, the development of his understanding of himself and his plight and his sharing of this with the audience, that lifts it to a higher plane. When the unforeseen consequences of his actions merge, the tragic hero questions what has happened to him, and through his questioning learns the vital truth about himself. This brings him around to facing his destiny and completing it by his death. It is through recognition that he reaches his tragic vision. His error was committed in blindness; recognition involves the intrusion of the light, the acknowledgement of the blindness. Recognition is not simply his knowledge of what has happened to him (in Macbeth's case, that he has been deceived by the witches). **It also involves the new awareness of the unalterably fixed pattern of the miserable life he has created for himself through his deeds, accompanied by a profound sense of loss at the thought of what he has sacrificed and forsaken. These elements are present in Macbeth's infinitely poignant soliloquy:**

> I have lived long enough: my way of life
> Is fall'n into the sere, the yellow leaf;
> And that which should accompany old age,
> As honour, love, obedience, troops of friends,
> I must not look to have; but, in their stead,
> Curses, not loud but deep, mouth-honour,
>   breath,
> Which the poor heart would fain deny, and
>   dare not.
>
> (5, 3, 22–8)

Macbeth arrives at the recognition of having irrecoverably lost, through his own blind deed, the things on which his happiness on earth depended. He discovers that he cannot arrest the processes he has set in motion and gains an insight into the workings of evil. He realises that evil isolates and that his deeds have cut him off from all that he treasures. He is alone in a hell of despair and is aware of the futility of all he has planned. It is the fate of the tragic hero to be finally isolated from the ways of men, but it is in his isolation that he grows both in stature and self-awareness, and consequently in the estimation of the audience, as he faces his destiny and confronts it. For Macbeth, this means dying valiantly in battle (5, 3,

32) rather than taking his own life, running away (5, 7, 1) or being taken prisoner (5, 8, 27–8).

In Macbeth's case, partial recognition comes comparatively early in the play. Disillusionment sets in long before his fortunes fail, indeed when he is at the height of his worldly success. Even before he has had Banquo murdered, he can face the prospect of having damned his soul ('mine eternal jewel / Given to the common enemy of man', 3, 1, 68–9). But if he does sense early on what is happening to him as a result of what he has done, he does not really *know* what kind of future is in store for him until the point at which he realises that it is as easy for him to go forward in crime as to go back. The recognition that he cannot control the processes he has set in motion or alter the course he has set himself is a tragic one: 'I am in blood / Stepped in so far that, should I wade no more, / Returning were as tedious as go o'er' (3, 4, 136–8). But the exact moment that Macbeth realises he is doomed is when Macduff relates that he himself was 'from his mother's womb / Untimely ripped' (5, 8, 15–16). Macbeth has earlier expressed a partial recognition of his fate at the news that Birnam wood is moving towards Dunsinane (5, 5, 42–6). It is the quality of his response to his destiny and the manner in which he confronts it that determines his essential worth as a tragic hero and gives him his ultimate tragic status. The physical death of the hero is a final symbol of his recognition: his former blind and ignorant self dies with him.

MACBETH AS POETIC DRAMA

Like all Shakespeare's other tragedies, *Macbeth* is a poetic drama, one of the supreme examples in literature of dramatic poetry. He achieves his characteristic effects by means of poetic language. He uses densely knit, recurring imagery to convey themes, distinctive character traits and the atmosphere unique to each play. Images and phrases constantly echo and anticipate each other. The imaginative use of imagery makes possible a richness of suggestion unavailable to the dramatist whose medium is prose. Some examples will make clear what is meant. Angus says of Macbeth:

> Now does he feel
> His secret murders sticking on his hands
> (5, 2, 16–17; my emphasis)

Here we are not merely told that Macbeth is suffering from pangs of conscience or that he is afraid. Instead, we are given an impressively concrete illustration of what it is like to be Macbeth at this point. 'Secret' suggests the attempts to conceal the murders; this is juxtaposed with an image suggesting that such attempts are futile: the blood will not go away, it persists in 'sticking' to his hands. The image is one in a long series, echoing Lady Macbeth's 'wash this filthy witness from your hand', 'smear / The sleepy grooms with blood' (2, 2, 50–1), 'A little water clears us of this deed' (2, 2, 68), and 'all the perfumes of / Arabia will not sweeten this little hand' (5, 1, 44–5), as well as Macbeth's 'Will all great Neptune's ocean wash this blood / Clean from my hand?' (2, 2, 61–2) and 'As they had seen me with these hangman's hands' (2, 2, 29). **The use of tactile imagery to make a more effective dramatic point than plain statement could possibly do is also found in the reference to Macdonwald: 'The multiplying villainies of nature / Do *swarm* upon him' (1, 2, 11–12; my emphasis), which evokes a picture of the man's vices swarming all over him like insects, with the further suggestion of a gathering around him of a swarm of villainous rebels.**

Macbeth's temptation on being greeted as Thane of Cawdor (1, 3, 105) is similarly presented with *concrete* force. **The rhythms of the speech suggest the pounding heart knocking at his ribs.** The thought of murder does more than elicit from him an abstract statement of his terror; instead, its 'horrid image doth unfix my hair' (1, 3, 135). We get the very *feel* of Macbeth's experience in what L.C. Knight has called 'the sickening see-saw rhythm' of the soliloquy ('This supernatural soliciting / Cannot be ill, cannot be good' (1, 3, 130–1).

In *Macbeth* we find a number of frequently repeated image patterns which help to express some of the major themes of the play. **One of its most frequently recurring ideas is that false appearance is inseparable from evil. This idea finds expression in a wide range of related images** and non-figurative statements. Duncan, having discovered Cawdor's treachery, moralises that 'There's no art / To find the mind's construction in the face' (1, 4, 11–12), while Malcolm, distrusting everyone after his father's murder, knows that 'To show an unfelt sorrow is an office / Which the false man does easy' (2, 3, 135–6). This commonplace notion is more effectively, because more concretely, expressed by Donalbain in 'There's daggers in men's smiles' (2, 3, 139). But the important images of disguise and concealment are used by Macbeth, and in relation to him. This is natural enough, since he acquires the habit of deception at the beginning and maintains it for a long time. His career is built on it. We are repeatedly reminded of his need to maintain a false appearance if his schemes are to succeed: 'To beguile the time, / Look like the time ... look like the innocent flower, / But be the serpent under't' (1, 5, 62–5); 'False face must hide what the false heart doth know' (1, 7, 82). **From this point until Act 4, when he drops all pretence at** concealment, Macbeth employs the masking images that have hitherto been a feature of his wife's speeches.

This may be interpreted in various ways. Shakespeare may be seen as employing imagery to show Lady Macbeth's ascendancy over her husband's mind. Macbeth's habit of using her kind of language betrays his readiness to learn from her. We may also choose to see his free use of masking imagery as evidence that the practice of maintaining a false appearance before the world has become second nature to him. He tells the murderers why he wants to be rid of Banquo without having to use barefaced power: friends whose support he finds necessary would react unfavourably, so he must resort to 'Masking the business from the common eye' (3, 1, 125). In the earlier scenes it was Lady Macbeth who used the most memorable images of concealment. By the time Macbeth has decided to murder Banquo without consulting her, it is he who takes the initiative in urging the need for dissimulation:

Let your remembrance apply to Banquo;
Present him eminence, both with eye and
*   tongue –*
Unsafe the while, that we
Must lave our honours in these flattering
*   streams,*
And make our faces vizards to our hearts,
Disguising what they are.

(3, 2, 30–5)

This is reminiscent of Lady Macbeth's advice to him before Duncan's murder (1, 5, 62–5). And in the final speech of Act 3, Scene 2, he longs that 'seeling night' may come to 'Scarf up the tender eye of pitiful day' (46–7), repeating almost exactly the night image used by both of them earlier (1, 5, 49; 2, 1, 50–1). After Act 3, there are fewer images of masking and concealment in his speeches. The banquet scene has

exposed his true character to the world. **A turning point is reached when he decides to take revenge on Macduff. From this moment, as he puts it, 'The very firstlings of my heart shall be / The firstlings of my hand' (4, 1, 147–8). The mask is finally off; there is no further point in disguise, and appearance and reality become one.**

MAJOR THEMES IN MACBETH

ISOLATION

Macbeth's movement from centrality to isolation is a major theme of the play. This pattern, which is progressive, encompasses the entire play and expresses an essential process in every tragedy: the hero must confront his destiny alone. Macbeth's role is that of a man who begins as the central and most admired figure in his society and ends by being totally estranged from it. His ultimate fate suggests that of a sacrificial victim. Having caused havoc in society and broken the bonds of nature, he must be isolated and destroyed so that natural and social order may be restored.

The early episodes of the play focus on Macbeth as the heroic object of everybody's admiration, a status he deserves since he is the saviour of his country. The Captain's account of his exploits in Act 1, Scene 2 and the king's lavish praise in Act 1, Scene 4 help to establish his heroic stature and his unique position in society before his fall. However, the images used in these places to convey Macbeth's prowess as a warrior have another, more disturbing, effect. There is a frightening savagery in some of the more memorable ones: the sword 'Which smoked with bloody execution'; the blood hero who 'carved out his passage' and 'unseamed' his enemy as if anxious to 'bathe in reeking wounds, / Or memorise another Golgotha' (1, 2, 18–22; 39–40). These reiterated images suggest Macbeth's natural capacity, even his relish, for destruction. Our first picture of him, as provided by the bleeding captain, is a faithful anticipation of our last one. The early image of the warrior carving up his enemy with a smoking sword is mirrored in the late one of the 'dead butcher' (5, 9, 35) whose severed head is carried onto the stage by Macduff. Echoes and anticipations of this kind are found everywhere in *Macbeth*.

Even before Duncan's murder we find both Macbeth and his wife taking the first decisive step which will isolate them from the process of normal living and break the bonds which bind them to human nature and society. With deliberate formality, Lady Macbeth dedicates herself to the powers of evil ('Come, you spirits / That tend on mortal thoughts', 1, 5, 39–40). Macbeth makes a similar prayer ('Thou sure and firm-set earth, / Hear not my steps', 2, 1, 56–7). His separation from God is implied in his 'But wherefore could not I pronounce "Amen"?' (2, 2, 32).

Duncan's murder hastens the process of Macbeth's isolation. Malcolm and Donalbain flee him (2, 3, 119–24) and Banquo suspects him (3, 1, 3). Even before Banquo's murder and the social debacle of the banquet scene, we have a glimpse of Macbeth estranged from his natural companions: 'How now, my lord! Why do you keep alone, / Of sorriest fancies your companions making' (3, 2, 8–9). **The banquet scene marks a decisive stage in his alienation from his subjects.** His gradual estrangement even from Lady Macbeth has already been suggested in his failure to let her share in his scheme to murder Banquo. **After her supreme efforts to save him from public disgrace in the banquet scene, she dwindles from being his 'dearest partner of greatness' (1, 5, 10) to a passive, listless, weary listener.** The last time we see her alone with him, at the end of Act 3, Scene 4, the collapse of their relationship is pathetically apparent.

The final movement of Act 3, Scene 4 has compelling visual images of Macbeth's separation from his subjects, who leave his feast in hasty disorder. This is not the only abandonment: in the same scene we learn that Fleance has escaped, that Macduff refuses to come at Macbeth's bidding and that Macbeth can depend so little on the loyalty of his followers that he must keep a paid servant in their houses.

The final movement of the play opens with news of growing opposition to Macbeth's rule and of intrigue and conspiracy against him. Macduff has fled to England (4, 1, 142). **In Act 5, Macbeth's isolation is made explicit in reiterated images of abandonment and loneliness.** He articulates this in some of the greatest poetry of the play, which is also the most profoundly pathetic: 'that which should accompany old age, / As honour, love, obedience, troops of friends, / I must not look to have' (5, 3, 24–6). The Doctor would desert him if he could (5, 3, 61–2). We are twice reminded that many of his soldiers have gone over to the enemy; first by himself ('Were they not forced with those that should be ours, / We might have met them dareful, beard to beard', 5, 5, 5–6), and later by Malcolm ('We have met with foes / That strike beside us', 5, 7, 28–9). There is an altogether appropriate image of his final isolation in his defiant 'They have tied me to a stake; I cannot fly, / But bear-like I must fight the course' (5, 7, 1–2). Macbeth should be shown on stage as a tired, angry, disarmed fighter, killed in full view of the audience after he has been encircled by the entire army and deprived of his weapons. **The transformation from cynosure to scapegoat, from leader to quarry, is here complete.** The pattern of Macbeth's isolation involves him in more than a physical and mental detachment from other human beings. He is in exile from the world of daylight, familiar with witches and apparitions unseen by anybody else, making discoveries about his predicament that he can never share with others who have never dared, as he has, to plunge into darkness.

KINGSHIP

In *Macbeth*, Shakespeare explores a number of models of kingship as these are exemplified in a variety of individuals: Macbeth, Duncan, Malcolm and the English king, Edward the Confessor. The three 'good' monarchs serve to throw Macbeth's unfitness for kingship into sharp relief in a number of ways.

Duncan represents a high ideal of kingship. The most convincing testimony to this is the appraisal of his character and reign by Macbeth, the man about to murder him. It is important to note that Macbeth's evaluation of Duncan is delivered in a soliloquy, where a character often tells the truth as he sees it. Everything Macbeth says about Duncan is an argument for not killing him. He acknowledges that the old king has been gentle and merciful in the discharge of his kingly duties and has, above all, been free from corrupt practices ('clear in his great office', 1, 7, 18). In action, Duncan displays authority, decisiveness ('Is execution done on Cawdor?', 1, 4, 1), and generosity of spirit: his gratitude to Macbeth for his services to the country finds expression in extravagant generosity when he tells him, with prophetic irony, that he cannot reward him enough ('More is thy due than more than all can pay', 1, 4, 21). Long after Duncan's death, his goodness is recalled by Macduff. 'Thy royal father', he tells Malcolm, 'Was a most sainted king' (4, 3, 108–9).

A parallel version of good, indeed saintly, kingship emerges during a telling episode of the longest scene in the play, where Malcolm and Macduff are in exile at the court of King Edward of England. Here **Shakespeare goes out of his way to emphasise the saintly, benevolent character of the English king, whose main function in the scene is to heal his sick subjects**. The illness afflicting these cannot be cured by medical science ('Their malady convinces / The great assay of art', 4, 3, 142–3) but heaven has given King Edward the power to cure them instantly. Apart from his power to heal the sick,

He hath a heavenly gift of prophecy,
And sundry blessings hang about his throne
That speak him full of grace.

(4, 3, 157–9)

Shakespeare's purpose in presenting Edward in the guise of saintly benefactor to his people is clear. By this point in the play, we have come to see Macbeth as Edward's opposite. **While Edward heals his subjects, Macbeth is engaged in killing those who dislike his tyranny:**

Each new morn
New widows howl, new orphans cry;
  new sorrows
Strike heaven on the face …

(4, 3, 4–6)

Edward is a saint; Macbeth is a devil whose very name blisters the tongues of those who pronounce it (4, 3, 12). When Malcolm lists the virtues proper to a king, he is implying that Macbeth lacks these, pretending at the same time that he himself also does:

… The king-becoming graces,
As justice, verity, temperance, stableness,
Bounty, perseverance, mercy, lowliness,
Devotion, patience, courage, fortitude …

(4, 3, 91–4)

We soon discover, however, that Malcolm shows every sign of exemplifying the kingly virtues of his father, Duncan, promising a reign of peace and harmony after Macbeth's reign of terror. Macbeth's conception of kingship is narrow and self-centred. He sees it primarily as a vehicle for the exercise of uncontested power: every threat to his power, real or imagined, is eliminated with the utmost ruthlessness (as in the case of Banquo). The innocent as well as those who may be conspiring against him are sacrificed to the maintenance of his rule: Macduff's wife and children must die in Macduff's absence. In the end, his power collapses because he has made too many enemies in striving to maintain it.

VISIONS

Tragic drama necessarily involves a look at the worst that human beings are capable of and the worst that can happen to them. In tragedy, human happiness is fragile and destructive forces, both within and outside the human agents, are readily set in motion. These forces work themselves out with terrible consequences for both the guilty and the innocent: virtue offers no exemption from pain and suffering once the tragic forces have begun to operate. The main focus in tragic drama is on the tragic hero, not on his victims, and it is in relation to him, and his concerns, that the tragic action is played out. The mysterious processes which are inseparable from tragedy lead, in *Macbeth*, to the corruption and degeneration of a heroic individual, the collapse of the social order he has originally helped to defend, the perpetration of unspeakable cruelties, the ritual destruction of the hero and the collapse of his wife into insanity. **Interpretation of the *Macbeth* universe will depend on whether we view it through Macbeth's consciousness or through that of his enemies**. Macbeth's tragic experience is ultimately a hopeless one. He finally comes to see his life, and life in general, as utterly devoid of meaning: it is, as he finds it, nothing more significant than 'a tale / Told by an idiot' (5, 5, 26–7). In the end, he can wish for the

destruction of the universe itself (5, 5, 50). **Macbeth's world is one without future hope, moral order or religious significance: nothing that can happen to or in it can make a difference**.

Macbeth's vision, derived from his own experience, is not shared by his enemies, whose role is to redeem society from what he has brought it to. **Malcolm, Macduff and those who are allied with them see meaning and value in human life**. Macbeth's tragedy is one of damnation. Those whose destiny is to overthrow him speak a language radically different from his; **their interpretation of the universe is a Christian one, reflected in their frequent reliance on Christian ideas and images, particularly those of redemption**. The anonymous Lord in Act 3, Scene 6 expects God to 'ratify the work' of those planning to invade Scotland (33). Lennox, developing the providential theme, prays that:

> ... Some holy angel
> Fly to the court of England and unfold
> His message ere he come, that a swift blessing
> May soon return to this our suffering country
> Under a hand accursed!
> (3, 6, 45–9)

Those who bring about Macbeth's downfall are motivated by similar sentiments and see themselves as instruments of a benevolent providence. As Malcolm puts it:

> ... Macbeth
> Is ripe for shaking, and the powers above
> Put on their instruments ...
> (4, 3, 236–8)

MAJOR RELATIONSHIPS IN MACBETH

The significant character relationships of the play focus on Macbeth: the other characters derive their interest and importance from their interaction with him. He and they are measured against each other. The Macbeth–Duncan relationship, for example, is marked by trust and confidence on Duncan's side and treachery and betrayal on Macbeth's. Duncan thinks he has learned from the activities of the disloyal Thane of Cawdor, on whom he built 'An absolute trust' (1, 4, 14), that appearances of loyalty can be deceptive. He fails to realise Macbeth's talent for plotting his downfall behind a mask of friendship and devotion. The relationship between Macbeth and Duncan is an unequal one. **Duncan's generous, trusting nature is no match for Macbeth's mastery of deceit.** Macbeth's relationship with Duncan is a relatively straightforward one. He has no personal animosity towards Duncan and has no reason to dislike him. Indeed, he has every reason to be grateful to Duncan, who has made him Thane of Cawdor and honoured him publicly in extravagant language (1, 4, 14–21). From Macbeth's point of view, however, Duncan represents a barrier to his ambition to become king and so fulfil the prophecy of the witches sooner rather than later.

Duncan erects a further, and more inconvenient, barrier to Macbeth's ambition when he nominates his son Malcolm as his successor. Macbeth's response to this announcement ('That is a step / On which I must fall down, or else o'er-leap, / For in my way it lies', (1, 4, 48–50) tells us all we need to know about his attitude to his greatest benefactor: his desire for the kingship is so overwhelming that it takes precedence over all human ties, whether of loyalty, kingship, duty or morality. **Duncan ceases to matter to him as a person and becomes merely an obstacle on his road to power, an obstacle that must be cleared.**

Having achieved power, Macbeth decides that in order to keep it he must eliminate another human obstacle and end his close personal relationship with Banquo, who has shared his trials and triumphs on the battlefield. He admires Banquo's personal qualities, as he admired Duncan's. Banquo is royal by nature and is brave, wise and judicious. These admirable qualities, however, are the ones that seal Banquo's fate because they seem to threaten Macbeth's security as king. When it comes to choosing between preserving his power and allowing Banquo to live as an annoying threat, Macbeth does not hesitate: **power comes before the claims of friendship and comradeship**. Ambition and the desire for absolute control have destroyed Macbeth's capacity for normal human relationships and Banquo must die. After this, Macbeth finds it progressively easier to classify those around him as facilitators of his power or as threats to it. Even those remotely belonging to the second category (Lady Macduff and her children, for example) are killed without mercy.

The relationship between Macbeth and Lady Macbeth, which dominates the play, helps to account in part for Macbeth's degeneration. The early scenes from the play reveal her as the more forceful of the two. Unlike the early Macbeth, she is unburdened by moral values, for which, it soon appears, she has total contempt. She recognises that, unlike her, he tends to consider issues in terms of right and wrong. Her approach to such matters is unambiguous. If his ambition is to be king, he must not allow human feelings (the 'milk of human-kindness', 1, 5, 16) to hinder him from seizing the throne. From her point of view, high ambition can only be achieved through wickedness ('illness', 1, 5, 19). It will be her task to work on his mind to make it free from whatever scruples of conscience might deter him from committing murder if necessary for the sake of the crown. This is why she is anxious for his return:

> *... Hie thee hither,*
> *That I may pour my spirits in thine ear,*
> *And chastise with the valour of my tongue*
> *All that impedes thee from the golden round ...*
>
> (1, 5, 24–7)

The final scene of Act 1 demonstrates her ascendancy over Macbeth. Her demonic forcefulness of character contrasts with his hesitant approach to what he is afraid to call murder, referring instead to 'this business' (1, 7, 31). He vainly tries to defend humane values, arguing that the murder of Duncan would put him outside the pale of humanity and make him no better than a beast ('I dare do all that may become a man; / Who dares do more, is none', 46–7). Her powerful verbal onslaught renders him helpless. She calls his manhood into question: when he was prepared to murder Duncan, he was fully a man; his hesitation shows him less than one. To refuse to murder Duncan now would be to break an earlier promise, something she would never do. At this point, she has undermined Macbeth's moral resistance to the murder. All that worries him now is the possibility that something may go wrong ('If we should fail?', 59). The completeness of her dominance is shown by his willingness to accept her gruesome plan to make the murder of Duncan easier by inducing a 'swinish sleep' (67) of drunkenness in his two chamberlains, and to involve him enthusiastically in her plot by adding a further refinement to it:

> *... Will it not be received,*
> *When we have marked with blood those*
> *sleepy two*
> *Of his own chamber and used their very*
> *daggers,*
> *That they have done't?*
>
> (1, 7, 74–7)

Within the space of 50 lines of this fateful scene, Lady Macbeth has converted her husband's determination not to kill Duncan ('We will proceed no further in this business', 31) to a firm resolution to commit the murder, whatever the consequences ('I am settled, and bend up / Each corporal agent to this terrible feat', 79–80).

Her dominance extends over most of the next two acts reaching its exhausting climax at the end of the banquet scene. After Duncan's death, however, this dominance is not total. Having become a murderer, Macbeth finds it much easier than he did to contemplate becoming one for a second time without prompting from his wife. She is not privy to his plan to have Banquo killed. This has been arranged with the murderers before he gives her a veiled hint of his 'deed of dreadful note' (3, 2, 44). **When she questions him about what he has in mind, he shows that it is he, not she, who is now making the terrible decisions:**

> *Be innocent of the knowledge, dearest chuck,*
> *Till thou applaud the deed ...*
>
> (3, 2, 45–6)

Macbeth, however, is not yet free from the need of her moral support and strength of character. She resumes her masterful role when the appearance of Banquo's ghost at the state banquet reduces Macbeth to a fearful, hysterical condition, in which he openly betrays his guilt. Her quickness of wit, presence of mind and decisive action save him from an even more damning exposure of his activities. **Her intervention in the banquet scene exhausts her moral and emotional resources and marks the end of her active role in the play and of her relationship with Macbeth.** When she next appears (5, 1) she is the passive victim of insanity, beyond the reach of effective aid.

As his wife declines into hopeless despair, Macbeth still asserts himself. Of the two, she has initially shown a much greater intensity of evil and a greater determination to pursue the initial evil deed. She has, however, been an effective teacher. **Macbeth learns to model his character and outlook on hers and proves more consistent and determined in the pursuit of crime than she does**.

HEROES AND VILLAINS

The heroes in *Macbeth* are found in the ranks of Macbeth's enemies. They are mainly middle-ranking or minor characters, not presented with any great depth or subtlety by Shakespeare. **They include Malcolm, Donalbain, Macduff and the other noblemen of Scotland. To the extent that Duncan and Banquo are Macbeth's victims, they may also be classified as heroes. Duncan has a better title to heroism than Banquo, since he is regarded, even by Macbeth, as a good and virtuous monarch.** Banquo is a somewhat different case, since the play seems to raise doubts about his character and motives. If we take the least favourable view of the evidence about his character in Act 3, Scene 1, we may feel that Banquo's nature has been tainted, if not corrupted, by ambition, that he has compromised with evil and that only death saves him from a dishonourable end. If this interpretation is correct, then his dramatic progress is parallel to Macbeth's, with the downward curve suddenly cut short in Act 3, Scene 3. His career would then illustrate the truth of Malcolm's later assertion that 'A good and virtuous nature may recoil / In an imperial charge' (4, 3, 19–20). On the other hand, **Banquo's innocence and funda-mental goodness are contrasted with Macbeth's guilt at various points: there is no evidence in the first two acts that Banquo is anything but honourable and high-minded.**

Lady Macbeth is the most extreme representation of evil in the play. She is characterised in terms of a few fundamental qualities: courage, determination, will power and a remarkable ability to focus all her resources of mind and heart on the matter in hand. **The evil she represents arises from her deployment of these moral qualities in the achievement of immoral ends.** Shakespeare presents her as a woman without a conscience for whom the end justifies the means and whose ambitions must be satisfied at any cost, even murder. She successfully induces her husband to abandon all his moral scruples and to divorce his desire to be king from the sanctions of the moral law. Her evil nature has a further dimension. **Her abandonment of conventional moral standards is underlined by her ritual dedication to evil and her plea to the powers of darkness to sustain her murderous intent ('Come, you spirits / That tend on mortal thoughts, unsex me here, / And fill me from the crown to the toe top full / Of direst cruelty!', 1, 5, 39–42).** Her involvement with the occult explains Malcolm's final comment on her as Macbeth's 'fiend-like queen' (5, 9, 35), which characterises her role as having more than human significance, suggesting a parallel with the 'secret, black and midnight hags', the Weird Sisters. There are few touches of humanity in the presentation of Lady Macbeth. Her one concession to humane feeling is her failure to kill Duncan because he reminds her of her father as he sleeps (2, 2, 14–15).

The extremity of Lady Macbeth's descent into evil brings with it its own frightful retribution. **She consciously suppresses pity, remorse and regard for a moral code, but punishment for this ultimately comes in the form of subconscious guilt leading to madness.** The central role of guilt in the genesis of her madness becomes clear in Act 5, Scene 1, when her hand-washing rituals are a symbolic enactment of her desire to remove the taint of guilt that refuses to go away: 'Here's the smell of the blood still: all the perfumes of / Arabia will not sweeten this little hand' (5, 1, 44–5). She cannot live with the evil she has done and generated within herself. It is perhaps fitting that her probable end should be in keeping with her role from Act 1, Scene 5 onwards. In the last speech of the play, Malcolm reports the belief that she has taken her own life 'by self and violent hands' (5, 9, 36–7).

Macbeth resists straightforward classification in terms of heroism and villainy. Our likely response to his career in the play might be summed up in a formula such as: 'Macbeth is an agent of evil, but ...' He commits monstrous deeds, but we cannot see him as a monster. On the one hand, we are made to feel that his death is justified and that his enemies triumph in a righteous cause; on the other, we are forced to acknowledge that **he never entirely forfeits our sympathy**. One general explanation for this sympathy is that we can understand such a character as Macbeth and pity him because he is doing on a large scale and with more appalling consequences for himself what we can at least imagine ourselves doing in a similar kind of situation.

It is interesting to study the methods used by Shakespeare in dealing with the major technical and artistic problems posed by the materials he has to handle in *Macbeth*. Given that tragedy demands our sympathetic interest in the fortunes of the tragic hero, Shakespeare was confronted with a major technical problem. How was he to command our sympathy to the end of the play for a hero who suffers a steep moral decline? He begins his career in the play as a brave and loyal general. Then he becomes a treacherous murderer and a hirer of assassins. He further degenerates into an employer of spies and further again into a butcher and a coward. He completes

his career as a man with no feeling for anything but himself – a monster and a hellhound, as his enemies and victims see him. This outline of Macbeth's progress through the play does not reflect the impression a theatre audience is likely to get from a good production. This is because Shakespeare employs a variety of dramatic techniques to lessen the impact of Macbeth's darker deeds.

In the early scenes Macbeth is generously endowed with the attributes of a hero. He is the man who matters in his society, having authority, passions and abilities far greater than those around him, easily earning respect and admiration. His good qualities are repeatedly underlined in the opening scenes. **What is emphasised most of all throughout Act 1 is how difficult it is to get him to come to terms with the evil he is contemplating. Lady Macbeth deplores his essential goodness ('what thou wouldst highly, / That thou wouldst holily', 1, 5, 19–20).** He hesitates, he agonises, he decides against the murder ('chance may crown me', 1, 3, 143). He is conscious of the moral, as well as the political, consequences of killing Duncan (1, 7, 12). This vacillation earns our sympathy. Again, he refuses to commit the crime ('We will proceed no further in this business', 1, 7, 31). It requires all Lady Macbeth's ingenuity, eloquence, demonic force of character, moral blackmail, even her jibes at his supposed unmanliness ('When you durst do it, then you were a man', 1, 7, 49) to make him proceed, and when he does, he is racked by guilt and terror (2, 2, 58–64).

If we approach Macbeth's initial crime in terms of guilt and moral responsibility, we find that the play confuses and blurs the issues to some extent. Macbeth is made to appear the victim of ignorance and blindness. He has had experience of many bloody executions in his career as a soldier;

he cannot foresee the fateful effect on his character of murdering his way to the throne. Two other factors tend to confuse the moral issue even more strongly. **The influence of the witches and their prophecies, however wilfully he misinterprets these, must inevitably appear to the spectator to mitigate his moral responsibility**. Almost anybody might be thrown off balance by the temptations presented by the witches. The other morally confusing element is Lady Macbeth, one of whose functions in the scenes leading to the murder is to distract her husband from weighing the moral issues involved by presenting the crime to him as a straightforward test of cowardice or courage.

It is worth noting how Shakespeare mitigates some of the worst horrors which Macbeth's career as a murderer must inevitably involve. **At all the critical moments, he dampens the unfavourable effects on our attitude to Macbeth of the atrocities for which he is responsible. For example, the murder of Duncan is not directly shown, nor is it narrated by any speaker sympathetic to the dead man**. No effort is made by Shakespeare to evoke sympathy for Duncan at Macbeth's expense. Instead of hearing the dying cries of the king, we hear instead Macbeth's heartfelt lament for what he has done. The crime is made significant for its effects on the conscience of the criminal, whose responses, compounded by self-torture, despair and regret, inevitably evoke pity for him. What we see enacted before our eyes is obviously far more telling in its effect than anything we are merely told. We know that Duncan is a good man: we are told of his generosity, while Macbeth pays tribute to his kingly virtues. But Shakespeare's Duncan is not a character who can engage our deepest feelings. We cannot, in light of Shakespeare's presentation of the two characters, feel the same kind of emotion

for Duncan as we do for the man who can heartily envy him in his death ('After life's fitful fever he sleeps well', 3, 2, 23), particularly after he himself has been haunted by the thoughts that having murdered Duncan in his sleep, he is now doomed to 'sleep no more' (2, 2, 44).

Banquo, unlike Duncan, is murdered in full view of the audience, who hear his dying words: these are concerned not with saving his own life, but that of his son. We have got to know Banquo better than Duncan, and most of what we know is appealing. As in the case of Duncan's murder, however, Shakespeare's representation of Banquo's is such that Macbeth is shielded from some of the condemnation he might otherwise attract. **Shakespeare minimises the adverse effects of Banquo's murder on our sympathy for Macbeth by ensuring that the deed is performed by hirelings**, and that Macbeth responds to it much as he did to Duncan's murder. Instead of seeing Macbeth perform a deed of wicked violence, we see him suffer spiritual and psychological torment, as well as social disgrace and embarrassment, in the banquet scene. **Our likely response to this is to feel that he is paying heavily in guilt and self-torture for what he has plotted against Banquo**.

Macbeth's acts become progressively more revolting to our moral sense. **It is obviously more difficult for Shakespeare to retain pity for him after the killing of Macduff's family than it was in the other cases: the presentation of the victims here is both sympathetic and detailed**. Lady Macduff and her children are helpless, blameless sufferers. In this case, pity for them threatens to eliminate whatever sympathy we feel for Macbeth and makes us desire his downfall. **Again, Shakespeare manages the circumstances surrounding this atrocity in such a way that the weight of emphasis on Macbeth's guilt is not at** all what it might be. He is nowhere near the scene of the crime and is shown as being more remote from Lady Macduff and her children than he was from his previous victims. Far from deriving any benefits from the deed of the murderers, Macbeth is once more shown to suffer. Lady Macduff's death is closely followed by the mental collapse of Lady Macbeth, as if Shakespeare wants to illustrate the working-out of the principle enunciated by Macbeth: 'We still have judgement here, that we but teach / Bloody instructions, which being taught return / To plague the inventor' (1, 7, 8–10). The essential point, then, about Shakespeare's presentation of Macbeth's worst acts is that his sufferings are made to appear almost proportionate to his crimes and are much more vividly realised than anything his victims undergo. Each stage in Macbeth's progressive moral degeneration is offset by a set of circumstances involving extreme suffering for him and inspiring pity at his predicament, however much this results from his own acts.

Sympathy for Macbeth is preserved in another significant way. Shakespeare ensures that we see most of the essential elements of the action of the play as these are filtered through Macbeth's consciousness. We are consistently taken into *his* mind, through soliloquy and dialogue, and hence we are obliged to share his point of view. The play is his tragedy, not that of Duncan, Banquo or Lady Macduff. Shakespeare also gives Macbeth the best poetry of the play, and in poetic drama this is a fact of the highest importance. Macbeth's supreme poetic gift ensures that we respond imaginatively to his speeches and enter into his feelings. We know that the enemies gathering to destroy him are virtuous, even exemplary, but they are too pallid and commonplace to be able to compel the kind of interest aroused by Macbeth's grand eloquence and heroic stance. Our moral sense may urge us to applaud Malcolm, Macduff and their allies, but our imaginations yield to the richness and beauty of Macbeth's despairing commentary on his altered circumstances in the final scenes of the play, his terrible sense that human life is nothing more than an absurd and meaningless procession of days:

> I have lived long enough: my way of life
> Is fall'n into the sere, the yellow leaf;
> And that which should accompany old age,
> As honour, love, obedience, troops of friends,
> I must not look to have ...
>
> (5, 3, 22–6)

> Tomorrow, and tomorrow, and tomorrow,
> Creeps in this petty pace from day to day,
> To the last syllable of recorded time;
> And all our yesterdays have lighted fools
> The way to dusty death. ...
>
> (5, 5, 19–23)

Macbeth is deeply compromised by evil, but Shakespeare maintains our lively interest in his concerns to the end. Had Shakespeare allowed our sympathy for Macbeth to ebb before the close of the action and encouraged an imaginative identification with Malcolm and his interests, he would have converted his play from tragedy to melodrama.

CHARACTER ANALYSIS AND KEY QUOTES

MACBETH

- The most unusual thing about Macbeth is that he has two roles in the play which are difficult to reconcile. He is its **tragic hero** as well as its **chief villain**. On the one hand, he is 'brave Macbeth', Duncan's 'valiant cousin' and 'noble Macbeth' (1, 2, 16, 24, 68). On the other hand, he is a **demonic presence**: 'Not in the legions / Of horrid hell can come a devil more damned / In evils to top Macbeth' (4, 3, 55–7). It is, however, worth noting that this comment is made by one of his enemies.

- He is most impressive when he is engaged in **violent action**. In Act 1, Scene 2 we find him in the thick of battle, wielding a sword which steams with the hot blood of his enemies ('with his brandished steel, / Which smoked with bloody execution', 1, 2, 17–18) and ripping one of them open ('Till he unseamed him from the nave to th'chops', 1, 2, 22). Such activity, it should be noted, is much admired by King Duncan ('O valiant cousin, worthy gentleman', 1, 2, 24).

- Macbeth's **courage** is evident in the reckless bravery he shows on the battlefield. When he is confronted by the King of Norway with his terrifying number of soldiers, he matches him in every respect and shows no fear, winning against the odds (1, 2, 51–8).

- He may be quick and decisive in action, but he **lacks patience**. When the witches greet him as the future King of Scotland ('All hail, Macbeth! that shall be King hereafter', 1, 3, 50), his response is: 'Stay, you imperfect speakers, tell me more', 1, 3, 70).

- Once he gets a promise of kingship from the witches, he is not content to look forward to being king at some future time. He is **immediately tempted to take fate into his own hands**, as his heart beats wildly at the prospect of murdering Duncan ('My thought, whose murder yet is but fantastical, / Shakes so my single state of man that function / Is smothered in surmise', 1, 3, 139–41).

- Macbeth displays supreme strength in the battlefield but **lacks judgement and**

moral courage. This is shown in Act 1, Scene 7, where his wife is able to overcome his opposition to murdering Duncan partly by suggesting that not to do so would show lack of manliness on his part ('When you durst do it, then you were a man', 49) and partly by reminding him that he had made a promise to her that he would murder Duncan. She would have been prepared to dash out the brains of her own infant rather than break the kind of promise he had made to her to murder Duncan ('had I so sworn as you / Have done to this', 58–9).

- The man who can destroy his enemies in combat is **no match for his determined wife, who takes charge of his mind** and deprives him of his power to resist. It does not take her long to achieve full control of his conscience and his judgement. Within a few minutes, following her vigorous verbal onslaught, she has moved him from firm resistance to murder ('We will proceed no further in this business', 1, 7, 31) to equally firm determination to kill Duncan ('I am settled, and bend up/ Each corporal agent to this terrible feat', 1, 7, 79–80).

- The best of Macbeth is shown before the murder of Duncan and immediately after this, when he is thinking in **moral terms and his conscience is still active**. The best illustration of this is found in his great soliloquy at the beginning of Act 1, Scene 7. Here he puts forward the standard moral arguments for not killing Duncan: fear of what may happen to murderers in the next life or what may happen to them in this life ('We still have judgement here', 8); the fact that Duncan is his cousin and his king; the claims of hospitality (he is Duncan's host, 'Who should against his murderer shut the door, / Not bear the knife myself', 15–16); and Duncan's virtues as a man and as a king ('this Duncan / Hath borne his faculties so meek, hath been / So clear in his great office', 16–18).

- What Macbeth provides in this soliloquy is a **clear-headed analysis of the morally correct way forward**.

- After he has killed Duncan, **Macbeth's conscience is still active and his sense of right and wrong as strong as ever.** It is as if the Macbeth who deplores his own crime is a different man from the Macbeth who has committed it. The voice of his conscience cries out 'Macbeth shall sleep no more!' (2, 2, 44). He cannot face the scene of the murder ('I am afraid to think what I have done', 2, 2, 52). His bloody hands terrify him ('They pluck out mine eyes', 2, 2, 60). He wants to forget who he is ('To know my deed, 'twere best not know myself', 2, 2, 74).

- His most powerful **moral insight** is his discovery that by killing Duncan **he has deprived his life of all its meaning** ('Had I but died an hour before this chance / I had lived a blessed time; for, from this instant, / There's nothing serious in mortality', 2, 3, 90–2).

- It does not take him long to put **his moral code, his humane feelings and his conscience to rest**. His soliloquy on his plan to kill Banquo expresses none of the strong moral objections to killing Duncan. Remembering that the witches have told Banquo that his descendants will be kings, Macbeth now concludes that no son of his will succeed him on the throne and that he has murdered Duncan and lost his own immortal soul only to 'make them kings – the seed of Banquo kings' (3, 1, 70). This is the basis of his decision to have Banquo and Fleance murdered.

- As he prepares to have Banquo murdered, Macbeth **decides that there is nothing to be gained by reflecting on his guilt and on threats posed by Banquo** ('on the torture of the mind to lie / In restless ecstasy' (3, 2, 21–2). Instead, having steeped himself in Duncan's blood, he will find it easier to proceed with further blood letting. Hence the announcement of a new phase, a turning point in his development: 'Things bad begun make strong themselves by ill' (3, 2, 55).

- The dream of freeing himself from Banquo and his issue becomes a nightmare when Fleance escapes. After his hysterical outburst on seeing Banquo's ghost at the banquet, he hardens his heart. **Fear, guilt, conscience and morality will have no place in his life:**

  > ... For mine own good
  > All causes shall give way: I am in blood
  > Stepped in so far that, should I wade no more,
  > Returning were as tedious as go o'er.
  > (3, 4, 135–8)

  Whatever evil deeds he will perform in the future, **the rights or wrongs involved will not matter to him**. He will convert his plans into immediate acts:

  > The very firstlings of my heart shall be
  > The firstlings of my hand ...
  > (4, 1, 147–8)

- Macbeth's evolution from the status of **heroic defender of his country** to that of **employer of spies and assassins** and **butcher of his subjects** may be thought of as arising from one of two kinds of cause or a combination of these: (a) forces operating outside Macbeth; (b) forces operating within Macbeth. The main external forces are the witches and Lady Macbeth. The prophecies of the witches provide encouragement for his ambition, while his wife impels him towards his initial crime.

- The forces operating *within* Macbeth are also significant. It is sometimes said that Macbeth's downfall begins as soon as he meets the witches and that his wife's mind-control techniques advance the process which they have begun. The problem with this analysis is that it fails to take account of an important aside towards the end of Act 1, Scene 3. Here Macbeth, who now knows that he is Thane of Cawdor, exposes his mind to the audience. The witches have merely given him three titles, the important one being 'King hereafter' (1, 3, 50), but make no suggestion that he should kill Duncan in order to become king. This suggestion comes solely from Macbeth himself: he wonders why his whole being is convulsed by the idea of murdering Duncan ('why do I yield to that suggestion / Whose horrid image doth unfix my hair?' (1, 3, 134–5).

- In Act 1, Scene 7, it becomes clear that **before he had even seen the witches he has discussed the possibility of murdering Duncan with Lady Macbeth** and has even made plans for this, as she reveals:

What beast was't then
That made you break this enterprise
*   to me? ...*
*   ... Nor time nor place*
Did then adhere, and yet you would make
*   both.*

(1, 7, 47–52)

This can only mean that **the witches have merely helped to reinforce an idea he has already entertained**.

- Macbeth himself suggests that the **only motive** he has for murdering Duncan is his ambition to replace him as king:

*   I have no spur*
To prick the sides of my intent, but only
Vaulting ambition ...

(1, 7, 25–7)

- After he has murdered Duncan, Macbeth suffers from **an overwhelming sense of insecurity**, and the **fear of** some unspecified form of **retaliation** haunts him. This paranoia can only be laid to rest when he has killed all those whom he sees as even remote threats to his position: Banquo, Fleance, Macduff and anybody associated or allied with these (Macduff's wife and children, for example). This is why Macduff can lament the fact that with Macbeth as king, 'Each new morn / New widows howl, new orphans cry' (4, 3, 4–5).

- As he acts more and more ruthlessly to quell the fears that will not let him sleep, we see an interesting process at work. At first, killing does not bring him peace. His half-dead conscience rises (after Banquo's murder, for example) to terrify him. But **gradually his conscience has less power and his will to suppress it becomes stronger**, and eventually his will prevails. The struggle between Macbeth's will and what remains of his conscience is evident in the banquet scene. When he no longer sees Banquo's ghost, his will takes over:

*   Why, so; being gone,*
I am a man again.

(3, 4, 107–8)

- Macbeth **deals his final blow at conscience and pity** with the purposeless butchery of Lady Macduff and her children, 'and all unfortunate souls / That trace him in his line (4, 1, 152–3)'. After this, his imagination troubles him no more and he has no more visions.

- The murder of Lady Macduff and her children lets loose all the evil in

Macbeth's nature. He becomes an **undisguised tyrant**, dreaded by his subjects, shedding blood everywhere in Scotland; in Macduff's phrase, 'an untitled tyrant bloody-sceptred' (4, 3, 104).

- What remains to admire in Macbeth as he nears his end is the sublime defiance with which he confronts his fate. He has conquered his fears and his nightmares:

*Direness, familiar to my slaughterous
  thoughts,
Cannot once start me.*

(5, 5, 14–15)

With no hope left, his old courage asserts itself:

*... Blow wind, come wrack!
At least we'll die with harness on our back.*

(5, 5, 51–2)

LADY MACBETH

- Lady Macbeth's outstanding characteristic is **her powerful, inflexible will** and her **fixed determination** that what she wills will come to pass:

*Glamis thou art, and Cawdor; and shalt be
What thou art promised.*

(1, 5, 14–15)

- Unlike Macbeth, she **lacks any moral sense**. It is significant that the thing she most fears about her husband is that he may seek to fulfil his ambition by fair and honest means:

*what thou wouldst highly,
That thou wouldst holily ...*

(1, 5, 19–20)

For her, on the other hand, **the end justifies the means**.

- Her role, as she sees it, is **to overcome whatever scruples Macbeth may have**

about taking the direct route to the kingship by killing Duncan ('Hie thee hither, / That I may pour my spirits in thine ear, / And chastise with the valour of my tongue / All that impedes thee from the golden round', 1, 5, 24–7).

- It is important to note that Lady Macbeth ceases to be a 'normal' character in Act 1, Scene 5. It is then that **she calls down evil spirits to take possession of her** and to deprive her of womanly feelings. The spirits she invokes are those which support people with murderous intentions. She asks them to suppress in her all feelings of pity and kindness which might weaken her determination to kill Duncan':

*... Come, you spirits
That tend on mortal thoughts, unsex me here,
And fill me from the crown to the toe top full
Of direst cruelty! Make thick my blood,
Stop up th'access and passage to remorse,
That no compunctious visitings of nature
Shake my fell purpose ...*

(1, 5, 39–45)

- Her prayer to the supernatural 'murdering ministers' (1, 5, 47) seems to be effective: Macduff pronounces her epitaph: she has been Macbeth's **'fiend-like queen'** (5, 9, 35).

- Shakespeare gives her one small human-ising feature. She would have murdered Duncan herself but for the fact that his sleeping form reminded her of her own father: 'Had he not resembled / My father as he slept, I had done't' (2, 2, 14–15).

- Lady Macbeth is involved in **the great character reversal of the play**. She is cool and practical after the murder of Duncan ('retire we to our chamber. / A little water clears us of this deed: / How easy is it then!', 2, 2, 67–9). Macbeth, shaken with terror, has his sleep troubled with nightmares. Later, however, it is Lady Macbeth who sleeps no more. Her mind is emptied of everything but the night of Duncan's murder; she cannot rid herself of the illusion that Duncan's blood is still sticking to her hands. She goes through the motions of trying to wash it off, but cannot imagine it gone: 'Here's the smell of blood still: all the perfumes of / Arabia will not sweeten this little hand. Oh! oh! oh!' (5, 1, 44–5).

- She has failed to dispose of her conscience and her guilt. Her suppression of these has been only temporary. **The terrible power of her subconscious mind destroys her**, leads to her madness (5, 1) and finally to her suicide (5, 9, 36–7).

- She tries successfully to maintain **an unbalanced relationship with Macbeth** at the beginning. In Act 1, Scene 5, when he enters, having braved great dangers and won endless praise, she ignores these triumphs and goes straight to her objective, taking on a position of superiority, breaking down his resistance and virtually preventing him from reflecting on the consequences for him of the murder she wants him to commit. Typical of her approach is her response to Macbeth's news that Duncan will be visiting them as their guest that very night and that he proposes to depart on the morrow:

    O, never
    Shall sun that morrow see! …
    … He that's coming
    Must be provided for; and you shall put
    This night's great business into my dispatch.
    (1, 5, 59–60; 65–7)

She does not allow Macbeth any say in what is to happen to Duncan. She will decide that, and she will present him with a prepared plan, of her own devising, for him to implement.

- She shows **perfect self-control** in circumstances of extreme horror and danger in both the murder scene and the banquet scene, keeping her head when Macbeth loses his and rebuking him for this:

    You do unbend your noble strength to think
    So brainsickly of things.
    (2, 2, 46–7)

She exerts **all her will power to control his ravings** when he see Banquo's ghost. He behaves like a woman, she like a man:

    O, these flaws and starts –
    Imposters to true fear – would well become
    A woman's story at a winter's fire,
    Authorized by her grandam.
    (3, 4, 63–6)

- The banquet scene (3, 4) marks **the end of her power over Macbeth**. She exhausts herself in a magnificent effort to restrain his violent outbursts and seems incapable of exerting her will any further. There was a time when she did the talking while he listened. After the guests have left, it is he who does the talking and directs events. She hardly seems interested in what he has to tell her. His news that Macduff has defied him elicits only a tired response from her ('Did you send to him, sir?', 129). She is unmoved when he tells her of his proposed visit to the Weird Sisters, telling him he needs to sleep (141). This is the last occasion in which we see her in a normal frame of mind. She disappears from the play until the beginning of Act 5, by which time she is insane.

- Her understanding of good and evil is as inverted as that of the witches, whose collective motto is 'Fair is foul, and foul is fair' (1, 1, 11). Good to Lady Macbeth seems the crown and whatever is necessary to obtain it, while evil means whatever stands in the way of this.

BANQUO

- Discussion of Banquo's character and role is frustrated by the obscurity of some of the exchanges in which he is involved (2, 1, 20–9, for example).

- Shakespeare has left some aspects of **his character and motives vague**, particularly at the beginning of Act 3, Scene 1.

- The most interesting problems associated with Banquo arise from his relationship with Macbeth.

- Banquo's **innocence** is strongly **contrasted with Macbeth's guilt** at several points. For example, his initial response to the witches is notably free from the guilty anxiety felt by Macbeth:

If you can look into the seeds of time,
And say which grain will grow and which
* will not,*
Speak then to me, who neither beg nor
* fear*
Your favours nor your hate.

(1, 3, 58–61)

This contrasts with Macbeth's:

Stay, you imperfect speakers, tell me more.
(1, 3, 70)

- When Banquo is later troubled by the witches' prophecies and **tempted by their incitements**, he freely acknowledges this, unlike Macbeth, who pretends otherwise:

Banquo: I dreamt last night of the three
* Weird Sisters:*
To you they have showed some truth.
Macbeth: I think not of them:
(2, 1, 20–1)

- Banquo, **whose conscience troubles him**, prays to the 'Merciful Powers' (2, 1, 7), whose function it is to restrain demons, for strength to resist evil:

Restrain in me the cursed thoughts that nature
Gives way to in repose!
(2, 1, 8–9)

- When Macbeth makes Banquo what looks like a treasonable proposal ('If you shall cleave to my consent ... It shall make honour for you', 2, 1, 25–6), Banquo refuses to consider anything **that might violate his honour or his duty** to King Duncan:

So I lose none
In seeking to augment it, but still keep
My bosom franchised and allegiance clear,
I shall be counselled.
(2, 1, 26–9)

- After Duncan's death, Banquo publicly adopts the stance of an **innocent, honourable man** and there is no reason to doubt his good faith or his willingness to combat 'treasonous malice' wherever he finds it. He places himself under God's protection:

In the great hand of God I stand, and
* thence*
Against the undivulged pretence I fight
Of treasonous malice.
(2, 3, 129–31)

- The fullest character sketch of Banquo is provided by Macbeth, who has a tendency to list the good qualities of those he is about to murder or have murdered (compare his comments on Duncan , 1, 7, 16–26). Macbeth draws attention to Banquo's **fearless temperament**, his ability to undertake **dangerous exploits** without risk to himself, and above all, perhaps, to **his kingly qualities**. These qualities make Macbeth fear him as a rival:

... Our fears in Banquo
Stick deep, and in his royalty of nature
Reigns that which would be feared: 'tis
*   much he dares,*
And, to that dauntless temper of his mind,
He hath a wisdom that doth guide his valour
To act in safety.

(3, 1, 49–54)

- **Doubts about Banquo's character arise at the beginning of Act 3, Scene 1.** These doubts stem from his soliloquy at this point, in which we are given a glimpse of his mind. Here he is convinced that Macbeth has become king by murdering Duncan ('Thou play'dst most foully for't', 3, 1, 3). He goes on to speculate that since the witches have told Macbeth the truth,

May they not be my oracles as well,
And set me up in hope? ...

(3, 1, 9–10)

This can only be interpreted as meaning that Banquo is **tempted by ambition** and that he is, like Macbeth, though to a lesser intent, the victim of the witches.

- If there is a case against Banquo, it has to be based on the fact that although he is convinced of Macbeth's guilt, **he takes no action**. Instead, he seems to have accepted Macbeth's accession as something to be lived with. He goes further: 'Let your Highness', he tells Macbeth,

Command upon me; to the which my duties
Are with a most indissoluble tie
For ever knit.

(3, 1, 15–18)

Macbeth points out that Banquo has been functioning as **one of his important advisers**. In that capacity, as Macbeth acknowledges, Banquo's advice has always been weighty and helpful ('grave and prosperous', 3, 1, 22).

- On the basis of such evidence, some critics have felt that Banquo **has yielded**

to evil and that he harbours a guilty hope of becoming king. It has even been suggested that Macbeth's action in having Banquo murdered saves the latter from a further deterioration.

- In defence of Banquo, it should be noted that **at no time does he think of acting to make himself king**. Also, while he is convinced of Macbeth's guilt, he is not in a position to prove it. If he were to declare his belief publicly, would anybody believe him, or even want to believe him? On the balance of evidence, the most Banquo can be accused of is **being prudent in the cause of self-preservation**.

DUNCAN

- Duncan is a generation older than the other main characters, but the text makes it clear that he should be played as a still active man, **able to lead and to command**. He shows himself to be decisive in dealing with enemies and the problems they cause:

No more that Thane of Cawdor shall
*   deceive*
Our bosom interest. Go pronounce his
*   present death,*
And with his former title greet Macbeth.

(1, 2, 64–6)

- He is quick to ensure that **his orders are swiftly carried out**:

Is execution done on Cawdor? Are not
Those in commission yet returned?

(1, 4, 1–2)

- The best, and probably **most objective, account of Duncan's character is given by Macbeth** in a soliloquy. There is every reason to believe all that Macbeth says here: there is no possible reason that he can have to deceive himself. It should be remembered that a soliloquy is, by convention, a speech shared only with the audience in which the speaker is telling the truth about his present state of mind and about his attitudes. In this soliloquy on Duncan (1, 7, 1–28), Macbeth identifies a number of Duncan's virtues as king, as follows:

- Duncan has been **gentle** and **merciful** in his use of his royal powers ('Hath borne his faculties so meek', 1, 7, 17).

- He has been **free from wrongdoing or corruption** in discharging his royal duties ('hath been / So clear in his great office', 1, 7, 17–18).

- In general, he is such a **virtuous** man that if Macbeth murders him, innocence, pity and the angels of heaven will ride on the winds and advertise the horror of the deed to all on earth (Duncan's virtues 'Will plead like angels, trumpet-tongued, against / The deep damnation of his taking-off', 1, 7, 19–20).

- Macduff confirms Duncan's **outstanding goodness** later in the play, telling Malcolm, Duncan's son and heir to the throne, that

  ... Thy royal father
  Was a most sainted king ...
  (4, 3, 108–9)

- Duncan is **the innocent victim of his own high expectations of Macbeth**, which are expressed in his plans to advance his career ('I have begun to plant thee, and will labour / To make thee full of growing', 1, 4, 28–29).

- Duncan's goodness of heart is such that **he is blind to the evil intentions of others**. He was badly deceived by the rebel Thane of Cawdor, as he admits:

  There's no art
  To find the mind's construction in the face:

He was a gentleman on whom I built
An absolute trust.
(1, 4, 11–14)

- Just as Duncan acknowledges that he **has been utterly mistaken in his judgement of Cawdor** and moralises on the difficulty of distinguishing between appearance and the reality beneath, Macbeth enters, already harbouring thoughts, not just of betraying Duncan, but of murdering him. Duncan, greeting his second betrayer with lavish praise ('O worthiest cousin', 1, 4, 14), **is about to be deceived a second time**.

- A major question is raised by Duncan's behaviour in Act 1, Scene 4. It may be felt that Duncan is **too extreme, too unrestrained, in his expressions of gratitude to Macbeth**, speaking as if he were a poor man thanking a wealthier one for being charitable to him. One passage is significant in this context:

  ... Thou art so far before
  That swiftest wing of recompense is slow
  To overtake thee. Would thou hadst less
  *   deserved,*
  That the proportion both of thanks and
  *   payment*
  Might have been mine! Only I have left
  *   to say,*
  More is thy due than more than all can pay.
  (1, 4, 16–21)

What Duncan is telling Macbeth here is that he cannot reward him in accordance with his merits and that he deserves more than he can ever hope to pay him. The problem here is that this can only lead Macbeth to expect more than the thaneship of Cawdor, and that he will now be entertaining hopes of being proclaimed Duncan's immediate successor.

- Then Duncan, having lavished praise on Macbeth, makes a proclamation that can **only anger Macbeth** and shatter whatever hopes he has:

We will establish our estate upon
Our eldest, Malcolm, whom we name
  hereafter
The Prince of Cumberland ...

  (1, 4, 37–9)

Duncan has chosen **a bad time to make his announcement**. As Macbeth's terrifying aside suggests, in making his son his successor, Duncan has **virtually pronounced his own death sentence**.

The Prince of Cumberland! That is a step
On which I must fall down, or else o'er-
  leap,
For in my way it lies.

  (1, 4, 48–50)

MACDUFF AND MALCOLM

Apart from Macbeth, Lady Macbeth, Duncan and Banquo, only two other characters make a strong impact, and their development is restricted. These are Macduff and Malcolm.

- The play has three movements. In the first, Macbeth confronts and murders Duncan. In the second, Macbeth confronts Banquo and arranges his murder, while in the third, **Macduff confronts Macbeth and kills him in battle**.
- Macduff is **less important for his qualities of character than for his role as leader of the forces of opposition to Macbeth** and as the restorer of lawful monarchy.
- It is Macduff who first discovers the murdered Duncan and who has the task of telling Malcolm the news (2, 3, 99).
- He **challenges Macbeth** as to why he has killed the grooms (2, 3, 107).
- He refuses to go to Scone to witness Macbeth's coronation, suggesting that **he may suspect Macbeth's involvement in the murder of Duncan** (2, 4, 36).
- Macduff's closing remark in Act 2,

Scene 4 implies that he has doubts about what Macbeth's reign may mean for Scotland: 'adieu! / Lest our old robes sit easier than our new!' (37–8)

- In Act 4, Scene 2, we learn that Macduff has fled Scotland, **leaving his wife and children unprotected in Fife**. His wife describes his flight as madness, while Ross tells her that she cannot know whether it was his wisdom that caused him to flee or his fear. Whatever the reason, Macduff's flight has a terrible cost: his family is destroyed, but not Macduff himself.
- Ross defends Macduff: 'He is **noble, wise, judicious, and best knows / The fits o'the season**' (16–17).
- Macduff's flight has one other consequence: Macbeth will be able to use it as **evidence of treason**.
- In Act 4, Scene 3, Macduff emerges as **the active champion of Scotland's freedom** from Macbeth's rule. While Malcolm wants to weep, he wants to act:

        Let us rather
Hold fast the mortal sword, and like good
  men
Bestride our down-fall'n birthdom.

  (4, 3, 2–4)

- Malcolm tests Macduff (4, 3, 13–114), who comes through the ordeal convincingly, and Malcolm pays tribute to his goodness of character: **his patriotic passion is the 'Child of integrity'** (4, 3, 115).
- It is appropriate that Macduff should be the one to kill Macbeth and **declare the liberation of Scotland** ('The time is free', 5, 9, 21).
- Malcolm, although he will succeed Macbeth, plays **a minor part** in the action. His big scene is Act 4, Scene 3. Here he feels it essential to test the honesty of Macduff and his reliability as an ally.

- By pretending to be an even worse individual than Macbeth, and therefore not an appropriate successor to him, he knows from Macduff's outburst of grief that Macduff is not Macbeth's agent and is not a danger to him.
- Malcolm **associates his cause with heavenly power** and feels that he and his allies are blessed by God ('Macbeth/ Is ripe for shaking, and the powers above / Put on their instruments', 4, 3, 236–8).
- Towards the end, Malcolm **takes on the leadership** of the invading army and gives orders ('your leafy screens throw down, / And show like those you are', 5, 6, 1–2).
- It is fitting that Malcolm is given the final speech of the play, as he **directs arrangements for the future**.
- Malcolm is **a worthy, blameless young man**, but he is pallid and tame compared to Macbeth. The audience will tend to be far more engaged with Macbeth's despair in the final scenes, conveyed in some of the most sublime poetry of the play, than with the forces of virtue gathering to destroy him. Pity for Macbeth at the end **deflects much of the glory won by the victors**, who could never hope to compete with him for attention. Corrupt as he is, Macbeth gains in heroic stature as the end approaches.
- **Macduff does not appear particularly intelligent**. Malcolm's deception of him in Act 4, Scene 3 is quite transparent. It is difficult to believe that anybody with a keen mind would be so **easily deceived** by such pretence as Macduff is.

- It seems surprising that Macduff should **turn a blind eye to the numerous sins which Malcolm pretends to be guilty of** in Act 4, Scene 3, sins which make him appear as wicked as both he and Malcolm think Macbeth is. If Malcolm were really as bad as he pretends he is, he would make a very poor successor to Macbeth.
- It should be noted that Macduff's image of Macbeth is not very like the real Macbeth as we see him in performance. **Macduff's Macbeth has little more reality than a phantom**, suggesting that Macduff's vision of reality **is extremely limited**. He sees Macbeth as a crude, devilish figure ('Not in the legions / Of horrid hell can come a devil more damned / In evils to top Macbeth', 4, 3, 55–7): such a character as he conjures up could never be the tragic hero Shakespeare has created and would be more suited to a melodrama.
- Macduff is narrowly focused on two interests: **the welfare of Scotland**, to which he is sincerely committed, and **the warrior's way of dealing with problems**, as revealed in his frequent reference to **the sword, through which he best expresses himself**.

Macbeth, the text

Every edition of *Macbeth* must be based on the text as printed in the First Folio of 1623. No earlier copy of the play in any form exists. Shakespeare's own manuscript has not survived, so it is impossible to discover how closely the First Folio text corresponds to Shakespeare's original version – or versions, since he may have revised his earlier draft or drafts. The First Folio text of the play contains obvious printing errors ('I' instead of 'Aye', for example), inconsistencies in spelling (the witches are sometimes the Weyward Sisters, sometimes the Weyard Sisters) and variations in the names of the characters (Banquoh, Banquo). Some words and phrases do not make sense or seem out of character, and editions since the early eighteenth century have been offering ingenious reconstructions and inspired guesses as to what Shakespeare actually intended in these cases. For example, the First Folio has Macbeth telling his wife:

> I dare do all that may become a man;
> Who dares no more, is none.
> *(1, 7, 46–7)*

Almost all editors agree that 'no' must here be changed to 'do', although a few believe that the second of the two lines belonged to Lady Macbeth.

Some have gone further than merely trying to remove such apparent errors and have suggested improvements. In Act 2, Scene 3, for example, the Folio text has the Porter say to the imagined farmer: 'Come in time, have napkins enough about you.' A modern editor, Dover Wilson, believed that Shakespeare must have written 'Come in time-server', as this matches other elements in the scene better than the Folio version does. Again, modern editors tend to

feel that the stage directions in the First Folio are neither detailed nor numerous enough and add many of their own for the sake of greater clarity. The First Folio does not indicate the location of scenes whereas modern editors almost always provide these.

Two more important problems presented by the text of the First Folio are that a few of its passages are almost certainly not by Shakespeare, and that one scene (Act 3, Scene 6) is in the wrong place. Scholars now agree that the Hecate scene (Act 3, Scene 5) and parts of the next witch scene (Act 4, Scene 1) are spurious. They are, however, almost invariably included in modern editions, as they are in this. It is now generally assumed that Act 3, Scene 6 was moved to where it now is from after Act 4, Scene 1. In Act 3, Scene 6 we find Lennox being told by a Lord that Macbeth's messenger has been repulsed by Macduff and that the latter has fled to England. But if we rely on the clear indications given in the next scene (Act 4, Scene 1), we are forced to conclude that Lennox and the Lord have, in Act 3, Scene 6, been discussing events that have not yet occurred. These difficulties would disappear if Act 3, Scene 6 were made to follow Act 4 Scene 1, and if the speeches of Lennox in one of the two scenes were assigned to some other character. In this, as in other editions, however, the order of the scenes in the First Folio has been followed.

The punctuation of the First Folio and the arrangement of its lines are generally altered significantly in modern editions, mainly in the interests of tidiness and consistency. Spelling is also standardised and modernised and capital letters reduced to lower case for common nouns. In this edition the two chief female characters are referred to as Lady Macbeth and Lady Macduff, in place of the First Folio's designation of the former as *Lady* and *Macbeth's lady*, and of the latter as *Wife*. In the First Folio text, the last act has seven scenes. This edition, in common with some others, divides it into nine.

The following are the main differences between the present text and that printed in the First Folio.

PRESENT TEXT			FIRST FOLIO	

Act 1, Scene 1

9	Second Witch:	Paddock calls.	All:	Paddock calls anon:
	Third Witch:	Anon.		faire is foul.
	All:	Fair is foul,		

Act 1, Scene 2

13	gallowglasses	Gallowgrosses
14	damnéd quarrel	damned Quarry
26	direful thunders break	direfull Thunders

Act 1, Scene 3

32	weird	weyward
39	Forres	Soris
57	rapt	wrapt
97–8	As thick as hail/Came	As thick as Tale/Can
135	unfix my hair	unfix my Heire

Act 1, Scene 4

1–2	Are not/Those in commission	Or not those in commission

Act 1, Scene 5

7	weird	weyward
16	human-kindness	humane kindness

Act 1, Scene 6

4	martlet	Barlet
9	they most breed	they must breed

Act 1, Scene 7

6	this bank and shoal of time	this bank and Schoole of time
23	sightless couriers	sightlesse curriors
47	Who dares do more, is none	Who dare no more, is none

Act 2, Scene 1

20	Weird	weyward
55	Tarquin's ravishing strides	Targuin's ravishing sides
56	sure	sowre
57	which way they walk	which they may walk

Act 2, Scene 2

19	Ay	I
64	Making the green one red	Making the Greene one, red

PRESENT TEXT		FOLIO

Act 2, Scene 3

5–6	come in, time – server	come in time
90	[Stage Direction]	[Stage Direction] Enter
	Re-enter Macbeth and Lennox	Macbeth, Lennox and Rosse

Act 2, Scene 4

| 7 | the travelling lamp | the trauling Lampe |

Act 3, Scene 1

2	weird	weyard
70	the seed of Banquo kings!	The seedes of Banquo Kings
110	Have so incensed	Hath so incens'd

Act 3, Scene 4

| 78 | The time has been | The time has bene |
| 144 | We are yet but young in deed. | We are but young indeed. |

Act 3, Scene 6

| 24 | The son of Duncan | The Sonnes of Duncan |
| 38 | Hath so exasperate the king | Hath so exapserate their King |

Act 4, Scene 1

59	all together	altogether
93	Dunsinane	Dunsmane
136	Weird	weyard

Act 4, Scene 3

4	Bestride our down-fall'n birthdom	Bestride our downfall Birthdome
14–15	something/You may deserve of him	Something you may discerne of him through me
	through me	
107	stands accused	stands accust
133	before thy here-approach	before thy heere approach
160	I know him not	I know him nor
234	This tune goes manly	This time goes manly

Act 5, Scene 1

| 1 | two | too |

Act 5, Scene 3

5	All mortal consequence	All mortall Consequences
21	or disseat me now	or dis-eate me now
39	Cure her of that	Cure of that
55	senna	Cyme

Additional study questions

Discuss the following:

1 'In *Macbeth*, the hero suffers ruin. He also brings ruin to many of those around him.' Write a response to this statement. In your response, you should refer to events in the play.

2 '*Macbeth* does evil things, but the play also shows him as a victim.' Comment on this statement, making suitable reference to the text.

3 In *Macbeth*, a noble and trusted general murders his benefactor, King Duncan. Using evidence in the play, why does he do this?

4 'In *Macbeth*, the "evil" characters are far more interesting than the "good" ones.' Argue for or against this statement, supporting your arguments with reference to the play.

5 *Macbeth* contains episodes of high dramatic tension. Choose two of these and discuss their impact.

6 Discuss the general vision and viewpoint communicated in *Macbeth*. Compare this vision and viewpoint with one other text you have studied as part of your comparative course.

7 Lady Macbeth excites pity as well as horror. Consider some relevant episodes in the play to show that both of these elements are part of our response to her character.

8 *Macbeth* features two of the most memorable characters in English drama: Macbeth and Lady Macbeth. Comment on some of the ways in which these characters contributed to your enjoyment of the play.

9 *Macbeth* would not be truly tragic if Shakespeare had simply made Macbeth a murderous villain. Suggest ways in which he avoids doing this and how he keeps our interest in Macbeth's fortunes alive to the end of the play.

10 Understanding the cultural context of *Macbeth* helps us to understand the values and attitudes of the characters. Develop this idea with reference to appropriate incidents, deeds and speeches in the play.

11 '*Macbeth* is the story of a soldier who sacrifices his moral principles to achieve his objective, but finds that what he achieves was not worth the sacrifice.' Examine the evidence for this statement.

12 'Lady Macbeth's major problem is how to get her husband to act against his own nature.' Agree or disagree with this comment.

13 'As Macbeth goes deeper into crime, he and his wife draw apart from each other, each dying, as they had come to live, in loneliness.' Comment on this statement, making suitable reference to the text.

14 In *Macbeth*, Shakespeare makes extensive use of parallels and contrasts between characters, themes, situations and incidents. Discuss the use of parallels and contrasts under two of these headings.

15   The sleepwalking scene (Act 5, Scene 1) is a dreamlike re-enactment of what has gone before. Develop this idea.

16   Guilt is a central theme of the play. How does Shakespeare develop this theme?

17   *Macbeth* has been described as a play of blood and darkness. Expand on this idea.

18   Macbeth is the tragic hero of the play. How, then, can he also be described as a villain by so many commentators and by some of the other characters?

19   If the play could be read as a moral fable, the moral might be 'never trust in appearances'. How do the events and images of the play, as well as the characters' behaviour, convey this idea?

20   Consider the idea that Lady Macbeth is mainly responsible for her husband's tragedy. What are the other possible factors?

21   The witches play a significant part in the events of *Macbeth*. Discuss their part with reference to the text. Do you think that their influence is decisive? Are other factors more important in shaping what happens in the play?

22   The relationship between Macbeth and Lady Macbeth changes significantly during the course of the play. Describe this change. Why do you think it happens? What do you think it reveals about the nature of the two characters?

23   Seen in terms of its major events, *Macbeth* is a particularly horrific crime story. Which events make it appear like this? Is it much more than a crime story? If you think so, explain why.

24   *Macbeth* dramatises a conflict between good and evil. Discuss the elements involved in this conflict.

25   It is not Macbeth's enemies who excite our imaginations, but Macbeth himself and Lady Macbeth who give us one glimpse after another of their tortured states of mind. Discuss this view, referring to examples from the text.

26   'Crime does not pay.' Could this be an alternative title for *Macbeth*? Support your discussion by reference to the text.

27   *Macbeth* is a play dealing with different versions of monarchy (Macbeth, Duncan, Edward the Confessor). Discuss the contrasts between these, with reference to particular events in the play.

28   Choose one theme in *Macbeth* that you consider to be particularly important and write about the development of this theme throughout the play.

29   In Shakespeare's plays, there are almost always two sides to the characters. Few of them are drawn in simple black and white. Show how this is true in the case of one of the characters in *Macbeth*.

30   Examine the role of Macduff in the play. What is his function as a character? What do we learn about the kind of man he is?

Bibliography

Lascelles Abercrombie, *The Idea of Great Poetry*, 1925

Wayne C. Booth, *The Rhetoric of Fiction*, 1961

A.C. Bradley, *Shakespearean Tragedy*, 1965

Stopford Brooke, *On Ten Plays of Shakespeare*, 1905

John Russell Brown, *Shakespeare's Plays in Performance*, 1966

E.K. Chambers, *Shakespeare: A Survey*, 1964

Samuel Taylor Coleridge, *Shakespearean Criticism*, ed. T.M. Raysor 1930

L Cookson and B Loughrey eds, *Critical Essays on Macbeth*

R.S. Crane, *The Languages of Criticism and the Structure of Poetry*, 1953

Patrick Cruttwell, *Hamlet*, Stratford-upon-Avon Studies, Vol 2, 1969

W.C. Curry, *Shakespeare's Philosophical Patterns*, 1937

David Daiches, *A Critical History of English Literature*, Vol. 2, 1969

D.J. Enright, *Shakespeare and the Students*, 1970

Helen Gardner, 'A Milton's Satan and the Theme of Damnation in Elizabethan Tragedy, English Studies, 1948

Northrop Frye, *The Anatomy of Criticism*, 1957

Alfred Harbage, Introduction to *The Pelican Shakespeare edition of Macbeth*, 1970

John Holloway, *The Story of the Night*, 1961

Maurice Hussey, *The World of Shakespeare and His Contemporaries*, 1971

L.C. Knights, *Explorations*, 1958

Oscar Mandel, *A Definition of Tragedy*, 1961

Kenneth Muir, *Shakespeare's Tragic Sequence*

Robert Ornstein, *The Moral Vision of Jacobean Tragedy*, 1960

J.I.M. Stewart, *Character and Motive in Shakespeare*, 1949

Kenneth Tynan, *Curtains*, 1961

John Wain, *The Living World of Shakespeare*, 1964